Mark Pearson's book is a necessary tool for anyone involved in the ministry of healing. His writing is clear and lucid. He speaks out of a wealth of personal experience and is firmly grounded in his own commitment. Above all, this book is theologically sound. It is one of the books the Order of Saint Luke has on its required reading list for new members. I wholeheartedly recommend it without reservation. Readers will be blessed, and others will then be blessed by them.

—THE REVEREND DONALD E. BAUSTIAN
NORTH AMERICAN WARDEN
THE INTERNATIONAL ORDER OF SAINT LUKE THE PHYSICIAN

In recent years scientists have proven the effectiveness of the power of healing prayer in more than 300 research studies. Now the challenge is to teach the Christian church how to harness the spiritual gifts, which can bring wellness. This new edition of Mark Pearson's book *Christian Healing* meets that need. All who seek healing for themselves or others will find it a rich source of knowledge and practical advice.

—BARBARA SHLEMON RYAN, RN
AUTHOR OF *HEALING PRAYER* AND *HEALING THE HIDDEN SELF*
PRESIDENT, BELOVED MINISTRY

Having blessed the Church of Jesus Christ for many years with his own healing and teaching ministry, Canon Mark Pearson now offers the Church a wonderful, healing gift. His book *Christian Healing* is an appealing, inspiring blend of encyclopedic, theologically sound, and carefully balanced scholarship and colorful, witty exposition, replete with evocative anecdotes from his own ministry experience. *Christian Healing* is a convincing, compelling call to action for the twenty-first-century Church to recapture and rejuvenate its first-century roots in the revolutionary healing mission and ministry of Jesus Christ.

—DALE A. MATTHEWS, MD
THOR, *THE FAITH FACTOR:*
EALING POWER OF PRAYER

D0595516

Christian Healing is a practical and comprehensive examination of God's ability and desire to heal people. Mark Pearson describes the history of healing in the Church and addresses difficult contemporary questions and concerns. He outlines how to foster a healing ministry and includes discussion questions and specific exercises to personally explore healing. Informative, challenging, and encouraging.

—CHARLES HUMMEL
FORMER DIRECTOR OF FACULTY MINISTRIES
INTERVARSITY CHRISTIAN FELLOWSHIP
FORMER PRESIDENT OF BARRINGTON COLLEGE, BARRINGTON,
RHODE ISLAND

Today, more than ever, there is a real and substantial need for healing. Many are looking in the wrong places—to self and New Age gurus. *Christian Healing*, on the other hand, points us to the Christian way of healing—through Jesus Christ, in the church, and by sacred action.

—ROBERT WEBBER
MYERS PROFESSOR OF MINISTRY
NORTHERN SEMINARY, LOMBARD, ILLINOIS

Mark A. Pearson's book *Christian Healing* is by far the best book on the topic. Nothing else comes close to providing the theological insights, practical advice, and comprehensive understanding of Jesus' gift to the Church. Every Christian should have a copy.

—DR. TED BAEHR
CHAIRMAN, THE CHRISTIAN FILM AND
TELEVISION COMMISSION
HOLLYWOOD, CALIFORNIA

Dr. Pearson in *Christian Healing* provides all Christians with a biblical mandate to fan into flame the gifts of God to heal the sick and to renew congregations into ministering true wholeness to those in need of God's touch.

—THE REVEREND GARY K. CLARK, DMIN
NATIONAL CHAIRMAN, AMERICAN BAPTIST HOLY SPIRIT
RENEWAL MINISTRIES

Pearson's *Christian Healing* examines what is essentially "Christian" about healing within an overall framework of the praxis. He offers an integrated, interdisciplinary approach, which takes seriously the Bible, Christian tradition, medical sciences, and human skills. Importantly, he does not discount the skeptical and awkward questions on this enigmatic phenomenon. Pearson shows how God's promise to heal has and can work today and warns against several compromises. Scholars, students, and ministers alike will find this classic on the subject useful. It will challenge the mind, warm the heart, and place healing where it rightfully belongs—at the heart of Christian missions.

—REVEREND DR. CHRIS GNANAKAN
PROFESSOR OF PASTORAL THEOLOGY
SOUTH ASIA INSTITUTE FOR ADVANCED CHRISTIAN STUDIES
BANGALORE, INDIA

Christian Healing by Mark A. Pearson is a comprehensive guide to healing. Pearson has a fine grasp of history and Scripture, a rare ecumenical sensitivity, and years of hands-on practice in the healing ministry. His approach skirts the New Age and overly therapeutic pitfalls, and gives a balanced and instructive course in healing. The book comes at an important time when there is a resurgence of healing gifts among God's people.

—KEVIN M. RANAGHAN, PHD
ROMAN CATHOLIC DEACON AND HEAD COORDINATOR OF
THE PEOPLE OF PRAISE, AN ECUMENICAL
COVENANT COMMUNITY

This guide is directed, at first, to the formation and practice of organized healing prayer groups within a Christian community, but it is (as the subtitle indicates) so practical and comprehensive that it can also be used effectively by informal groups of praying believers and even by individuals who seek healing for smaller issues, physical or otherwise, on their own. While warning against some of the pernicious fads in contemporary thought and practice, Canon Pearson has an admirable capacity to draw from the full range of Christian traditions. The text is both friendly and direct; seekers as well as professionals can use this book as a truly spiritual resource.

—VICTOR E. HILL IV, PHD
THOMAS T. READ PROFESSOR OF MATHEMATICS
WILLIAMS COLLEGE , WILLIAMSTOWN, MASSACHUSETTS
ASSOCIATE OF THE (ANGLICAN) SOCIETY OF ST. MARGARET
ARCHIVIST OF THE ASSOCIATION OF ANGLICAN MUSICIANS

The possibility of healing through the power of Jesus Christ is part of the very texture of Christianity, but it has too often been misunderstood or exploited. It takes a wise guide with years of practical experience to show us how to cooperate with God in this great gift, and Mark Pearson supplies that guidance.

—FREDERICA MATHEWES-GREEN
AUTHOR OF THE ILLUMINATED HEART
COMMENTATOR, NATIONAL PUBLIC RADIO'S
"MORNING EDITION"

Mark Pearson's Christian Healing is an excellent, comprehensive presentation of the way God works to restore our physical, psychological, emotional, and spiritual health. Informed and inspired by his words, readers will find themselves well disposed to receive God's gracious touch.

—BERT GHEZZI
AUTHOR OF SACRED PASSAGES

Since the western Church only recently rediscovered the ancient Christian practice of the ministry of healing, a book that combines balanced insight, careful pastoral direction, and solid biblical teaching is all too rare. Mark Pearson's lovely book meets the need for such a treatment. I pray that a new reformation will include this important element of healing ministry in both liturgy and community life. I believe this book should become a reliable guide for those who desire a holistic biblical reformation.

—JOHN H. ARMSTRONG
PRESIDENT, REFORMATION & REVIVAL MINISTRIES
CAROL STREAM, ILLINOIS

Mark Pearson has produced the definitive work on Christian healing. He has not only inquired into the history of the ministry of healing in the Church, but he has also looked at the reasons for its neglect by the Church after the Christianization of the Western world. He makes a biblical case for the reinstitution of healing as a ministry today and tells us how to do it. I am in complete agreement with all that he wrote. He has written truth that is supported biblically and experimentally. God is still in the business of healing, so we should not neglect the power He has given us to attend to the problems of people in the world. I cannot recommend this book highly enough.

—WILLIAM P. WILSON, MD
PROFESSOR EMERITUS OF PSYCHIATRY
DUKE UNIVERSITY MEDICAL CENTER
DISTINGUISHED PROFESSOR OF COUNSELING
CAROLINA EVANGELICAL DIVINITY SCHOOL

Having been in the healing ministry for twenty-five years, I have found *Christian Healing* to be a necessary "textbook" for those beginning and continuing in the healing ministry. It is extremely helpful to all denominations and to all types of people.

—RUTH D. URBAN
RECTOR OF ST. PETER'S BY THE LAKE CHURCH,
BRANDON, MISSISSIPPI
FOUNDER, HEMS MINISTRY
(HEALING, EVANGELISM, MINISTRY, AND SPIRITUALITY)

In this balanced and well-argued book by Mark Pearson, filled with practical guidelines and recommendations from an experienced practitioner on the field, all Christians, whether ministers, lay leaders, or students, will find an essential guide to healing ministry in the church and parachurch organizations. Rarely does one find a manual that is so comprehensive and practical in its orientation, and yet so well aware of the potential pitfalls and weaknesses of healing ministry. A must-read for all Christians interested in the power of the gospel to bring about wholeness and recovery.

—Veli-Matti Kärkkäinen
Professor of Systematic Theology,
Fuller Theological Seminary
Pasadena, California

This is one of the most balanced and important introductions to the Christian ministry of healing ever written.

—Lyle W. Dorsett
Professor of Christian Ministries
Wheaton College and Graduate School,
Wheaton, Illinois

I want to *highly* recommend this book to you as a book of sound scholarship, inspiration, and practicality. It may not be the best work out there on healing, but it is the best I have come across. Mark Pearson deals very well with the fact that we are living between the two comings of Christ, and while we should expect healing in this age, the resurrection of the body at the Second Coming is the fulfillment of perfect healing. He also deals very well with some of the recent movements that have caused damage in the body of Christ. He deals with the importance of the sacraments in healing.

—L. Dayton Reynolds
Former General Overseer of Elim Fellowship

In this book, all who are engaged in healing humans will find helpful answers to key questions concerning theoretical and practical aspects of healing. The author leads us to an expanded view of health and healing and to a new understanding of Jesus' ministry of healing and of God's healing presence today. By his vision of a multidisciplinary approach to healing, Mark Pearson counteracts each one-dimensional understanding of healing and is able to bridge the gap between the healing disciplines, especially between theology, psychology, and medicine. This book is of high value, especially for those cultures that lost the biblical holistic idea of man and neglected the spiritual dimension of health and healing for so many centuries.

—Dr. Beate Jakob
German Institute for Medical Mission
Tuebingen, Germany

I find *Christian Healing* a thorough and unusually balanced effort to answer the questions so many ask. If there is a God, why is there suffering and pain? If God loves us, why don't all get healed? What is the role of medicine in Christian healing? This book is unusual in that it actually tackles such issues head-on and in humility brings God's answers to a waiting world. We long for that day when Jesus returns and all healing is complete, and until that day may we know substantial healing, as Canon Pearson teaches.

—Bob Mendelsohn
Australasian Director of Jews for Jesus

I have had the pleasure of knowing and working with Mark Pearson for many years. His book *Christian Healing* is one of the best books on the subject in recent years. It wonderfully combines balanced theology with practical guidance. I heartily recommend it!

—Dr. Vinson Synan, Dean of the Graduate
School of Theology
Regent University, Virginia Beach, Virginia

Ring the bells for this one—set them to pealing—for Canon Pearson, out of his long, direct experience, has distilled godly wisdom, salted with wit, to give us a sane, sure guide to the accessible mystery of Christian healing. His book is sensitive, intelligent, biblically authentic, and buoying. If *Christian Healing* eludes perfection on its topic, it does so by a hairsbreadth. Read it and see.

Who reads this book without blessing is blessing-proof. Who reads it without edification is stone. Who reads it without tears is a desert. Open these pages and let ancient truth, experienced as reality in our generation, stride into your comprehension.

To state that a book is "balanced" seems the tamest of commendations, but on this subject, where fanaticism and fakery make their claims, it is utterly requisite, and Canon Pearson's welcome text is beautifully balanced throughout. It points a plain path between extremism and skepticism, where all who regard the Scriptures may safely, and gladly, walk.

—JOHN MCCANDLISH PHILLIPS
AUTHOR AND CELEBRATED JOURNALIST
FOR THE *NEW YORK TIMES*

A really practical, balanced, and useful book on healing. I recommend it for all who explore the healing ministry.

—REVEREND DR. OPOKU ONYINAH
RECTOR OF PENTECOST COLLEGE
ACCRA, GHANA

Sadly, when it comes to the Christian healing ministry, we, like Kipling's blind men and the elephant, incline to lay hold of just a bit of truth and defend it against all comers. But here we find no narrow spotlight beam, but a broader illumination of the Christian healing ministry. It encourages, informs, and unites, keeping Christ at the center. We need encouraging, teaching, and God's anointing; this book provides all but the anointing as well as any I have found.

—Dr. Michael Harper, Director
Burrswood Christian Hospital and
Place of Healing, England

This great book cured me of the habit of underestimating what God's healing touch can do today. And I am certain it will do that for other believers, too. Mark Pearson not only tells why we should rely on God for healing but also how to go about as an individual or a church. *Christian Healing* is powerful, practical, and highly readable.

—Frederic Barnes
Executive Editor, *The Weekly Standard*
Fox News Commentator and Co-host of
"The Beltway Boys"

CHRISTIAN HEALING

A PRACTICAL & COMPREHENSIVE GUIDE

MARK PEARSON

Charisma
HOUSE
A STRANG COMPANY

Most STRANG COMMUNICATIONS/CHARISMA HOUSE/SILOAM products are available at special quantity discounts for bulk purchase for sales promotions, premiums, fund-raising, and educational needs. For details, write Strang Communications/Charisma House/Siloam, 600 Rinehart Road, Lake Mary, Florida 32746, or telephone (407) 333-0600.

CHRISTIAN HEALING by Mark A. Pearson
Published by Charisma House
A Strang Company
600 Rinehart Rd.
Lake Mary, FL 32746
www.charismahouse.com

Unless otherwise noted, all Scripture quotations are from the Revised Standard Version of the Bible. Copyright © 1946, 1952, 1971 by the Division of Christian Education of the National Council of the Churches of Christ in the USA. Used by permission.

Scripture quotations marked KJV are from the King James Version of the Bible.

Scripture quotations marked NAS are from the New American Standard Bible. Copyright © 1960, 1962, 1963, 1968, 1971, 1972, 1973, 1975, 1977 by the Lockman Foundation. Used by permission. (www.Lockman.org)

The Bible study questions in Appendix 4 are printed with permission of the International Order of St. Luke the Physician.

Appendix 8 is adapted from the booklet "May Christians Judge?", copyright © 1978 by Mark A. Pearson.

Previously published by Chosen Books, first edition, copyright © 1990, ISBN 0-8007-9165-7; second edition, copyright ©1995, ISBN 0-8007-9221-1.

Cover design by Karen Grindley

Library of Congress Control Number: 2004107773
International Standard Book Number: 1-59185-629-9

04 05 06 07 08 — 987654321
Printed in the United States of America

This book is dedicated to my parents, The Reverend Deacon Hedley A. Pearson (1922–2000) and Beverly L. Pearson.

Acknowledgments

I WOULD LIKE TO thank all those who have helped me in the writing of the first edition of this book. In particular, special thanks to my colleague-in-healing Mary Shelton, who made many valuable suggestions for the whole book, but especially for the chapter on the healing of memories; and to my wife, Mary, who, in the midst of a demanding medical internship, always found time to comment on each chapter and, more importantly, give me lots of love and moral support.

Much of the material in this book was fleshed out, theologically and practically, during the seven years (1982–1989) I was part of the fellowship of St. Paul's Church, Malden, Massachusetts. Special thanks go to two men who were then the full-time clergy of St. Paul's: the Revs. Jürgen W. Lilas and Roger W. Wootton, who always provided wise, godly reflection as concepts were being pondered and ideas were being tested. I wrote portions of this book while "in residence" in three different churches. Thanks to the clergy and people of St. Paul's Church, Malden, Massachusetts; the Church of St. Michael and St. George, Clayton, Missouri; and St. John's Church, Sharon, Pennsylvania, for their spiritual blessings and practical assistance.

In this revised edition, I have added at the end of most chapters several suggested discussion questions and an "experiment." The purpose of these is to make the book more usable as a healing team training manual. The questions and experiments at the ends of chapters one through twelve were thoughtfully crafted by Harry Camp, a Christian attorney from Tennessee. Harry has served his Lord faithfully for many years and has been a leading figure in the United Methodist Renewal Services Fellowship/Manna Ministries, a ministry working for spiritual renewal in the United Methodist Church.

Contents

Foreword

I WILL BE HONEST with you. When I picked up this book to read, I intended to skim it. This rapid approach was not because I did not think Father Pearson's book would not be excellent. I knew Mark was well educated (an Oxford graduate) and brilliant, and I realized that anything he wrote would be worthwhile. It was just that I was swamped with work and manuscripts, and thought I had best scan it rapidly and gather the gist of all he said. Instead, I found that I was drawn into the book, and I took the time to read it because, although I have had twenty-five wonderful years in the healing ministry myself, I found that God has gifted Mark with some important insights that I had not seen before.

In chapter twelve, for example, on setting up a prayer team, he says that the person he chooses for the team does not necessarily have a healing gift! Instead, he looks for such qualities as having a strong spiritual life, a loving disposition, and being teachable. At first that surprised me. Then I realized Mark is probably right.

Another important insight I had never seen before: the mighty works of God are not described as miracles in the New Testament, but as signs and wonders. To call them miracles would imply both that they are somehow violations of the natural order and that they are rare. Rather than violating the order of things, God's intervention in people's lives when they pray is the natural order.

Father Pearson does an excellent job bringing together the basic truths about healing prayer from three streams of Christianity: the sacramental, the evangelical, and the charismatic/Pentecostal. What characterizes his presentation is balance. He is especially helpful, for instance, in presenting a brief, succinct account of the New Age movement and precisely where its dangers lie.

Whatever religious background you come from, I believe you will find *Christian Healing* an excellent introduction to the healing ministry if you are just getting started, or an important addition to your library even if you have been praying for the sick for many years.

—DR. FRANCIS S. MACNUTT
DIRECTOR, CHRISTIAN HEALING MINISTRIES
JACKSONVILLE, FLORIDA

Introduction

THE TWENTIETH CENTURY saw a marvelous renewal of the healing ministry of the Church. This resurgence in our time of a significant part of Jesus Christ's own ministry finds a major impetus with the extraordinary explosion of Pentecostalism throughout the world, a movement maintaining that healing is integral to the evangelical message.

In the mainline churches, spiritual healing has been courageously pioneered by such persons as Agnes Sanford and Glenn Clark, and it has been respectfully promoted by the Order of St. Luke. Healing services have become a normative part of the life of many traditional churches and are included in their liturgical forms (for example, the Episcopal *Book of Common Prayer*). Since Vatican II in 1962, the Roman Catholic Church has transformed the sacrament of unction from a rite for the dying (extreme unction) to a sacrament of healing.

The Charismatic Renewal throughout all the churches has brought a renewed sense of the immediate experience of the Holy Spirit into the life of the believer with a rediscovery of many of the more "miraculous" gifts of the Spirit, including healing. Evangelical Christianity, though historically ambivalent about spiritual healing, has seen a wondrous opening to the biblical command to heal, thanks to the work of pastors like John Wimber.

Finally, even secular medicine has become a strong advocate of the extraordinary power of faith and hope in the healing process. As the Church rediscovers this vital part of her commission and seeks to empower clergy and laity to exercise this ministry, there are many areas of concern, both theological and pastoral. My former parish, St. Paul's Episcopal Church, Malden, Massachusetts, and the Institute for Christian Renewal developed over the years a unique training program of teaching and practicing the art of Christian healing, from which this excellent book has evolved. It is both a theological-biblical primer on the principles of Christian healing and a practical instruction manual on the art of spiritual healing, useful to individuals and especially parishes.

I pray it will be a most useful resource for Christians to discover and share the awesome joy of healing in the name of Jesus.

—THE REVEREND JÜRGEN LIIAS
CHRIST CHURCH
SOUTH HAMILTON, MASSACHUSETTS

CHAPTER ONE

The God Who Heals

O**NE OF THE** great blessings to occur in the life of the Church in recent years is the revival of the ministry of healing through prayer. As recently as thirty years ago, relatively few churches conducted healing services; now many do, and the number is growing. Truly this ministry is being restored to its rightful place in the life of the church.

And why not? Healing is at the very heart of who God is. The Bible tells us repeatedly that God is all powerful and all loving. These words remain platitudes, and God remains an abstraction, until they are applied to real situations. To say that God is love and yet not see Him at work in people's lives is a cruel contradiction. The God we worship is not an absentee landlord, but a loving, caring Father who ministers to His children at their points of need. Sometimes the need is for healing.

The second Person of God came to earth in human form, in part, to make more widely known and more easily available God's manifold blessings. Not surprisingly, healing was a major part of the ministry of Jesus. His very name means "salvation," a word connoting more than forgiveness of sin unto eternal life. The word literally means "wholeness." Our Lord's earthly ministry was to minister this wholeness in every area of our lives. God invested Christ in us when He sent Him to die for our sins. And He intends to keep up His investment! Put another way, God, who loved His enemies so much as to send Christ to die for us, will certainly not abandon us in our needs now that we are His friends (Romans 5:8–10).

The ministry of healing leads people to God. Some, like the nine lepers in Luke 17:17, will not return to give thanks. Others, having received the healing, fall in love with the Healer. For many this is the first time God has seemed real.

To be sure, there were healings in Old Testament times, but they were occasional and done through a few extraordinary prophets. But then, because of Jesus' message and ministry, healing became widespread and happened through the prayers of simple fishermen and other ordinary folk. In Old Testament times an incident or two of God's healing would be reported, then none for a long time. But from Jesus' day onward, healing was deemed a regular part of the life of the Church.

The Gospels describe our Lord as going about teaching, preaching, *and healing* (Matthew 4:23; 9:35). One-fifth, or 727, of the 3,779 verses in the four Gospels concern healing in some way or other, a significant amount considering all the various doctrinal and ethical matters that had to be addressed.

Jesus trained His followers in the ministry of healing and sent them forth to heal in His name (Matthew 10:1, 8). Jesus told them they would continue this ministry after His return to heaven, when He said:

> Truly, truly, I say to you, he who believes in me will also do the works that I do.
>
> —JOHN 14:12

In the Acts of the Apostles we see the young Church effectively ministering healing just as Jesus had done (Acts 3:1–10; 8:7; 9:33–34; 14:8–10). Their ministry of healing helped authenticate their message. (See Mark 16:20.) Although their Holy Spirit-inspired and empowered preaching won many to the faith, many others were convinced only when they saw the signs and wonders that attended their ministry (Acts 8:4–7; 9:32–35). While other religious leaders might merely have talked about what they believed, the followers of Jesus demonstrated that, in Christ, a new order had begun. What they said—that the kingdom of God had been inaugurated through Jesus of Nazareth—was happening for all to see.

The mighty works of God are described as signs and wonders in the New Testament. A sign does two things: it gives both information and direction. We look for signs when we travel to tell us how far a distant city is and which of the various roads we should take to get there.

People may call such divine interventions "coincidences," but these events increase dramatically when God's people turn to Him in believing prayer. William Temple, Archbishop of Canterbury during the Second World War, used to say that the more he prayed, the more the "coincidences" happened. Healing—and other blessings—are not rare, except to those who do not ask God to go to work in human lives.

Healing, as with other signs of the kingdom, gives us information as to what God is like and points us to where abundant life is found. Healings, important as they are, point past themselves to the Healer Himself.

Healings are wonders as well. As we see a loved one helped by divine intervention, or a life set free from a bondage or an illness, no matter how many times we have seen God at work before, we marvel at both His majestic power and the fact that God, "who has so much to do," would take the time to care about ordinary persons in need.

Therefore, the healing ministry of Christ and His Church is not optional. It is one of the ways people get from God the help they need so very much. God wants His people made whole, and people today, in spite of advances in medicine and counseling, still need the direct intervention of God for healing.[1]

How wrong is the statement that the Church's ministry of healing might be OK "if you are into that sort of thing." To keep the ministry of healing from God's people, because it happens not to interest the leaders of a given congregation, is as much spiritual malpractice as it would be medical malpractice for a hospital to refuse to treat heart attacks because its staff preferred only to treat pneumonia. But why the need for healing in the first place? If God loves us so much that He will send healing, then why did He ever allow us to get sick in the first place?

The answer is that the human race has been given free will, and that our misuse of it—corporate and individual—has brought on the consequences of sin. These include sickness in body, soul, and spirit. In fact, the human race has been under a curse since Adam's sin.

We can see the extent of the curse in the early chapters of Genesis, where we read how Adam and Eve disobeyed God: in the aftermath of their sin, they hid themselves from Him—a sign of their spiritual sickness and sense of estrangement from God (Genesis 3:8–9). Adam blamed his wife for the temptation—illustrating emotional sickness and disintegration of relationship (Genesis 3:12). Adam and Eve became subject to physical sickness, pain, and death—which we likewise suffer (Genesis 3:16, 19). Cain killed Abel—illustrative of societal sickness (Genesis 4:8). The ground yielded thistles and thorns, demonstrating how even creation became skewed through human sin (Genesis 3:17–18). The healing Christ offers is as extensive as the damage done.

There is spiritual healing through forgiveness of sin and the promise of eternal life, offered to all and experienced by those who receive Christ as Savior (John 1:12). Our chief sickness is alienation from God. In Christ, the curtain of estrangement is torn down between God and us (Mark 15:38). As a result, we can become His sons and daughters, live in fellowship with Him now, and enjoy eternal life in heaven with Him when we die.

There is healing for the turmoil within people and between people as the Lord sets the captives free emotionally and behaviorally. As an evangelist once put it, Christ wants not only people taken out of the slums, but also the slums taken out of people.

There is physical healing through science and through the ministry of the Church, sometimes instantaneous, sometimes gradual. There is societal healing, as God works in the hearts of groups of people and nations. There is a renewing of the earth as God restores what we need to survive. Total environmental healing will come when, in the new heaven and earth, the lion will lie down with the lamb, and disorders and disasters of the environment will be put in order. Until then, creation stands on tiptoes waiting for it (Romans 8:19–22).

These are all foretastes for now. When Jesus Christ returns to make the heavens and earth new, the very presence of sin, with all its harmful consequences, will be removed. At that point believers in Christ will experience perfect healing. For now, while we do not experience healing perfectly, we can experience healing substantially. To accomplish this in us, God works in several ways.

FOUR WAYS GOD WORKS HEALING

1. Through skill and science

God has given us minds to unlock the secrets of creation through skill and science. When God told Adam to subdue the earth, He was not giving him permission to pollute or despoil (Genesis 1:28). Rather, He was saying that one of the ways we discover His provisions for us is through human skill and science. Doctors, nutritionists, trainers, and counselors make mistakes and do not know everything, yet they are intended by God to bless us and promote our well-being.

Luke is honored as "the beloved physician" (Colossians 4:14). Nothing in Scripture indicates that Jesus wanted Luke to abandon his craft and simply pray for his patients. Paul instructed Timothy to "use a little wine for the sake of your stomach and your frequent ailments" (1 Timothy 5:23). Although using a little prayer for healing would also have been appropriate, Paul encouraged Timothy to make use of a substance that, when taken in moderate amounts, can have a healing effect.

2. Through the clergy, rites, and sacraments of the Church

Services of worship often are occasions for physical, emotional, and spiritual healing, even if they are not intentionally healing services. I will just say for now that the sacraments, like Jesus, incarnate, which is to say they "flesh out," the spiritual reality of God in material ways. God uses the elders of the Church by virtue of their office (James 5:14). The oil of anointing is not just a visual aid. It is a "delivery system," to use Oral Robert's phrase, for God's healing. While we can go too far and turn sacraments into superstitions, we must not neglect the sacraments as a means that God uses to bring His healing to us.

3. Through the various spiritual gifts God has given the Church

Some people have been specially gifted by God to heal in a way that is dependent entirely on His grace and not on human skill or science (1 Corinthians 12:9). Others have received gifts that augment or assist the ministry of healing.

4. Through the prayers of Christians

The Church ministers healing corporately through the members' love for one another. In addition, any individual Christian, whether or not an elder of a church or the possessor of healing gifts, can pray for the sick. Jesus said:

> These signs will accompany those who believe…they will lay their hands on the sick, and they will recover.
>
> —MARK 16:17–18

These last three ways in which God works to minister healing could be given the descriptions Catholic, Pentecostal, and evangelical. It is easy to see why. Catholic Christianity stresses the importance of liturgical rites, orders of ministry, and the sacraments. Pentecostal Christianity gives special emphasis to the various spiritual gifts, which are often manifested in powerful and spontaneous ways. Evangelical Christianity, in addition to holding before us the primacy and authority of Scripture, upholds the ministry of all believers.

THREE STREAMS, ONE RIVER

Half a century ago, a bishop in the (interdenominational) Church of South India named Lesslie Newbigin described in his book *The Household of God* how important it is for the Church to incorporate all the riches God has given it. He saw three streams—Catholic, Pentecostal, and evangelical. In order to let the Church be the mighty river God wants it to be, the three streams, so often kept apart, must flow together. As a bishop in the Church of South India, which was the product of the merger of many denominations of different traditions, Newbigin saw the possibility of the streams coming together and feeding each other.[2]

Sadly, though offered this mighty river, most Christians have contented themselves with just a rivulet. We in the healing ministry would do well to resist this tendency. We need all of the four ways mentioned above for healing, for two reasons:

1. We dare not insist God go about His work only in the ways we prefer while refraining from helping us in ways we do not. If we truly believe God is the sovereign Lord of our lives, we will receive what He wants us to have in the way or ways He wants us to have it.

2. Each one of the four ways, when held together, keeps the others from going off into imbalance.

The mind orientation of skill/science and of preaching the

Word needs the balance of the supernatural nature of sacrament and of spiritual gifts. The mind is a wonderful gift of God, but it is only one way to know Him, hear Him speak, or receive His blessings. God comes to us in ways beyond our understanding, as anyone who has encountered Him in worship or in a sunset can attest. Encountering God in such mystical ways, however, has its dangers. We must make sure that any so-called experience of God conforms to what He has revealed in Scripture. Otherwise we will be at the mercy of accepting anything as long as it "feels good" or seems "otherworldly."

Additionally, the stress on one's personal faith in God, so emphasized in evangelical Christianity, has to be balanced by a similar stress on the sovereignty of God. While our grasp of God is important, so is His grasp of us. When our faith is weak, it is good to know that through the sacraments and spiritual gifts, God is reaching out to us, even apart from our ability to respond. Our faith ebbs and flows. How good it is to know that God remains constant! While personal feelings of faith are subjective, the sacraments and spiritual gifts are objective, available to us even when we are weak.

Yet without a personal relationship with Christ, we can easily become passive recipients of ministry. We might receive a specific blessing at a point of need, while not knowing, or knowing well, Him who is the source of all blessings. If our personal relationship with God in Christ is nonexistent, we are still dead in sin.

Furthermore, individualism, as seen in each-member ministry or in persons exercising the spiritual gifts, has to be balanced by the sense of the corporate, as represented by skill/science and by a catholic sense of the corporate Church. Professional practitioners of medicine or nutrition are not free to act in accordance with their own whims, but they must act in accordance with generally accepted standards of medical science or nutrition. Their understanding and adherence to such principles is monitored, and they are accountable to their fellows. The Church over the centuries has formulated theology and liturgy according to what people of many cultures and temperaments heard God saying. They worked to preserve the truth and hold their teachers accountable. This tended to weed out individual quirks of understanding.

Yet neither science nor the Church is infallible. Science is often improved when a solitary voice challenges that which has been accepted. Reformers, often speaking alone, have repeatedly called the Church to rediscover parts of the biblical message that have been misunderstood or neglected.

The "routine" of science and sacrament has to be balanced, moreover, by the fresh, new, and often dramatic inbreaking of God as individual Christians minister through the spiritual gifts. The love of God is ever fresh. He who does not make two snowflakes alike ministers to His people in a variety of creative ways. God, who made the exciting phenomena of earth and sky, often ministers in ways that are stupendous.

Yet God is also a God of order. We do not have to wonder if summer will be followed by autumn, or if gravity is operative on a given day. God too wishes us to know that His healing is regularly available through skill/science and through sacrament. Dramatic actions, when God is their author, can be thrilling, but sometimes people seek not the Lord, but the phenomena. And one can be so busy focusing on the uniqueness of how the ministry is taking place that the content of the ministry is lost.

All the streams, therefore, are needed, because they help keep each other, and us, in balance. Even though each stream is given by God and of great importance, individuals sometimes turn off to one of the streams. This can happen for several reasons.

REASONS FOR NOT ACCEPTING "FULL GOSPEL" CHRISTIANITY

One reason is bad theology. If the only way a particular stream of Christianity has been presented to us is in the context of bad theology, we may indict the stream itself and not the bad presentation of

11

it. If the way we have encountered the sacraments is in the context of a theology that makes them sound as though they are magical ways to manipulate God, we might reject the sacraments entirely or relegate them to mere symbols.

If the people who have spoken to us about spiritual gifts also try to convince us that for us to experience them, we must have a dramatic encounter with the Holy Spirit and immediately start speaking in tongues, we may disagree with their theology and subsequently reject the whole idea of spiritual gifts. If those who tell us about the ministry of each member of the Church also assert that there is no special role for the doctor, the clergy, or those with spiritual gifts, we may reject the idea of lay ministry.

The second reason is wrong practice. Sometimes the theological understanding of the stream is correct, but the manner in which it is carried out is wrong. The sacraments can be offered in a way that is dull and boring or in a way that looks like hocus-pocus. The spiritual gifts can be used in a way that burns, not warms, people. Lay ministry can be incompetent.

Third, foreign "packaging." It is a fact that we often judge something more by its cover than by its contents. Each of us has a certain cultural way we like our Christianity to be packaged. This depends on our upbringing, our personalities, what we value in music or art, and so on. If the style in which one of the streams is offered is not valued, we may reject the stream itself.

If our image of a sacramental church is an ethnic, blue-collar Roman Catholic parish, what we think about that subculture will strongly influence what we think about the sacraments in general. Or, if someone mentions spiritual gifts, and what comes to mind is a wild Pentecostal tent meeting, and this is not our style, then we may reject the spiritual gifts. Or, if the term *lay ministry* implies pouring out our private business to our peers who will then spread it around town, then we will not let anyone except "the professionals" help.

Fourth is prejudice. Our prejudice against Roman Catholics

or Pentecostals, or the idea of our waitress or auto mechanic ministering to us, may keep us from receiving the help from God we need.

If we can overcome these pitfalls, we will be the richer for it. Additional sources of grace will be available, for our sake and for the sake of those to whom we minister. And if discovering other streams via the ministry of healing has proven a blessing to us, we can integrate these streams into all other aspects of our walk with Christ and come to enjoy a fuller, richer discipleship. Over the years, I have seen many move to a full gospel faith because the ministry of healing was presented to them in a full gospel way.

While skill and science, the sacraments, the spiritual gifts, and the ministry of fellow Christians may be the means God uses to bestow healing, it is vitally important to remember that the source of all healing is Jesus Christ. We must ever keep this before us for at least two reasons.

JESUS, THE SOURCE OF ALL HEALING

First, seeking and receiving a healing without seeking and finding the Healer is settling for much less than is offered. The most important healing anyone can ever have is to be healed spiritually by reconciliation to God through Jesus Christ. Kathryn Kuhlman once said, "I do not care if I never see another physical healing as long as people keep coming to Jesus Christ. That's the greatest healing." Assembly of God pastor Tommy Barnett points out, "Miracles are so mighty that often we are tempted to glorify them rather than get on with the work of the Kingdom. Miracles are meant not to dazzle us, but to help us carry out the Great Commission of Jesus Christ."

This is not to say, of course, that physical or emotional healing is not important. Kathryn Kuhlman continued her own gifted ministry of healing. It is, however, to place things in proper priority. As a historic Communion liturgy puts it, "Through faith in His blood, we…have remission of our sins and [then, and secondarily] all other benefits of His passion." Jesus said:

> Seek ye first the kingdom of God, and his righteousness;
> and all these things shall be added unto you.
> —MATTHEW 6:33, KJV

For this reason, a ministry of healing is better identified as a ministry of *wholeness*. We want, for ourselves and others, not just to look at the specific physical, emotional, or spiritual problems, but at whole lives in light of what God wants for us. Whether healing comes through medicine, "miracle," or help through counseling, we are doing a disservice if we do not bring our entire lives before God—and help others do the same.

The second reason it is important to remember that Jesus Christ is the source of all healing is that many methods of healing are now being offered that are either based on humanistic techniques or that seek help from spiritual powers or beings. At best, these are foolish, for they press people to look for cures that cannot provide wholeness. At worst, these methods put people in touch with spiritual entities that are not surrendered to God, that are condemned by God, and that seek to harm the creation of God, however friendly they may first appear. Although people sometimes receive healing through these spiritual beings, often the end is worse than the beginning since these beings are spiritually, emotionally, and physically harmful, and now have special access to those who invited them to come and heal. Any spirit not of God is demonic and therefore highly dangerous.

There is much we do not know about the ministry of healing. But for now, our less than perfect knowledge should not stop us from making use of this rich ministry of blessing called healing. God wishes to bless us more than perhaps we had once expected. As He blesses us, let us love Him for who He is and ask Him to use us as His blessing to others.

DISCUSSION QUESTIONS

1. List New Testament examples of restoration to wholeness.

2. What does all this reveal about God? About yourself?

3. Of what significance is healing to the church?

4. List the different types of ailments.

5. List four basic procedures for healing.

6. Discuss the limitations inherent in each procedure.

EXPERIMENT

Select a person with whom to share that you are studying a book on Christian healing. Tell the person you need help, that you would like to pray for someone to be healed, and ask if he or she will cooperate. If so, ask the person to tell you of a physical problem or broken relationship that needs healing. Pray, and invite the person to pray also. In a notebook begun for this purpose, record information similar to that kept by a doctor, including at least the date, the person's name, the ailment, how you prayed, what you told God, what you asked God, what, if anything, you felt God saying to you, your physical posture and that of your "patient" during prayer (if you laid your hands on this person, and if so, how), if the patient prayed also, if you agreed to have additional sessions, and any discernible results.

You may want to make an appointment for further prayer. Keep a meticulous record. After about four weeks, talk with the person; evaluate and record the results. Critique your procedure. This will help you measure your growth as you continue in the study of this book.

CHAPTER 2

Why Did Healing Decline?

T**HE MINISTRY OF** healing occupied an important place in the Church in the first three hundred years of her existence. In the fourth century, however, a serious decline took place, and the focus shifted. It was not that God intended for healing to be part of the Church only in her infancy and then disappear once the Church had gained a firm footing. Rather, other factors came into play that caused the decline in this ministry.

These factors, having nothing to do with the purpose of God, are still with us. It has often been said that history repeats itself. As we examine the various reasons for the decline in the ministry of healing in the fourth century, we see striking parallels as to why the ministry of healing is downplayed or even rejected by some in the Church today. Let's look at the reasons.

THE CHURCH AS PART OF THE ESTABLISHMENT

Prior to the fourth century, Christians were persecuted for their faith, and many were martyred. The only ones who identified themselves with Christ and His Church were the ones who meant business. Those early disciples believed the Christian message and knew that nothing else could compare even remotely with it. Thus, they received the promises about healing and obeyed His instructions to minister it to one another.

In the fourth century, however, much of the Church lost this fervor. In A.D. 313 the Emperor Constantine's "Edict of Milan" gave official tolerance to Christianity. Although a brief return to persecution occurred later in that century, before long Christianity was not only tolerated, but it also became the established religion of the Empire. The Church was soon flooded with nominal believers for whom the radical centrality of Christ was secondary to social acceptance and career advancement.

Are things so different today? Are there not a variety of lesser motivations for church membership than the gospel call to die to self and live to Christ? I know of many churches in which a committed core of believers desires to receive the blessings of Christ and follow Him wherever He leads. But they are thwarted by others who do not want their church to challenge them to have a relationship with God, to make demands on their lifestyles, or to do those things that would make them look odd to their peers.

Many want just enough religion to make them look respectable or feel good, but not enough to force them to change. The ministry of healing startles nominal Christians in much the same way as Jesus' walking on the water startled the disciples. A rabbi who goes around telling people to be good threatens no one. But when that rabbi walks on water, those watching know immediately the old ways are gone forever. They are faced with three logical choices: deny what they see, passing it off as a hallucination; try to kill that rabbi in a desperate attempt to cling to the status quo; or respond in faith, significantly advancing their commitment. One thing they cannot logically do is shrug off the event.

Methodist leader John Wesley noted the correlation between the decline of the various gifts of the Spirit and the deadness of the church.

The causes of their decline were not as has been [commonly] supposed, because there was no more need for them.... [T]he real cause was: the love of many, almost all Christians so called, was waxed cold.... [T]he Christians were turned heathen again and had only a dead form left.[1]

FALSE ZEAL AND FANATICISM

While we strive for a true, self-surrendered zeal for Christ, some fall into a false, out-of-balance zeal. Even prior to the fourth century was the unfortunate appearance of the Montanists, a group in the Church that emphasized the miraculous workings of the Holy Spirit far out of proportion to everything else in the faith. Later, as nominal believers started to determine the depth of discipleship, some of those who were keen for the Lord reacted further still. We recall the misplaced dedication of one Simon Stylites. Simon, recalling the scripture "At the name of Jesus every knee should bow" (Philippians 2:10), climbed a stylite, or column, and recited the Lord's name over and over again, genuflecting as he did so.

For many, including many of the truly devout, such excesses tended to have an overly tempering effect. The powerful move of God and the dramatic operations of the Holy Spirit became somewhat suspect, even when done in scriptural balance. Many dedicated believers became cautious, and the ministry of healing (as did other good things) suffered.

The unfortunate excesses of a small minority in the Charismatic Renewal of today have made some people similarly wary. In addition, certain emotionally troubled individuals who have gravitated to the ministry of healing have discredited legitimate expressions of Christian healing in the eyes of some. Obviously the bizarre and the unusual garner the headlines and make those of us who want a balanced healing ministry suspect. There are just enough examples of churches divided and individuals harmed to make many who believe in Christian healing overly cautious.

ASCETICISM OR RIGORISM

While some reacted to the growing nominalism of the fourth-century Church with a false zeal, many others adopted a rigorist posture. Some fled to the desert, there better to confront the devil and purify their souls. Rejecting many of the creature comforts of the city, they felt free to focus on becoming like their Lord who had nowhere to lay His head. In contrast to this, healing, especially physical healing, seemed a self-pampering compromise.

Today many react to expressions of Christianity that seem to be self-indulgent. The wealth of the Church in this country, in the face of world poverty, racism, and oppression, strikes many as obscene. People have commented, "We have too much as it is; why should we ask God for yet more?" Others have stated that what we need is revolution, not pietism.

The enticements of the "prosperity gospel," encouraging people to grab on to as much comfort as God will provide, strike many as bearing little resemblance to the model of Jesus, the "Man for others." In short, prayers for healing seem, to some, selfish.

I maintain that receiving a blessing often equips and motivates one better to be a blessing to others. Had it not been for my sudden healing from chronic bronchial asthma in 1979, I would not have been able to make several ministry trips to those Third World places where a severe asthmatic response would have been likely. Part of the motivation behind my going on these trips, moreover, was gratitude to God for His healing me.

Additionally, asking God for a much-needed healing is different from asking for material wealth. And for some, the inability to ask God for help is not a sign of embracing evangelical poverty, but of either proud self-sufficiency or neurotic self-abnegation.

A PHILOSOPHY THAT DEEMS THE BODY TO BE LESS IMPORTANT THAN THE SOUL

In the fourth century, a popularly held philosophy was Neoplatonism. This view, which gained a strong influence on the life and thought of the Church, held that the body was irrelevant to the all-important soul. What God really cared about was our inner spiritual life. It was, after all, the soul that lived on. Why bother with the body, which would perish anyway? This belief failed to take into account the numerous examples of our Lord's healing bodies, or the fact that Christianity is based not on a Greek body-soul dichotomy but on a Hebrew psychosomatic unity. It failed to understand that Christianity affirms the resurrection of the body, not just the immortality of the soul. It forgot that God deemed the physical creation "good" (Genesis 1:31) and that the problem with the world is sinful rebellion, not physical existence.

Some people today understand these things intellectually, but they maintain an often subconscious separation between the physical and the spiritual. "Do not pray for my arm to be healed; pray that I grow to be more like Jesus," I was once told. No matter how hard I tried to convince this person that one could indeed pray for both, the lingering notion prevailed that any blessings the body received would somehow be at the expense of the soul.

SICKNESS AS A PUNISHMENT FOR OUR SINS

As the western part of the Roman Empire crumbled in the fifth century, the Church took on a more pessimistic stance. As life became rougher, people were encouraged to look for blessings chiefly in the world to come. Sometimes pagan tribes, with their views of a vengeful, wrathful God, were only partially converted as they were incorporated into the Church. Their views influenced the attitude that no one should ask God for anything except His tolerance of us wretched children of Eve. For a long time physicians were not allowed to treat the sick until the priest had first heard the sick person's confession, for it was felt that sickness was always a direct punishment for sin. Many today have a vague feeling that we are too unworthy to ask God to heal us. We may avail ourselves of medical science, but we should come to God only to beg His mercy, not seek His blessings. One man questioned me thus: "God heal me? But I do not deserve a healing, given all I have done wrong." It did no good to remind him that Jesus came for the sick, since the well have no need of a physician, as Mark 2:17 states, or that the gospel message is that God wishes to bestow grace on the undeserving.

THE SPLIT OF THE CHURCH

In the first few centuries of the Church, much interplay of thought existed between the Eastern (or Greek) and Western (or Roman) halves. Eastern Christianity was more mystical, while Western Christianity more duty-oriented. As East and West increasingly went their own ways, two different styles of Christianity emerged. Healing, more akin to the Greek half of the Church, was less at home in the Roman half.

In today's Church we see similar splits into groups that have little influence on each other. Pietists and social activists, traditionalists and renewalists, intellectuals and mystics, all reflect various aspects of the whole. But the various streams come together all too infrequently to form that mighty river of comprehensive, full-gospel experience of which Bishop Newbigin wrote. Individuals growing up in one Christian subculture may live their whole lives without firsthand knowledge of other expressions of the faith. Certain aspects of Christian life may actually be considered to belong exclusively to one or another of the Christian subgroups, having nothing to do with us and our part of the body of Christ.

Forty years ago in the Episcopal Church, someone interested in anointing with oil for healing was immediately deemed an "Anglo-Catholic." Today that person is immediately labeled a

21

charismatic. Given the fact that anointing with oil for healing is a sacrament of the Church with its own service in the *Book of Common Prayer,* an Episcopalian believing in this ministry should simply be called an Episcopalian. More importantly, with the weight given this ministry in Scripture, such a person should simply be called a Christian. The healing ministry, in other words, is "generic" Christian.

Many of the Christian churches of today's West—whether fundamentalist or liberal—are still centered in correct performance of duty, however that may be defined. It is still difficult for many to conceive of the faith as personal encounter with God through which lives are transformed and healed. And there is little regular communication between those churches and the others—largely charismatic or Pentecostal—in which healing is a regular part of church life.

THE CULT OF THE SAINTS

"Healing miracles," when they did happen, were associated for many centuries with great figures like St. Francis of Assisi. Given their unique sanctity, it was not hard to understand healing occurring at their hands. It was considered presumptuous, however, for anyone else to attempt to perform such works or to expect them to occur in general. Thus, in spite of our Lord's direction in John 14:12 that all of us should do the works He did, the experience of healing was restricted to those fortunate enough to be helped by a "saint."

Such an attitude remains with us today. Many Roman Catholics who save up for a trip to the shrine at Lourdes, France, hoping to be healed, deem foolish the suggestion that a healing could occur in their own parishes. Others petition a deceased holy person for help (witness the prayers to St. Jude regularly printed in newspapers), but they will not ask a fellow Christian to minister healing to them. Many Protestants flock to healing crusades conducted by well-known evangelists, not realizing that God can also use the prayers of the folks in their own church. Every congregation should have a regular ministry of healing. All Christians should pray with expectation for the sick to be healed.

A BAD USE OF SCRIPTURE

Since the early days of the Church, there have been those who get from Scripture a message far different from its plain, simple meaning. Whether this stems from blinders put on by the intellectual outlook of the day, a proud desire to be clever, a refusal to believe something they have not experienced, or from a desire to rewrite Scripture to their own liking, the result is the same—a portion of God's Word lost to His people.

In the early centuries of the Church, passages were sometimes "spiritualized"—that is to say, a word was thought to be a symbol or even a code for something else. When it came to healing, some saw references in the Gospels as parables, not literal accounts. For example, the man healed of blindness was not *physically* but *spiritually* blind. I wonder how much of this was an excuse to cover the fact that the Church at that time lacked the faith to believe in and experience healing from physical blindness?

Another blow to the ministry of healing came when Jerome translated the Bible from Greek to Latin, the Vulgate edition, which was, in his day, the common language of the educated of the Western Empire. The Greek *sozo*, or "save," and *soteria*, or "salvation," are rich words speaking of deliverance from a wide spectrum of danger or harm. In the narrow sense, the words mean deliverance from the danger of eternal damnation, much as people today use the word when they say, "So-and-so went to an evangelistic crusade and got saved." That is not, however, the only meaning in Scripture. The word can mean "healed," as James 5:15 indicates. Here, however, Jerome rendered the word as "save," in the narrow sense of the term, not "heal." Thus, a key text for the church's ministry of healing was lost to the Western

23

Church. Many church people today are bewildered by the various theologies, which go in and out of fashion rapidly and serve to undermine confidence in God's written Word. It seems that every time we turn around we are told that Paul did not write a particular epistle attributed to him, that Jesus did not utter this or that word the Gospels quote Him as saying, that our Lord's doing of one or another deeds was the invention of the early Church, that a given verse does not mean what it says, or that it no longer applies. In their confusion they miss out on much of what God wants for them. Besides theologies that undermine confidence in Scripture as the trustworthy Word of God, there are theologies that, while claiming to uphold the authority of Scripture, misinterpret it. Scripture tells us that we must suffer with Christ (Romans 8:17). This is often interpreted to mean that we should endure our pain or disease stoically. Yet the sufferings Jesus endured were persecutions, not illnesses (Matthew 16:21).

Yes, healing declined in the early centuries of the Church and continues to be in short supply in some segments of the Church today. But that is due to the ignorance, fear, laziness, and sin of its members, not the desire or purpose of God. When church members submit to God's will and trust His promises, healing happens. May God give us His grace to be part of the restoration process of this much-needed ministry.

DISCUSSION QUESTIONS

1. Identify modern examples of the spirit of:
   a. The Church, as part of the establishment
   b. False zeal and fanaticism
   c. Asceticism or rigorism
   d. Neoplatonism
   e. Sickness as punishment for sins
   f. Brokenness in the body of Christ
   g. The cult of the saints
   h. Use of Scripture to deny healing

2. What has been the greatest obstacle to your own participation in the healing ministry of the Church?

EXPERIMENT

Select a person as at the end of chapter one. Ask him or her three questions, and record these in your healing notebook:

1. Do you believe the Church should be involved in the healing ministry?

2. Why or why not?

3. Why, in your opinion, is healing in the Church so rare?

CHAPTER 3

Objections and Answers to the Ministry of Christian Healing

EALING IS A significant part of the Gospels, was a regular component of the life of the early Church, is a sacrament of the Church, and is a reality experienced by many people today. In spite of this, objections are lodged against it, even by some in the Church. I am happy to say that each of these objections has a solid answer.

Objection 1: With all the problems in the world, isn't being concerned with healing selfish?

Personal healing could become selfish, but is not an individual's sickness one of those "problems in the world"? To be concerned with personal needs does not mean one is concerned *only* for oneself. Many people are not concerned with helping others—nor are they able to be—until their own problems are dealt with. Many individuals, out of gratitude to God for healing them, give themselves in service to others in a way they would not have considered had Jesus not healed them. (Note Jesus' call to Peter in John 21:15–17 to manifest his love toward his Lord by serving others.)

Do those who make this objection not seek medical help

when they are sick? If they do, why is *that* not selfish?

Objection 2: Aren't there frauds and moneygrubbers in the healing ministry?

Certainly, but point to a profession or calling where that is not the case! We read periodically about a physician who has bogus credentials or who, in spite of several serious blunders, is still practicing medicine. Do we reject the whole profession of medicine because of those persons?

While the televangelist scandals of the 1980s focused on a few individuals who lived in luxury, most ministers of healing are either unpaid volunteers or, if Christian ministry is their full-time work, are paid very little.

Objection 3: Healing is so rare. Why get people's hopes up only to disappoint them and hurt them emotionally and spiritually?

Who says healing is so rare? Stories abound, some with physicians' statements included or told by physicians themselves, of people being healed through prayer. To declare that "healing is rare" says much about how little investigation the objector has done. I have heard people state flatly they knew of no one who was ever healed through prayer, when I knew several in their own communities whose healings were dramatic and lasting.

Even if healings were rare, that would be a statement about what currently is and not about what is supposed to be. If healing is rare, could it be traceable to a lack of vital faith on the part of the Christian community? Often, revival occurs when a remnant few in the Church study the promise of Scripture and the experiences of the Church in previous periods of fidelity, and start praying for whatever is missing to occur again.

As for emotional or spiritual hurt, we can encourage people without setting them up for hurt. Physicians and therapists acknowledge how important in the healing process is one's belief in the possibility of getting better. Do physicians not encourage people, with the same possibility of emotional hurt if the patient is not cured? Whether done by physicians or healing team members, an encouragement to believe in the possibility of getting well can be accomplished without manipulation or excess. Part of the purpose of this book is to ensure a good and growing number of ministers of healing who are capable, effective, balanced, and humble.

We also need to ask how much damage is done by the opposite extreme. How many fewer healings would take place if the physician or therapist counseled a patient not to expect anything to happen? Yet how many in the Church counsel people regularly not to expect anything from prayer? Such people are sharing their own doubts and lack of experience, not the truth of Scripture and the historic experience of the Church. No wonder healing in those places is rare!

One Sunday I filled in for a priest who was away. At both services I preached on healing. After the eight o'clock service, four women out of the seventeen people who had been present related that they had been healed through various ministries of healing in the area. Each woman shared in a whisper after making sure no one else could hear, apparently believing she would be deemed odd for making such a claim! I wonder how many more in that congregation might have experienced healing had there not been such a climate against sharing what God wants to do for His people.

Objection 4: Wasn't healing just for the purpose of getting the early Church going and not to be expected today?

Jesus ministered healing out of compassion for hurting individuals (Matthew 9:35–36; Luke 17:13). He also did it to symbolize and effect the breaking in of God's kingly rule on earth. Although some who were healed became disciples, healing was not a come-on to get the ball rolling. (See John 4:46–53; 9:38.) Jesus' compassion does not change. He is the same yesterday, today, and forever (Hebrews 13:8).

The decline in healing did not occur because Jesus withdrew an inducement to faith; it occurred because the Church, having eventually become established, cooled off in fervor. The progressive unfolding of God's compassionate, kingly rule will continue until the Lord's return.

Often those who so gullibly state that healing was withdrawn once the Church got going overlook one significant fact: healing continued! Healing died down, but it did not die out, and it died down for the reasons we have already examined, not because God withdrew it. As Church history illustrates, whenever vital faith flowered, healing—and indeed all kinds of divine blessings— became much more in evidence.

Further, we find no time limitations on the ministry of healing set in Scripture. When Scripture says in Mark 16:17, "These signs will accompany those who believe," there is no phrase adding, "... until such-and-such a time." When James exhorts the sick person to call for the elders of the Church in James 5:14–15, he does not hint that this is a limited time offer.

First Corinthians 13:9–12 is sometimes misunderstood to mean that when the founding of the Church, or the writing of Scripture ("the perfect"), was completed, the various gifts of the Spirit ("the imperfect") would come to an end. These interpretations are faulty. The Church, with all of us imperfect people, can hardly be seen as perfect or complete. And although Scripture is perfect and complete, we are not; we continue to need the gifts of the Spirit to help us understand and minister.

Many commentators believe that a more accurate translation of "when the perfect comes" is "when the perfect one comes," that is when Jesus returns. Then, and only then, will we see "face to face" and "understand fully." Then, and only then, will Jesus make the new heavens and new earth, eliminating all disease. Until such time as the Lord returns, we need all the gifts and operations of the Spirit, including the ministry of healing.

Objection 5: Doesn't healing lead to easy Christianity? Doesn't Jesus want us to bear our crosses?

In one sense, why *not* easy Christianity? Jesus came to give us abundant life (John 10:10). The Lord, our Shepherd, gives us green pastures and still waters, and He restores our souls (Psalm 23:1–3). The attitude that we should feel guilty for being blessed is psychologically unhealthy and theologically unsound. God does not bless reluctantly. He blesses in abundance. (See Matthew 7:11; 2 Corinthians 9:8; James 1:5.)

As we are blessed, God invites us to work for the betterment of humanity, the building up of His people, and the extension of His kingdom. Being healed frees us to complete our tasks. When Jesus healed Peter's mother-in-law of her fever, she got up and waited on them (Mark 1:30–31).

When it comes to bearing one's cross, as Jesus spoke of in Matthew 16:24, the context is the persecutions one suffers for standing firm for Christ, not enduring illness. If it were otherwise, then why did Jesus heal people? Did Jesus ever tell a sick person that illness was a good thing? Although God can bring good out of anything, including illness, Jesus saw illness as an enemy to be defeated, not a virtue to be desired.

Once again we would ask the objector if he also refuses all medical attention. If the answer is no, then what happens to this objection? If we should not seek healing through prayer because God wants us bearing our crosses of sickness, why should we seek a medical removal of those crosses?

Objection 6: If we establish a healing team, doesn't that imply that some people have gifts and others do not? Doesn't it set up an elite?

Each believer, according to 1 Corinthians 12:4–7, is given one or more gifts for use in gospel service. These gifts are to be used (Romans 12:6; 1 Timothy 4:14). Those whose gifts are not in the area of healing have gifts in other areas. As a church establishes a healing team, it should also establish other ministries if it does not already have them and encourage all the members to take part. It is true that some have gifts of healing and others do not, just as it is true that some can preach, counsel, play or sing, evangelize, or teach Sunday school.

Any ministering group or individual could, of course, succumb to pride. Part of the ongoing supervision of the healing team by those in leadership is to encourage both confidence and humility. No, we should not wait until we are free of pride before we minister—otherwise, no one would ever minister anything. Rather, to be preferred is the attitude of Cliff Barrows toward Billy Graham when Dr. Graham's ministry was just beginning in the early 1950s: "Lord, if You keep him anointed, I'll keep him humble."

Objection 7: Isn't healing associated with spiritual fringe groups? We have seen healing done in bizarre ways.

Some groups have overemphasized the dramatic and spectacular, the miraculous and otherworldly. The response to those groups that wrongly minister healing (or, indeed, anything) is not to turn away from it, but rather to do it better and more wisely. Would we, for example, refuse to eat just because there are obese people? The key, of course, is balance.

Dr. Charles Hummel's phrase "fire in the fireplace," also the title of an excellent book on the history and theology of Charismatic Renewal, has been very helpful to me over the years. According to this analogy, the fire represents God's rich activity in the life of believers. This includes answered prayer, the gifts of the Spirit, a personal relationship with Him, enthusiasm for God, and so on. The fireplace is careful biblical scholarship, the doing of things decently and in order, the consensus of the faithful over the centuries, and the structures and rules of the Church. The fire and the fireplace need each other! A fireplace without the fire—the danger established, traditional churches often fall into—may be beautiful, cultured, and safe, but it is also cold, dark, and powerless. The fire without a fireplace, a danger in Pentecostalism, can do much, but it can also burn the house down. The answer, obviously, is to build fires in the fireplaces and fireplaces around the fires. It is in this way that a healing ministry should be conducted.

Objection 8: Why should we have a separate ministry of healing? Doesn't God know who is sick already, and doesn't He heal as He chooses?

Yes indeed, God heals in a variety of ways, including sovereignly with no input on our part. But we have a separate, intentional ministry of healing for two reasons:

One, we are told to. In James 5:14, the sick in the church are told specifically to send for the elders who will anoint them. Jesus sent His disciples out to heal (Luke 9:1–2). Since our Lord's example and direction, and Scripture's command, include healing, who are we to ignore or disobey?

Two, a healing ministry makes intentional that which may otherwise only occur coincidentally, and specific that which is general. God ministers to our problems, but we do not rule out pastoral counseling. God exhorts us in many ways, but we still have sermons. So too with healing. While there are many avenues by which God ministers healing, we need an intentional ministry of healing, a ministry in which healing is the central theme, the chief focus.

Objection 9: Didn't God use healing through prayer then because medical science had not advanced to the place it is now?

First, physicians understand that the etiology, or cause, of the majority of sickness is emotional or spiritual. In these cases, while physicians treat symptoms, medical science is useless to cure root causes. How many people do we know who have come away from their physicians shrugging their shoulders, saying, "He said it was stress"? Many physicians, referring to their patients, have said to me, "They need you more than they need me."

Nor is the solution to be found in psychological counseling

alone. People face many problems because their lives are not in order as God has established it. As Blaise Pascal pointed out, we have a God-shaped void in us. We will try to fill that void with all sorts of things—some good, some not good—but nothing will fill it except God. As St. Augustine put it, "Our hearts are restless until they find their rest in Thee, O God."[1] I do not deny the value of psychological counseling, but sometimes it too treats just the symptoms.

God has made us to live in personal, obedient relationship with Him. As we depart from that relationship through ignorance, laziness, or willfulness, we suffer. God is not harming us for this; we are harming ourselves. Any form of healing by medicine, counseling, nutrition, or even religion, that does not center on God and His will is inadequate to make people whole. It is often inadequate even to make them physically well.

Second, although medicine has come far, especially in the last one hundred years, there is much it cannot do. Antibiotics can do a great deal, but the common cold is still with us. Medicine is a good friend and part of the multifaceted approach to wholeness God provides, but it fails miserably as an infallible, all-providing master.

Objection 10: Isn't healing antiscientific?

First, many nurses and doctors believe in and practice Christian healing in addition to their work in medicine.

Second, just because something cannot be proven in a laboratory experiment does not mean it is false. Many things that are true and dear are proven by other means. Can we weigh 6 ounces of patriotism? Can we produce the scientific formula for love? Scientific experiments rarely explain how or why certain events always seem to work in a certain way, only that they do. A laboratory scientist once told me, "We do not know why this medicine seems to produce good results in patients. But in about 72 percent of the cases, it yields noticeable improvement. So, since there seem to be no bad side effects, we use it."

I would ask that no more "proof" be required of healing. If all we can say is that many people experience noticeable improvement by praying with believing Christians, often when medicine or surgery has not helped, then fine! Why should we ask of Christian healing greater proof than we do of medicines or medical procedures?

Third, a growing number of experiments have demonstrated the reality of prayer in the process of healing. Dr. Randolph C. Byrd, a physician on the staff of San Francisco General Hospital, decided to conduct such an experiment. He had a computer divide the names of 393 patients admitted to a coronary care unit into two sections, equal in terms of illness and likelihood of recovery. The names and problems of the people in one section were sent to intercessory prayer groups. The second section was not prayed for in this way, although doubtless some of the people were prayed for by friends and loved ones. No one in the hospital knew who was in which group, lest there be any compromise of the integrity of the experiment. After a certain period of time elapsed, and all the relevant data was collected, a comparison was made. This medical conclusion was drawn: prayer to God has a positive impact on the healing and recovery of patients admitted to a coronary care unit. (This is documented in "Positive Therapeutic Effects of Intercessory Prayer in a Coronary Care Unit Population," *Southern Medical Journal* [July 1988]: 826–829.) Given this and other evidence, could we not validly reverse the question and say: can the biases of some physicians not hurt the recovery process of their patients by their unscientific prejudice against prayer for healing?

Fourth, during the last few decades there has been a profound shift in the philosophical underpinnings of science. While still believing in the validity (within its proper place) of scientific experimentation, few people now hold to a Newtonian-Cartesian view of "fixed laws of nature." The universe is seldom seen anymore as a machine operating within specific rules, most of which we know. Rather, the universe is seen more in spiritual terms, and observers are humbled by how much we do not know. As John Polkinghorne expressed it in *Science and Creation*:

> The very transition from the naïvely objective world, as perceived by Newton and Maxwell, to the elusive quantum world of Heisenberg and Dirac, is a tale of the often reluctant recognition by physicists of the strangeness of what actually is. If encounter with the physical world can so sharply revise our understanding of what can rationally be said about its nature, it would scarcely be surprising if the pursuit of the divine required openness to the unexpected.[2]

Recent scientific discoveries and theoretical postulations have discredited, at least among some of the learned, belief in a closed, mechanistic universe with no room for divine intervention. The view of science held by the proverbial "man in the street," however, is often from the pre-Einstein "dark ages." In the days of Copernicus and Galileo, it was the Church that needed to be corrected by the discoveries of science. Today, ironically, when it comes to a belief in the direct intervention of God in human lives, it is science that is finally catching up with the Christian faith. (For a succinct statement of the issue, see Appendix E, "Natural-Supernatural Distinctions," in Charles E. Hummel's book *Fire in the Fireplace: Charismatic Renewal in the Nineties*. For a more thorough treatment, see *The Galileo Connection: Resolving Conflicts Between Science and the Bible* by the same author.)

Objection 11: Isn't a healing ministry likely to disrupt the good order in our church? Our service is long enough as it is without adding more!

Much depends on what is meant by *disrupt* and *long enough*. If someone is fearing wild, out-of-control zealots or services that go on and on, then I can understand the objection. I am not advocating that.

But if the objector really means that he wants a Christianity that makes no demands on him, that does not interfere with his life, or is confined to one hour (and no longer!) on Sunday morning, then I would say he woefully misunderstands what Jesus' call to discipleship is all about! Jesus did not come to be fourth in our lives behind the things we really like. He came as Lord. As the experience of the rich young ruler in Luke 18:18–23 shows, Jesus offers only one category of discipleship—committed discipleship.

Yes, a healing ministry will cause some disruptions. An effective ministry of healing will attract people who are hurting physically and emotionally. Some of them may dress strangely, act oddly, or smell bad. But did not Jesus come for these? (See Luke 5:30–32; 7:36–50.) And is not part of our task as a community centered in Him to reach out and welcome into our midst such as these? (See James 1:27; 2:5.) A local church is a community responding to God's call—called out from the world, called to faith in Him, called together as a body, and called forth to do His work. It is not a gathering of the self-righteous who want "God on retainer fee" or who want God to give sentimental feelings on demand.

Yes, as we claim more of our privileges as believers and own our duties as disciples, the service of worship will grow longer. But those who have tasted the beauty of the Lord and surrendered to Him want it that way. To someone who hates baseball, being dragged to a game can be agony. But to someone who likes it, a game that goes into extra innings is a bonus!

A FINAL POINT

The objections examined above can be honest difficulties on the part of committed disciples. These people rightly do not wish to rush into anything while there are roadblocks in their minds. I hope we have seen that we need to take these objections seriously and that there are answers to them.

Other objectors do not really want the roadblocks removed. A man once told me, "If God heals, then God is real. And if

God is real, He probably wants me to change. I do not want to change; therefore, I wish to keep Him at arm's length. I come to church because I enjoy the music, I meet interesting people, and it is good for the kids. But I do not want God to be at the center of my life. Anything that may indicate His power and reality, or anything that reminds me of any claim He might have on my life, is too threatening. Therefore, healing or any other kind of spiritual fervor is to be blocked."

I must admit, I seldom hear such an honest, articulate statement as this man gave on why some oppose healing. This is the attitude, to a greater or lesser degree, consciously or unconsciously, held by many people in the Church. While respecting them as individuals, we cannot let such faithless objections deter us from starting or expanding the ministry of healing (and anything else the Lord wants us to do). The program of the Church must be based on the revealed will of the Lord, and the agenda set by those who wish to know and do His will, not by those who do not.

DISCUSSION QUESTION

State in your own words how you would respond to a fellow church member who raised each of the eleven objections stated in this chapter. If you are in a group, you might even consider role-playing.

EXPERIMENT

Block out at least twenty minutes of private prayer time. Take at least five minutes for quiet, thoughtful, verbal thanksgiving and praise. Read Isaiah 53:1–9 slowly until a thought arrests your attention. Stop and ask God for enlightenment on that thought. If you finish reading without stopping, start over; read more slowly and thoughtfully. Record your thoughts, meditations, and conclusions.

CHAPTER 4

Why Are Some People Not Healed?

HE OBVIOUS FACT is, not everyone ministered to is healed. Why not? It is a good question. Some try to duck it, but that is foolish. If the ministry of Christian healing is nothing more than a pleasant, but ineffectual ritual, we should stop it immediately. It would be dishonest to continue and harmful to the emotions and faith of those we have deceived. If, on the other hand, there is something to this ministry of healing, if God actually does wish people to be healed, we need to identify and remove whatever barriers are blocking the healing from taking place. Look at a medical analogy. If a person has a medical problem and one series of tests does not reveal the identity of the illness, does the doctor stop there, or does he run further tests? If one kind of treatment proves ineffective, do we give up trying to get well, or do we try something else?

There are a number of reasons why a person ministered to is not healed. (This fact alone should keep us from making snap judgments or giving simplistic, across-the-board answers.)

1. A wrong diagnosis of the problem

While God sometimes heals a foot when we pray for an arm, or honors a generalized prayer of "Lord, please heal Jim; You know the need," it is often important to know the problem and its root cause.

When time allows, a conversation with the person to whom we are ministering can help us ascertain the problem and its root cause(s). In addition, we should spend time asking God to give us supernatural discernment, for it may be that we cannot know what the problem truly is unless God tells us. When we do not have the luxury of lengthy conversation before ministering to a sick person, such as at a public service of healing, we can pray for discernment while the ministry is being carried out.

We should always remember the dangers of attributing every problem to only one factor and of emphasizing only one aspect of healing. Sometimes a person's problem is traceable to unrepentant sin, sometimes to a biochemical disorder, sometimes to a bad emotional experience in one's youth, sometimes to a bad diet, sometimes to demonic activity, and sometimes to several causes at once. Healing painful memories of the past will not heal someone who needs to repent of a certain sin, nor will deliverance from evil spirits help someone who needs to alter his diet. Although we should not push this point too far, many evangelical and fundamentalist churches tend to see every problem as sin-caused and every solution as repentance; many Pentecostal and charismatic churches tend to see every problem as demon-caused and every solution as deliverance; and many liberal churches tend to see every problem as psychological or emotional and every solution as counseling or inner healing. If we have diagnosed incorrectly, we will often be ineffective in prayer and can even do harm.

2. Limiting God to one method

God has many ways to bring us to wholeness. If we try to limit Him by insisting He heal us in a particular way, we might block a healing from happening. Remember Naaman the Syrian, whom the prophet Elisha told to bathe in the Jordan River in order to be healed? (See 2 Kings 5:1–14.) Imagine the shock to his pride for a Syrian military commander to have to wash in a Jewish river. But he did, and he was healed. Had he insisted on a method other than the one God told Elisha to use, he would have remained ill. Also, Timothy's stomach troubles were alleviated by moderate drinking of wine, not by prayer (1 Timothy 5:23). I believe Jesus varied His methods of healing each time so people would center on Him, not on a method.

Some Christians rule out confession of their sins; others see no value in nutritional programs; a few rule out doctors; others refuse to go to healing services. If someone refuses to use a particular legitimate method of healing because of pride or prejudice, God may well insist on that method as the—or at least a—key to healing, because pride may be the real root problem.

The ministry of healing is better and more fully described as a ministry of *wholeness*. In order for a person to be whole, God must be sovereign over that person's life. A stubborn refusal to cooperate with God in the manner in which a healing occurs may be symptomatic of the need for a spiritual healing.

3. Counteracting God's work

If we are praying for healing but indulging in things that hurt us (bad diet, lack of exercise, letting emotional hurts eat away at us, holding on to a root of bitterness), we may be blocking the healing or else reinfecting ourselves.

Several years ago I had an ongoing stomach problem. At each "team prep" meeting before our Friday evening healing service, I asked our team to pray for me. They did, and the problem went away—until Monday afternoon. The next Friday they would pray again, and I would be healed again—until Monday afternoon! Eventually somebody suggested we pray for divine wisdom. Soon, one of the team members received a "word of knowledge" (information about something that comes directly from God; see

1 Corinthians 12:8, NAS). "This may be nothing," she said, "but what comes to mind as we pray is a picture of a giant coffeepot. Canon Mark, how much coffee do you drink in the course of a day?" I was shocked when I added up the number of cups! God was not punishing me or removing my healing—I was counteracting His work.

4. Holding on to sin

Closely related to this is the refusal to let go of a particular sin or attitude that may block wholeness. Although it is obvious that persevering in sin blocks our fellowship with God, and therefore our wholeness, sin can also harm us physically.

I once ministered to a man who was contemptuous and abusive of store clerks. On those days that he ran an errand during his lunch hour, and inevitably got into an argument, he came down with a headache during the afternoon. While aspirin alleviated the symptoms, it also masked the cause. He consulted pharmacists for stronger medication. One of them, with whom he had an argument, tried to point out that the answer was not in a pill, but the man did not want to discuss it. Finally, when the pain got much worse, he was ready to listen. By God's grace he was able to face the problem, ask forgiveness of the many people he had wronged, and take steps to change. Eventually the arguments ceased, and so did the headaches.

The psalmist noted, "There is no health in my bones because of my sin" (Psalm 38:3). Jesus' ministry of healing often involved forgiving sins. (See Mark 2:5; John 5:14.) Articles are being published both in medical journals and in the popular press demonstrating the relationship between sickness and the inappropriate handling of emotions. Bitterness, resentment, anxiety, inappropriately expressed anger—all of which Scripture calls sin—besides harming others, harm ourselves spiritually, emotionally, and physically. While this is not a license to tell people their faults indiscriminately, we can follow the Lord's leading and confront people lovingly, but firmly, with sin and its consequences to themselves and to others.

Some people, operating out of a misunderstanding of what it means to accept and affirm others, refuse to make the connection between sin and sickness, repentance and healing. This is because of an attitude of permissiveness, or a codependent need of people's approval, or a theology that lets us do whatever we want regardless of what God has said.

To be sure, there is a wrong way to confront that is judgmental, self-righteous, and condemnatory. Jesus ruled this out when He said, "Judge not, that you be not judged" (Matthew 7:1). But there is a right way, a way that is discerning, caring, and helpful. This is what Jesus meant when He told His followers to "judge with right judgment" (John 7:24). The popular term today for judging in a right way is *tough love*. It is the secret behind an "intervention" to confront a substance abuser with his addiction, and the accountability in which Alcoholics Anonymous members hold one another. (See Appendix 8.)

5. A secret desire to stay sick

There are people who would rather stay sick because their illnesses give them power over others. I once heard a mother tell her teenage daughter, "You can go out Friday night with your friends if you want. But just remember, they do not have a bedridden mother as you do, one who took care of you when you were little, one who needs you now." That woman was using her illness to manipulate her daughter. Physicians had said repeatedly that, although her symptoms were real, there was no physical cause for them. She was sick because she wanted to be sick, because it gave her power.

Other people desire to stay sick to have an excuse to avoid work, responsibility, or good behavior; to attract pity; or to be the center of attention. I remember how much more quickly I recovered from an illness when my mother told me, "I do not care how sick you are, you will no longer get away with that kind of behavior!" Jesus' perceptive word to the man at

Bethesda was, "Do you want to be healed?" (John 5:6).

Others desire to stay sick because they believe they are unworthy of health, of love, or of anything good. This can be traced, variously, to parental upbringing that demeaned or abused, to neuroses of various kinds, to a theology of a punitive, vengeful God, to an overdose of the hard knocks of life, or to other causes. They just cannot believe that things could be better. Anything good that comes their way is pushed aside. Even the thought of being healed and the new lifestyle it would bring is scary to them. This secret desire to stay sick might be conscious, or it might be buried deep down inside. But it is real and keeps some people from becoming whole.

This is not to say we do not have a ministry to such people. It is to help them see either that they do not have to stay sick or that their sickness, far from warranting their being excused, warrants their being confronted. This attitude must be one of compassion and genuine understanding of the repressive faculty of the psyche and of neurosis. In doing so, the sufferer must not be made to feel ashamed of needing his illness as a way to cope with the emotional traumas of life. It was what allowed him to survive emotionally until he could be brought to a different way of living that allows him to be healthy.

6. Not seeing healing as gradual and progressive

Sometimes God works gradually. We see this in Mark 8:22–25 with a blind man who was healed in two stages.

Sometimes the healing is gradual because several pieces of the puzzle need to fit together in a certain order. I ministered to a woman who had a number of serious problems, all of which were rooted in an abuse during her childhood. I ministered inner healing until her growth into wholeness eventually plateaued. At that stage, I had to shift from inner healing and start dealing with her anger toward her abusers. Forgiveness had not been possible in her until then, but from a certain point onward no further inner healing could take place until she started to forgive. Then we went back to work on inner healing.

During her childhood she had sought solace in food that was nutritious enough in proper amounts, but that could be harmful if a diet is centered in them. She eventually became healed enough emotionally to let go of them, but then had to learn about nutrition. As she rearranged her diet, certain physical problems went away. The healing progressed, it seemed, at a pace she could handle and integrate into her life. It was a long time before she was healed of the major problems, physical, emotional, and spiritual. We worked hard, but it was well worth it.

While thanking God for, and marveling at, the powerful, dramatic, instantaneous healing I witness, I often wonder if the immediate removal of a painful physical problem does not sometimes short-circuit this gradual process of going deeper into a person's life and bringing before the Lord all the pieces of the puzzle. (This danger is eliminated if the person, besides attending healing services, is also receiving ongoing discipleship training or spiritual direction.) Sometimes the healing is gradual because God is using the healing process to work in the lives of other people.

I was privileged to be part of a large healing service for a few years in the mid-1970s at St. Timothy's Episcopal Church in Catonsville, Maryland. Led by the Rev. Philip C. Zampino, now a bishop in the Charismatic Episcopal Church, this service attracted several hundred people each week, and many healings took place. One evening, a blind girl was brought by her father. Father Zampino ministered to her, and there was some slight improvement. Near the end of the service at the altar call, which afforded people the opportunity to receive or rededicate themselves to Jesus, the girl's father came forward. His conversion seemed real, and subsequent events proved it to be both genuine and lasting.

For several weeks he brought his daughter to the services. Each week her eyes got a little bit better. And each week her father—who was taking in all he could in terms of his new relationship with the Lord—grew spiritually. Then one week he asked his wife to bring the girl. At the altar call she went forward. Soon the three of them were in church every Tuesday night. Other family members started noticing both the growing physical improvement in the girl and the profound change that had come over her parents. They started coming, too, and some of them found the Lord. The girl continued toward full sight, and the revival in her family spread.

Sometimes God allows healing to unfold gradually, and we should trust His sovereign wisdom when it does.

7. Healing is not God's immediate will

It could be that in the short haul, God is using the illness for a purpose, perhaps to get our attention, perhaps to remind us of our mortality or to teach us what is important in life. How many people have recovered from a brush with death to reorder the priorities in their lives? How many relationships have been strengthened when an illness forced people to look at what really matters? Perhaps God has urgent things to do in us before attending to our physical or emotional distresses.

However, do not overdo this point. If God is allowing the illness to continue for a reason, we need to do everything possible to find out that reason! If God wants us to learn a lesson, we need to learn it and not just remain sick. Then, once the lesson has been learned, the needed change implemented, the new attitude owned, and the new behavior begun, we should expect the healing to occur, sooner or later.

According to Victor Frankl, a therapist imprisoned in a Nazi concentration camp who lost his family in the Holocaust, suffering can be tolerated only when we can find meaning in it. The challenge for sufferers is to find a purpose deeper than the hurt itself. When we are sick or when we minister to someone who is sick, we need to direct effort toward learning whatever lessons await us as we pray for healing. Otherwise, should healing not come, we may turn bitter toward God, toward life, or toward others.

8. An "illness unto death"

If God is taking a person home through an "illness unto death," which Jesus mentions in John 11:4, our ministry should not be as much for restoration to health as it should be for spiritual and emotional preparation for death. Has the person made peace with God by receiving Jesus Christ as Lord and Savior? This is crucial. Where we will spend eternity is the most important matter we will ever face. The opening of the kingdom of heaven to all believers was the chief reason God the Father sent His Son to earth (John 3:16–18). However uncomfortable it may be to them and to us, we must speak clearly about eternal destiny, for the repeated teaching of Jesus is that not all will go to heaven when they die. How grateful I am that I did so with my maternal grandfather shortly before his death, and that he is now eternally safe in Jesus' arms!

Next, have they reconciled with loved ones? Are wills drawn up? Is there any other "unfinished business" that needs to be done?

Yet, we do pray for their physical well-being. I have seen many instances in which the patient remained ill, but was relieved of pain and discomfort, and died peacefully and lucid in conscious fellowship with God and loved ones.

What about those cases when we are not certain whether it is an illness unto death or not? It may be obvious with someone who is elderly, but what about someone much younger who suffers from a so-called terminal illness? Should our efforts be toward spiritual preparation for death or for physical healing?

The answer is both, but it takes a careful balancing of the two. We may have to contend with the denial of family members—and even physicians—who cannot face someone's death and who selfishly think it wise that the sick person "not be told" of his condition. In fact, most people nearing death know or suspect the seriousness of their conditions and want someone—anyone!—to talk with them about it. While we certainly want to express hope, we do not want to be swept up into the game many play, denying the severity of the illness. We are under no obligation to go along with family or medical staff admonitions not to tell the person of his condition. We do not want our conversations about death, on the other hand, and the necessary preparations for it to dash faith and hope for healing.

Let me illustrate how we can minister in that balanced way by telling you the story of someone I ministered to, a young woman I will call Kristi, who had terminal cancer. Kristi knew she was very sick. Fortunately, no one was hiding this from her.

Her parents asked me to minister to her. I asked Kristi how she was feeling. "Terrible, Father," she said. "It sounds like I am going to die. I do not want to, but some days the treatments make me so sick, I would like to die and get it over with."

We talked about her relationship with the Lord to make sure she understood the way of salvation. I discovered that she was trusting Jesus Christ as her Lord and Savior. With that most crucial issue resolved, we talked a bit about God's love, heaven as a place where there is no pain, and so on. We talked at some length about what unfinished business might be between herself and loved ones, and we worked out some plans as to what to do.

As I noticed she was tiring, I knew I should bring my visit to a close. "Kristi," I said, "we've been talking about your preparation in case you are going to die soon, but I don't know that this is what is going to happen. I don't know everything about why God does things one way one time, another way another time. But I have seen God heal people of cancer like yours. Will you pray with me for your healing?"

"I can't," she said. "I believe God can do anything, and I have seen answered prayer, but I have never seen anything like this happen."

"Well, Kristi," I replied, "if I can't pray *with* you, I would like to pray *for* you right now. And I am going to get a number of 'prayer warriors' to intercede for you. OK?"

"OK."

That was several years ago. Not only is Kristi in a wonderful relationship with God, but she is also close to her loved ones and still here with us.

"Spontaneous remission," the doctors called it.

"Yes, certainly," we responded. "And we know who caused it."

9. Not enough power in the ones ministering

If being an instrument of grace can be likened to holding God with one hand and the sick person with the other, our usefulness as an instrument depends to some degree on our grasp of both God and the sick person. If, through ego, condemnation, superiority, or laziness, we do not care about people, we will have a "faulty connection" on that end. It will be difficult for blessings to flow through us into them. If, on the other hand, our grasp of God is weak, little or no blessing will flow into us in the first place. The "power shortage" can exist for several reasons.

We are faithless. We do not think God really wants to heal people or use us to do it. We have taken a God-centered ministry of power and turned it into mere human love and sympathy, woefully short of the fullness of what God wants for people and what He can do through His yielded vessels. When the disciples asked Jesus why they could not cast out a demon, He responded, "Because of *your* little faith" (Matthew 17:20, emphasis added). Jesus did not just comfort people in their illness—He healed them!

We are lazy. Spiritual growth demands work, sacrifice, and surrender. Many are willing to follow Christ at a superficial level, but they hit a plateau when much else is demanded. Although God can, and often does, use us in spite of our inadequacies, the person God uses best, regularly and most powerfully, is the one who takes time to work hard on spiritual growth. Think, if you need convincing, about your golf game (or your equivalent of it). While even a duffer can hit the occasional great shot, it is best described as a fluke. Those who do well consistently are those who work at their game.

We are proud. We think we can effect healing by our own willpower or by checking in with God occasionally. This is especially likely if we have been used by God previously. After a while we start to think we are "good at healing" and forget we need His moment-by-moment empowering. There have been times in healing services when I noticed a drop-off in "results." I realized that, while I had started the prayer time for others with abject dependence on God, as the service progressed, and especially as things were happening, I relied less on God and more on my experience, knowledge, and stamina.

We are embarrassed. For many of us, speaking of the things of God is embarrassing, no matter how deeply we believe them. Or we forget that, while Christianity is personal, it is not private. We must overcome this reticence, lest our ministry become merely armchair psychology.

Those of us ministering healing need humbly to acknowledge that part of the problem may be ours and not the person's to whom we are ministering. Yet, how often have we been to healing services in which people were told, "If you are not healed tonight, it is because you do not have enough faith"? That may well be true, as we will see shortly. But it may be true that the problem lies with the one(s) ministering.

No, we should not allow Satan to condemn us when we fall short, or be deeply distraught at every failure. But at the same time, we may need to confess we have let people down. Our attitude should be that of my physician-wife: "Many people are depending on me. By God's grace I have to do the best job I can."

10. No perseverance

Most people have no difficulty understanding the need for a lengthy course of medical treatments. But many expect God's healing always to be immediate. If nothing happens or seems to happen, they give up. Since some healing is gradual, and perhaps involves a variety of factors coming into play, perseverance is necessary. Do not give up! God is just beginning to work.

This is why a church healing ministry that concentrates only on the occasional big healing mission fails to bring healing to more than just a few people. Much better, in addition to such missions, is faithful, week-by-week ministry in Sunday worship services. The ongoing "cure of souls" through confession, counseling, spiritual direction, preaching, teaching, prayer, worship, the sacraments, and intentional, specific prayer for healing yields great fruit in people's lives.

Furthermore, those who avail themselves regularly of all these aspects of spiritual growth find them also to be preventive medicine. As emotional and spiritual problems are nipped in the bud, or even prevented from budding, many of the diseases that might have occurred are prevented.

11. Negative thinking or not enough faith

It is perhaps here that the greatest controversy about healing occurs. For some, "not enough faith" is an easy solution to the problem of not being healed. For others, the idea that God would withhold a blessing because of some lack on our part is inconsistent with their view of God.

In fact, the Scriptures, illustrated in human experience, present a picture that is more complex. Our Lord performed hundreds of healings. We see this reflected in such statements as "many followed him, and he healed them all" (Matthew 12:15; see also Luke 4:40). We have, however, specific information about slightly more than three dozen individuals healed by our Lord. These "case histories" present a wealth of information. (See Appendix 3.) From them, we see the relationship of faith and healing. We discover that sometimes faith, or its lack, is a key in healing. At other times faith does not seem to be a factor.

Let us look first at faith, or more precisely, faith in Jesus to heal, as a factor on the part of the sick person.

On several occasions Jesus ministered in response to a person's faith. In Matthew 9:29, Jesus said, "According to your faith be it done to you. (See also Matthew 9:22.) On the negative side we read the sad notation, "And he did not do many mighty works there, because of their unbelief" (Matthew 13:58).

Why is faith so important? First, we know the value of a positive mental attitude. Two people can be suffering from the same illness, have the same bodily strength to recover, yet one dies and the other lives. Physicians often use the phrase "the patient's will to live" to describe that intangible, yet real, component in the recovery process that is akin to faith. The placebo effect is one reason (the other being satanic counterfeits) why there are cures in all sorts of religious healing services, sane or wild, Christian or otherwise. We Christians need not make ourselves look foolish by denying either the reality or the value of such recoveries. It is obvious that sick persons have recovered, and we should be glad they are better—though we should inform them that beyond cure of what ails them, the greater blessing of wholeness is found only in Christ. We should also warn them that certain non-Christian healing practices, though obviously effecting something good in the short run, can do damage down the road, whether to their wallets, their emotions, or their spiritual lives.

But faith is much more than positive mental attitude. It is trust in the Lord—in who He is, what He does, and what He wants to do for us. Faith does not mean just believing certain doctrines (although this is important, for Jesus said in John 8:32 that it is the truth that sets us free). Faith is also trust. Faith is entrusting ourselves, our hopes, our fears, our needs, and our hurts to God. Further, faith is "trust in motion." It is trusting God enough for us to act, knowing He will give the increase.

God is respectful of our personhood. He has given us free will to accept or reject Him. He allows the believer to turn various parts of his life over to Him or keep control over them himself. This is illustrated in the story of the rich young ruler in Matthew 19:16–22. Jesus wanted him as a disciple, but the man chose not to pay the price. Although Jesus encouraged him and warned him of the consequences of not following Him, the choice was ultimately the man's.

Faith as applied to healing means, "Jesus, I give You permission to go to work on my life. Fix what is broken. Point out to me what I have to do, and show me where my sins are blocking what You want to do. I trust You to do Your part. Please teach and empower me to do mine."

Always remember: faith is not an emotion. Nor is it something a few people are lucky enough to have while others do not. Nor is it the possession of those with a certain personality type. *Faith is firm, confident trust in God who has proven Himself trustworthy.*

How, then, is faith engendered?

We can ask God for faith. We can be like the man who said to Jesus, "I believe; help my unbelief" (Mark 9:24). It is a request God delights to answer.

Faith also grows as we meditate on who God is, what He has done for others in the past, and what He has done in our own lives. As we pray—unless our prayers are rote recitation or merely a list of wants—we learn about Him. As we read Scripture and Christian biographies, we see in a variety of people, many like ourselves, how God works. As we recall what God has done for us in the past, we remember His love and provision.

One aid to this, one practiced by many of the great saints of God throughout Church history, is to keep a diary, a journal, or what I call a "miracle notebook." Whenever our faith wavers in God's ability or desire to bless us and help meet our needs, we can turn to page after page of accounts how at various times, in various needs, and in various ways God answered our prayers. The result? Firmer confidence—*faith.* As we thus focus on God, we emulate the psalmist who said, "I will call to mind the deeds of the LORD; yea, I will remember thy wonders of old" (Psalm 77:11).

And yet, it is not the amount of faith that is important, but rather in whom our faith is placed. We do not have to have great faith in God. What we need is faith in God who is great. Jesus told us our faith needs only to be as a mustard seed, the tiniest seed in the garden (Matthew 13:31–32). But for that seed to grow, it needs to be watered, fertilized, and protected from predators.

Our devotional lives, practiced regularly and devoutly, water the seeds of faith so they will be sufficient when we need them.

What about times when faith is not present in the person who is sick? At times, personal faith falters, often when we need it most. The devil has snatched it from us, the busyness of life has choked it out, or the bad experiences we are going through have acted like hard soil to keep faith from sprouting. (Compare this with the parable of the seeds and soils Jesus told in Matthew 13.) In times like these, it is so good to be part of a community of faith upon whom we can lean. While obviously we cannot presume upon this—if everyone were always leaning on everyone else, the whole pile would soon topple or the one or two whose faith remains strong would soon be exhausted—what a joy it is for the faith of others to help us!

Roughly half of the accounts of our Lord healing specific individuals illustrate the results of such vicarious faith. Jairus, by seeking out Jesus, exercised faith on behalf of his daughter (Mark 5:22–23). The centurion did the same on behalf of his servant (Luke 7:2–3). Four men acted on their faith by raising a roof and lowering their paralyzed friend into Jesus' presence (Mark 2:2–5). In each case, Jesus healed the hurting person in response to the faith *of others.*

As priestly people of God we can intercede for others, taking them to God's throne of grace. (See Hebrews 4:16; 1 Peter 2:5, 9; Revelation 1:6.) What a responsibility, but what a privilege as well!

While the sick person may not need faith to believe that anything good will happen, he must allow God to work. In other words, while the sick person does not necessarily need to have positive faith in Jesus for healing, he does need to cooperate, however passively. Active "negative faith"—refusing to let Jesus go to work, or dismissing anything good that starts to happen—can be a barrier to healing. This is not out of divine anger or punishment, but out of respect for the freedom God has given us.

What about the role of emotions? If faith is confident trust in God, where do the emotions fit in? As with so many things in the Christian faith, a fine balance is the answer. We know how music, worship, and a beautiful sunset can engender a religious encounter with God. No doctrinal content is imparted, but something powerful is experienced, often to the strengthening of our faith. Affective—that is, nonrational, noncognitive—learning is important.

Let us use music as an example. Music can soothe, as we see in 1 Samuel 16:23 when the young David played the lyre for Saul. Music can inspire. The psalmist wrote in Psalm 22:3 that God dwells in the praises of His people; as He dwells there, music can release faith or deepen it. I know someone who was healed physically at an organ recital I once gave. A simple worship service can bring us face to face with Jesus and His love. An ornate liturgy can let our spirits soar as we enter into the lofty transcendence of God's majesty. A service beside a lake can minister peace to us, as can a candlelight service. All these things can help faith.

A few words of caution. Any experience of God must be checked against the truths of Scripture. Just as not all spirits are of God, neither are all religious experiences. (See 1 John 4:1.)

Nor are all uses of emotion-filled services wise. Joseph Goebbels used martial music and pageantry to manipulate the German multitudes into a frenzied desire for war. I have been at services in which people have been worked into a froth. Some healings occurred, but they were generally transient ones. The persons seemed to be healed, but a few days later, when the emotional rush subsided, the problems came back. Emotion is good when it enhances faith, but not when it manipulates the worshiper.

What about the phrase "Please heal me if it be Your will"? While this sounds like a good prayer, a humble waiting on God's sovereign will, it sows seeds of doubt.

God has amply demonstrated His desire to heal us in what His Word says and in what Jesus did. Although there may be exceptions, we should not center our theology on the exceptions but in the dominant teaching of Scripture: God wishes to heal. To pray "if" bespeaks a rejection of Scripture. It is no different from praying, "Lord, give me Your grace to keep the Ten Commandments, if it be Your will." Such a prayer undermines belief.

We must be careful, on the other hand, not to tell God exactly what to do, when to do it, and how. In the so-called "positive confession" theology, one is encouraged to make a positive confession: "I am being healed," or even "I am healed right now." Not to believe that, or to give any regard to remaining symptoms of the problem, is, according to followers of positive confession teaching, a faithless "claiming" of the problem.

A fuller discussion of the theological difficulties we should have with such teaching will have to wait until chapter eight. Suffice it to say, such a belief is not faith but presumption.

If the prayer "Lord, heal me if it be Your will" is a prayer of doubt, and the assertion "I am healed right now" is a statement of presumption, where is the balance? I believe the best prayer we can offer for healing is something like this: "Lord, confident in both Your promise and Your example, I know You are on the side of health and of my being healed. I pray, then, heal me *in accordance with Your will.* I affirm Your loving power and powerful love, and I leave the details up to You." This balanced prayer affirms confidently the fact that God wants to heal us while it honors His sovereignty in allowing Him to determine when and how.

So what should we conclude about the relationship between faith and healing?

1. Faith is confident trust in God, who has proven trust-worthy.

2. Faith involves emotions, but it does not center on them.

3. Faith is not a product of manipulation. Rather, it is a gift of God for which we can pray, and it is strengthened as we meditate on who God is and what He has done, as recorded in Scripture, in our lives, and in the lives of others.

4. Faith helps us be healed in the sense that it gives God permission to work in our lives.

5. As the priestly people of God, we can pray effectively for others, especially to help those with weak or nonexistent faith.

6. Not everyone need have faith in order to be healed, but those who deliberately set up barriers seriously diminish the likelihood of being blessed.

7. To avoid the extremes of doubt and presumption, the best attitude to express is, "Please heal me, Lord, *in accordance with Your will.*"

12. God's kingdom realized only partially on earth now

The birth, life, death, and resurrection of Jesus Christ began, in a new and special way, the kingly rule of God on earth. The rule of Satan, the prince of demons and the prince of this world (as described in Matthew 12:24 and John 14:30), is being rolled back. Even a cursory glance at the world situation will remind us that the defeat of darkness and the establishment of light is not yet complete.

I use the term *kingly rule* rather than *kingdom* because it is a better translation of the New Testament Greek and because the word *kingdom* implies a settled territory under the control of a particular ruler. The reality is quite different. As with many a country involved in civil war, people in the same community, even the same family, give allegiance to different leaders, and the final victory of one group over the other has not yet occurred. Those following the Lord and those following the evil one, including the spiritually indifferent, are still caught up in the raging spiritual warfare (2 Corinthians 10:3–4; Ephesians 6:12). The beachhead of God has been established, but the final victory has not been secured. How, then, should we live, and what should we expect in terms of the pervasiveness of God's healing?

Perhaps I can illustrate by a comparison with the latter days of the Second World War in Europe.[1] On June 6, 1944, when the invasion of Normandy established the Allied beachhead in Europe, British Prime Minister Winston Churchill said, "The war is over." Churchill knew much fighting and dying still lay ahead. But he also knew that, because the Allies were now established firmly in Northern Europe, and other Allied soldiers were working their way up through Italy, the outcome of the war was no longer in doubt. The only unknown was when. On May 8, 1945, Victory in Europe Day, or V-E Day, was celebrated. On that day, the war in Europe was literally over, and the blessings of peace could be celebrated confidently.

What would a wise sergeant say to his soldier during that "in-between time" between June 6, 1944, and May 8, 1945? It would depend on the soldier's attitude. If the soldier were despondent, weary from fighting, and longing for a decent meal, a warm, dry bed, and reunion with loved ones, his sergeant might say, "Chin up! The war rages on, but victory is in sight." Sad to say, some soldiers gave up emotionally just as the war was concluding.

But if the soldier were cocky, presuming on the military successes just secured and running around foolishly, the sergeant might say, "Head down! The victory is in sight, but the war rages on." Sad to say, some soldiers moving about without their helmets died just before V-E Day.

In the spring of circa A.D. 30, Jesus established the beachhead on earth. His cry was, "It is finished" (John 19:30). This was not an agonized cry of despair; He did not say, "*I* am finished," but, "*It* is finished"—the work of redemption. His atoning death on the cross marked the beginning of the end for Satan. Historically, the Church has described this as our Lord's wrestling Satan and winning, though momentarily dying in the process (Colossians 2:15; see Gustav Aulen's *Christus Victor* for a good expression of this understanding of the atonement). It has also been described as Jesus giving Himself as a ransom payment to free souls locked in Satan's prison (Mark 10:45; see

Leon Morris' masterful exegesis of the word *ransom* in *Apostolic Preaching of the Cross*).

At some time in the future, a time Jesus said even He did not know, He will return (Matthew 24:36). His Second Coming will be the ultimate V-E Day, Victory-Earth Day, for at that time the kingdoms of this world will become the kingdom of our God and of His Christ, and He shall reign forever (Revelation 11:15).

What might a pastor say to the Christian community as we now live between the times? To the despondent, to those believers burdened with their struggles against sin, the fiery darts of the enemy, and recurrent sickness of body and soul, he would say: "Chin up! The victory is assured. We are no longer in darkness. Messiah has come. 'The people who walked in darkness have seen a great light' (Isaiah 9:2). 'Greater is He who is in you than he who is in the world'" (1 John 4:4, NAS).

But to the cocky, to those who, because Christ has come into their hearts, expect that all should be well, the battle against temptation easy, every prayer answered immediately, and all sickness taken away quickly, he would say, "Head down! The battle is still on. We still wrestle against principalities and powers. We still succumb to sin. Some sickness still occurs, and some even remains. So be sober, be vigilant. Your adversary the devil still prowls around like a lion seeking someone to devour." (See Ephesians 6:12; 1 Peter 5:8.)

What does this have to do with the question of why some remain sick? Simply that for all our prayers and faith, for all our making use of the various means God has given us for our healing and ruling none of them out, some believers will still get sick, and a few will even stay sick. (While the health of Christians, especially those who believe in and pray for healing, is better than the general populace,[2] and while Christians experience remarkable healings when they get sick, we are not immune to sickness, and the road to healing and wholeness is long.) Sometimes it is because of a lack in the sick person or in the community of faith, but sometimes it is because Satan is not yet totally conquered. Sometimes he wins a little victory in us. It is important to acknowledge, in the interest of balance, that we are living between the times. Some churches act as if the Messiah has not yet come. They *say* that Christ has come, two thousand years ago in Bethlehem, but they *act* as if the kingly rule of the Lord has not begun and that the blessings of His kingly rule are not yet available. As a result, they have no confident expectation that healing will take place. Other churches act as if He has already returned in His Second Coming. They *say* that the Second Coming is in the future, but they *act* as if all God's blessings occur now, unsullied by any lingering satanic action or human sin.

We can remind both groups that in Communion, we have a powerful, effectual sacrament, the appetizer course to the Messianic banquet, the "Marriage Supper of the Lamb" John wrote about in Revelation 19:9, but God and His people are not yet at that banquet. We can remind them that while the teachings of Christ are known, and the barrier between us and the Father has been rent in two, we still know only in part and see through a dark glass (Matthew 27:51; 1 Corinthians 13:12).

Wonderful healing blessings are available now, but to expect total healing is as presumptuous as sitting prematurely at the heavenly banquet table, claiming to have complete understanding or imagining we know God perfectly.

Failure to grasp the significance of living between the times for Christian healing has serious consequences for the Church community. Churches that are like the despondent soldier do not offer healing. If they do, it is with little encouragement, expectancy, or seriousness. Parishioners miss out on blessings they might otherwise receive. Churches that are like the cocky soldier offer healing confidently and frequently, but woebetide those who are not healed! Something must be wrong with the person, they figure, or he would be healed.

While this is sometimes true, it is not always. Too many people are still sick whose faith is strong, whose sins are confessed and repented of, and whose compliance with everything that makes for healing is strong. The result? On top of their sickness come the judgment and condemnation, however masked with politeness, of their fellow Christians. Another result: they have to live in denial of the problem to others and perhaps even to themselves.

I met a woman once who was obviously physically sick, yet she said she was fine. When I commented that she did not look fine, she told me that in her church she had learned to say she was fine even when she was not. If she told them her problem, they would scold her for "claiming" her illness and accuse her of having some deep, unconfessed sin, a rebellious spirit, laziness about the things of God, or worse.

"Then how do people get others to pray for their real needs?" I asked her.

"They don't. Everyone has to present a happy face at all times."

Sooner or later that church will collapse. The question is, how many people will be seriously hurt, emotionally and spiritually, in the meantime?

There is mystery here. We affirm the beautiful testimonies of healing from many people, yet wonder why the Rev. Canon David C. K. Watson, one of the leaders of renewal and healing in the Church of England, who followed all the "rules" of what one should do when falling sick, died in his early fifties of cancer. We can also cite as example the early death of charismatic author Jamie Buckingham and that of John Wimber, founder of the Association of Vineyard Churches. There is much we can affirm, yet much we do not know. Let us celebrate the blessings of healing, remove the roadblocks that are observable and removable, and live in the mystery that only in heaven will it all be explained.

DISCUSSION QUESTIONS

1. Use one or two sentences to paraphrase the essence of each of the twelve reasons why some are not healed.

2. A respectable scholar, seeking a precise, linguistically
    correct definition of the biblical word *faith*, as used in
    the context of healing, declared it to be *chutzpah*. What
    do you think he was saying?

EXPERIMENT

Repeat the experiment at the end of chapter one, but with a new
"patient." Use new ideas from your study so far.

CHAPTER 5

Sin, Sickness, Repentance, Healing

ONE OF THE reasons people get sick and stay sick is sin. I am not saying that every time a person is sick, it is because God is punishing him or her.[1] What I am saying is that there is often a connection, a cause-and-effect relationship, between sin and sickness, between repentance and health.

We read in the second chapter of Mark that the forgiveness of the paralyzed man led to his healing (Mark 2:5–12). We discover our Lord's admonition to the man at the pool of Bethesda in John 5 that he should "sin no more, that nothing worse befall you" (John 5:14). We find a connection in James 5 between the elders' healing ministry of prayer and anointing, and the call to confession of sin (James 5:14–16).

Why this connection between sin and sickness, between repentance and health? God has given us principles for living. These principles work. As Jesus said:

The truth will make you free.

—JOHN 8:32

God has given us the free will to go against what He has told us, and when we do, we sin. When we disobey, we are not so much breaking God's laws as we are breaking ourselves, or others, against them. When we sin against God, we remove ourselves from the place where the shower of divine blessings falls. God has promised us abundant blessings and new life (John 10:10; 2 Corinthians 5:1–7), but we cannot always experience the blessings of health when our spiritual laziness or deliberate disobedience removes us from the place God has chosen to put the blessings. God has not proven unfaithful; we have (2 Timothy 2:12–13). In short, when we sin, God does not harm us; rather, we place a barrier between God and ourselves.

Let me give a few examples. If we smoke four packs of cigarettes a day, we should not be surprised that we suffer from shortness of breath or develop lung cancer. If we are promiscuous, we should not be surprised if we contract a sexually transmitted disease. In both cases, the negative consequences to our health are self-inflicted.

The harm of sin can be seen in three kinds of relationships: with God, with others, and with ourselves. Please remember: this division of sin into three categories, while useful for discussion, should not lead us to believe things are divided this neatly in life. Still, all sin is in some way sin against God, against others, and against ourselves.

Sins Against God

The most fundamental sickness a person has is estrangement from God. God is holy, and our rebellion against Him has placed a barrier between us (Isaiah 59:2). Ever since the sin of Adam, people have bumped up against this barrier that keeps them from enjoying perfect fellowship and a life free from difficulty. When Adam hid himself from God, he demonstrated his awareness of how sullied his relationship with God had become (Genesis 3:10). Adam's new propensity to sin and his instinctive urge to run away from God have been part of the human condition ever since. From Adam we inherited spiritual estrangement and a desire to disobey. This is what theologians call "original sin." To that inheritance we add our own individual sins.

The consequence of sinning, according to Scripture, is physical and spiritual death (Genesis 3:19; John 3:18; Romans 6:23). When confronted with this divinely issued death sentence, many of us want to protest that our sins "are not that bad." But the truly holy person, the one whose chief aim in life is to please God, is usually most aware of how much he or she is still fallen. To object that God is wrong in issuing this sentence against us is, in itself, a sign of how much we want to be in charge of our own lives and deny God that right. It is not against the prevailing standards of society that we compare our own behavior, but against God's will for us. As Jesus pointed out in the Sermon on the Mount, we might not be committing adultery literally, but anyone who lusts after another in his heart has, in God's eyes, committed that sin (Matthew 5:27–28).

Because God is holy, no sin is excused. And yet, is there no hope? Because God is loving, He opened a way that upholds both punishment of sin and forgiveness of the sinner. He sent His Son to pay the penalty of our sins for us. Throughout the Old Testament we see God preparing His people for Jesus by instructing the Jews to sacrifice unblemished lambs as offering for their sins. They came to see that sacrifice for sin is necessary, and that unless they were going to suffer the consequences themselves, they needed someone or something to do it for them. Year by year the sacrificial lambs were offered to prepare God's people for the coming of Jesus, "the Lamb of God, who takes away the sin of the world" (John 1:29). By offering Himself on the cross as a pure sacrifice for sin, Jesus became the Savior of those who would put their trust in Him (Romans 5:8; 1 Peter 2:24; 3:18; 1 John 3:16). Those who receive Him are given forgiveness of sins and adoption as sons and daughters of God (John 1:12).

God's upholding of both His holiness and His love is the model the Church is to follow. Some churches, usually extremely conservative ones, uphold God's standards in such a way as to bring condemnation on those who fall. They not only hate the sin; they hate the sinner. The problem rampant in the mainline denominations is the opposite. In an attempt to be accepting and inclusive, they allow all manner of perversion. They not only love the sinner; they allow various kinds of perversion.

We find New Testament balance in the way Jesus reached out to the woman caught in the act of adultery (John 8:3–11). While He refused to condemn the woman, He exhorted her not to sin again.

The apostolic Church debated whether or not to include Gentiles. (See Acts 15.) They concluded that Gentiles could be admitted, but only if they forsook pagan practices and immorality. For the Church today to be true to the teaching and example of her Lord, we must demonstrate a similar "love-the-sinner-hate-the-sin" attitude. We are to reach out with love to those who are marginalized by society and call them, as the Lord calls everyone, to forsake their sin and turn to Him.

In addition to being the Savior of individuals, Jesus inaugurated the kingdom of God. Although its completion comes at His Second Coming, we taste substantial fruits of it now. While emotional turmoil rages around us and within us, it is still possible on earth to enjoy "the peace of God, which surpasses all understanding" (Philippians 4:7). We may get sick, but healing is available. Our human bodies are subject to decay, but believers in Christ will rise to newness of life with Him.

As for this latter point, it is wrong, theologically and pastorally, to encourage someone by saying that in death God took a loved one home. Rather, *death* took the loved one from us, but God has taken away death from those who have put their trust in Christ.

How do we receive Christ's free gift of eternal life, this now-and-forever healing of the most fundamental of all sicknesses— estrangement from God? We receive it as we do any other gift:

We simply take it with thanks. If you have never done this, or if you are not certain that Christ has taken the penalty for your sins, you might offer a simple prayer to God like this:

> *Heavenly Father, I admit to You that I am a sinner. I have sinned in thought, word, deed, and by what I have failed to do. I acknowledge that I cannot earn my salvation, but I need Jesus to be my Savior. I know that He died on the cross to pay the penalty for my sins. I now ask Jesus to be my Savior, to take the penalty of my sins away so that I can have fellowship with You, both now and in heaven. Thank You, Jesus, for being my Savior. Amen.*

When we receive Jesus as Savior, we also promise to receive Him as Lord of our lives. It is not possible to separate the two. No Christian believer will ever be free from committing sin. But what God wants when we ask Jesus to be our Lord and Savior is, first, our desire to surrender to Jesus as Lord, and second, a regular, good-faith effort to do our best, instructed by the Scriptures, aided by the Holy Spirit, and in active participation in a church.

Even after a person has received Jesus as Lord and Savior, there can be spiritual sickness from time to time. To be sure, it is far less serious a problem than before he came to salvation. But it is a problem nonetheless. Suppose I were adopted into a family and had a fight with my adoptive father. I would still be his son, but our relationship would be impaired.

The degree to which a Christian is aloof from or rebellious toward God is the degree to which the relationship with God is sick. God did not send Christ to die for our sins only to have us accept salvation but reject a personal relationship with Him. God made us to know Him, to enjoy Him, to glorify Him, to be beloved by Him, and to live according to His commandments.

As for aloofness from God, we must remember that, while our good behavior is important, *God first wants us*. Let me give you an example.

When I was doing my graduate work in England, I stayed with a number of families during vacations. One was a working-class family living in Birmingham. There was a lot of noise and confusion in the home, the children did not always do everything they should, and harsh words were sometimes exchanged. Apparent immediately, though, was a deep and abiding love between children and parents. Another family with whom I stayed was upper class and lived in a posh section of London. There was wealth and luxury, even "hot and cold running servants." The children were polite. They observed all the social graces. They never seemed to do anything wrong. But it became obvious that their relationships with their parents were built on formal politeness, not love. Any love they had was for the nannies and governesses who reared them.

I have often asked parents which sort of children they would like. Nearly everyone opts for the children who, despite their faults, are in a relationship of closeness and warmth. Is God any different from this?

As for rebellion against God, spiritual sickness can also come through slipping back into spiritual lethargy or by an intentional refusal to make Jesus Christ sovereign over one's life. The earliest creedal formula in the Church was the simple statement "Jesus is Lord" (1 Corinthians 12:3). Many Christians are quite willing to worship God, do things for God, and ask favors of God. The stumbling block is obedience. Jesus saw that many followed Him for whatever they could get out of it. They did not want to obey. "Why do you call me 'Lord, Lord,' and not do what I tell you?" He once asked (Luke 6:46). Our love of God, while involving thoughts and emotions, includes much more. "If you love me," Jesus said, "you will keep my commandments" (John 14:15).

Keeping the commandments is much more than dos and don'ts. (See Matthew 23:23.) Fundamentally it is attitude or disposition. Do I want to do just what is socially respectable, or is my fundamental desire to please by comparing every aspect of my thoughts, words, and deeds against His revealed will?

Community standards of what is acceptable have changed considerably in the past few decades. Some etiquette writers have revised their works to supply "proper" ways to do various things that God calls sin. Several etiquette books, for example, now list the "correct" way to address an invitation to two people living together apart from marriage. Apart from a careful examination of the revealed will of God in Scripture, it is likely that we may be approved by others in polite society while breaking many of God's commandments. God wants more than believers—*He wants disciples.* We are to observe everything He taught (Matthew 28:20). To do less is sin.

In identifying our own sins for the purpose of amending our lives, I find it helpful to study Scripture with Christian believers who come from different cultural or political backgrounds. Why? No matter how committed we are to the Lord and to His written Word, no matter how much we ask the Holy Spirit to guide our understanding, we read the Bible with blinders on.

Several years ago I spent some time teaching clergy in various locations around Kenya. Toward the end of my stay in one location, I pulled aside the local bishop, a man I had known when he studied in Boston, and told him that while there was much admirable in the spiritual life of Kenyan Christians, I was puzzled at how these otherwise obedient disciples could be so unobservant of the Lord's clear teaching in certain matters.

"It is our cultural legacy from the days before we knew Jesus," he said. "In spite of a century of teaching, our people are still blind to what God's Word says about these things."

I was feeling smug until he continued, "When I studied in America, I noticed that while there was much that was admirable in the spiritual life of American Christians..."

One of the ways we can overcome cultural blinders is by studying Scripture with believers from other cultures, with the understanding that we will set aside superficial politeness and lovingly hold one another accountable.

We can note the same blindness when it comes to ideology. Simply put, biblical Christians who are "conservative" by nature tend to be more attuned to some scriptural commandments than others, while biblical Christians who are "liberal" by nature tend to do the same thing with different scriptural commands. Although this is a generality and exceptions are many, "conservative" Christians tend to be acutely sensitive to sexual sins and drug and alcohol (ab)use, while less concerned or even indifferent to matters of racial justice and environmental stewardship. "Liberal" Christians tend to be the opposite. Once again, the solution is the same: study Scripture with people who uphold the authority and reliability of all of God's Word, but who come with a different ideological makeup.

SINS AGAINST OTHERS

Such sins as resentment, bitterness, jealousy, and unresolved anger hurt us spiritually, emotionally, and physically. Let me give you an example. I was once leading a conference at a church in New York. The rector asked if I would accompany him to visit a sick woman bedridden with paralysis. I was not in the woman's room for more than a minute before she launched into a stream of angry invective against her sister. I tried to suggest gently that God's will is forgiveness, and that sometimes paralysis comes from our attitudes. This was nothing original with me, nor was it particularly a Christian insight. Medical people say the same thing. Nor was I being judgmental. I was simply diagnosing the situation.

"I would rather be bedridden than forgive that no-good sister of mine!" she shouted at me. I tried to tell her that that might be exactly what would happen.

I had occasion a year later to speak to her rector again. "Is so-and-so still angry?" I asked him.

"Yes," he replied.

"Is she still bedridden?"

"Of course."

Another year passed, and I was invited back to the church to teach. I made sure I visited the woman.

"I suppose you are going to try to convince me to forgive my sister, aren't you?" was how she greeted me when I entered her room.

"No, actually, I am not," I replied. My thought was that nothing short of a dramatic confrontation would get through, much as an intervention of tough love is sometimes the way to get the message across to an alcoholic. "You can be bitter, or you can forgive. It is your choice, not mine."

After a very long pause, she looked at me through heavy eyes and said, "I am tired of being bedridden. I am tired of being angry. I know I should forgive, but how? I do not feel it, even though I know I should."

Forgiveness, I told her, is not a matter of feelings. Forgiveness is a choice we make, and it involves several steps.

First, she should ask God for grace, for we cannot do this without His help.

Second, she should confess her own faults—not just the sin of bitterness, but also every sin in her life she could remember. Part of the reason for this was to remind her that she was no better, sin-wise, than her sister. (See Matthew 7:5.)

Third, she should pray blessings for her sister. Often when we "pray" for others, we are really telling God how to change them. It is an attitude of judging, of superiority; hardly the framework for forgiveness. Positive prayers are prayers that God will bless them, make things go well for them, and so on. I have found it difficult to stay angry with someone for whom I am regularly positively praying. These prayers may at first be offered out of sheer duty, but eventually our feelings will mellow. The *feeling* of forgiveness follows the *action* of forgiveness.

Fourth, as these things were underway, she should start praying for reconciliation. One must be very careful to make sure the motive for this is correct. To call up someone, no matter how badly he or she treated us, and say, "I am calling to tell you I have forgiven you for all the bad things you have done to me," is hardly going to affect reconciliation. A better attitude and approach is to say, "We have been estranged for some time now. I know that I have done and said things that have been wrong. I know I have hurt you. I ask your forgiveness."

Some people use the word *sorry* when asking forgiveness, as in "I am sorry we had a fight." Sometimes all that does is express regret without actually admitting fault. While it is certainly unhealthy to wallow in guilt or blame oneself for everything, neither is it enough just to say, "Sorry." Far better is to say, "I was wrong, please forgive me."

Often, something wonderful happens. Humbling ourselves and asking for forgiveness can release the other person to do the same. So many times in asking forgiveness I have been told, "Mark, I do forgive you. But part of the fault lies with me. Please forgive me for how I treated you." Not only does such reconciliation remove a barrier and reestablish a relationship; often the relationship is much stronger.

But a note of caution. Asking for forgiveness is not always met with a reciprocal request. Sometimes we hear, "Well, I should certainly hope so, after the way you behaved!" In cases like that we are not to say, "Wait a minute! I did my part; now it is your turn!" That would nullify the step of asking forgiveness. We would be building the wall of estrangement back up again. Even if only 10 percent of the sin that led to the initial estrangement was our fault, we are responsible for that 10 percent. We are not responsible for the other person's part. Let God deal with him or her on that.

There may be little else we can do about another's attitude except to pray. Realize, however, that feelings of anger may well up within us because of his refusal to be reconciled or to ask our forgiveness. These feelings have to be dealt with. Otherwise, if repressed or denied, they will lead to bitterness and resentment.

Forgiving others does not mean that we have to allow inappropriate behavior to continue. Forgiving a spouse who beats you does not mean returning home for more. Forgiving an alcoholic family member does not mean continuing to cover for him or her.

The spouse returning home for another beating may be evidencing a subconscious self-loathing attitude of "I am a nobody and worthy only of more abuse." More appropriate is this response: "I will forgive and pray for you, but I will no longer submit to beatings. I will work on my own inadequacies, and until you get serious, sustained help, I will not return to you." Making excuses for an alcoholic, far from being an act of Christian love, may be an expression of codependent "enabling." While we are to love alcoholics and let go of any bitterness or judgment, we must let them take responsibility for their behavior. Such "tough love" may be the only way alcoholics will face the truth about their problem.

Just as we can sin against others, the sins of others can harm us. If an unscrupulous company dumps its toxic waste near a water supply, the local residents might become physically sick. Or if a person has been molested in his youth, he might grow up with various emotional disorders, some of which might cause physical illness. Here too is a critical factor in our search for healing. We will examine it more fully in the next chapter.

SINS AGAINST OURSELVES

Our bodies are the temples of the Holy Spirit (1 Corinthians 6:19). They do not belong to us, but are God's property. We are called to be good stewards of them. If we harm them by wrong actions or by neglect, we are damaging what belongs to God, and we render ourselves less able to do His work. Here is yet another example of how sinning against ourselves is sinning against God and others. Under this heading of the stewardship of our bodies come exercise, the right amount of sleep, diet, weight, rest or playtime relative to work, and so on.

Unfortunately, in some Christian circles this has been expressed in a selective legalism against certain "taboos," while other harmful practices are not mentioned. I once heard a fiery Pentecostal preacher rail against tobacco and the harm to one's body it causes. My concern while listening to him, though, was whether this 300-pound man would make it through his sermon without suffering a heart attack! His harangue against the "demon weed of tobacco" was based not so much on a consistent theology of turning from that which could harm the body as it was on specific taboos in his denomination. He should have been more comprehensive in his understanding of what harms us. As good Christian stewards, we need to examine carefully how we take care—or do not take care—of our bodies. Not to do so is sin, and it can hurt us.

Similarly, we sin against and harm ourselves by wrong attitudes. The stressed, hard-driving, impatient, anxious person is more likely to be ill. Jesus tells us, "Do not be anxious" (Matthew 6:25). While our Lord did not say, "Be irresponsible," He does want us to let the burden of the solution to things rest with Him. Long before the phrase "Stop and smell the roses" became popular, our blessed Lord invited us to "consider the lilies" (Matthew 6:28). He considered foolish the stress-producing—and therefore disease-producing—rat race to achieve and acquire. (See Matthew 6:25–33.)

The body, via what medical people call the sympathetic nervous system, turns attitudes and emotions into chemicals, many of which can stress the physical body. As my father's doctor once told him, "Hedley, your ulcer is not caused by what you are eating, but by what's eating you." While continuing to be responsible, we are to cast our care on God, who cares for us (1 Peter 5:7).

We are not talking here just about eating less red meat and more turkey, or taking an occasional extra day off, although these are not bad ideas. Rather, we are talking about a major reorientation of lifestyle, of values. No wonder Jesus described it as being "born anew" or "born again" (John 3:3). Jesus is not asking us merely to believe in Him. The evil spirits did that (Luke 4:34; James 2:19)! Nor is He asking us to become more "religious." The Pharisees were that, and more!

Rather, He is asking us to have a new way of life—one based on trust in and dependence on God, one of gentleness, different goals, and different means to those goals. No wonder the rich young ruler would not become a disciple. More than his riches needed to go. He needed to change his whole attitude about life (Mark 10:17–22). The cost is great, but eternity is at stake, and for many people, their health is, too. Does it take a heart attack before you will reorder your life? Do you have to be knocked flat on your back before you will look up?

SIN AND SICKNESS: A PLEA FOR BALANCE

To sum up, sometimes getting sick and staying sick is our own fault, and sometimes it is the fault of others.

Another factor deserves mention, of course: sometimes sickness is rooted in the activity of the evil one. The man born blind in John 9 was not blind because of any sin in his or his parents' lives. Job was certainly a godly man, yet he was sorely afflicted (Job 1:1). On occasion Jesus described an illness as being caused directly by Satan (Luke 13:16). My experience confirms this. I have seen several people released from various physical, emotional, and spiritual sicknesses as I ministered deliverance to them. We will discuss this in more depth later.

In the matter of sin and sickness, biblical balance is sorely needed. When sickness is our fault, we need to take responsibility. Yet it is surprising how many people are ready to attribute sickness to anything but sin. Why is this true in the face of overwhelming biblical and medical evidence?

One reason is the confusion between affirming people and agreeing with them. Many people confuse confrontation with judging, condemning, or rejecting a person. Since we are not to stand in judgment of others, so this argument goes, we must never imply that a person is in the wrong or in any way responsible for his sickness. Is not this belief farfetched? What would you think if your physician tested your blood pressure and refused to tell you how high it was for fear of being deemed judgmental?

Some ways of presenting information are demeaning. Your physician could say, "Are you ever a no-good reject! Just look at that blood pressure!" To speak in this manner would, of course, be wrong. But to simply state that there is a problem with the blood pressure and that something must be done about it is not. It is necessary for treatment to begin. Of the same order is informing people that certain behaviors or attitudes, which are out of line with God's will as revealed in the Scriptures, are sin and that they cause unwellness in body, soul, and spirit.

In order to understand better the difference between "tough love" confrontation of a person in sin, and judging or condemning that person, consider the differences between how God and Satan speak to us about our sin.

First, God speaks to us at appropriate moments, when we are able to listen and to respond. He does not ruin every moment of our day with a barrage of accusations. Satan, however, is a constant accuser. He will whisper insinuations at times when we can do nothing about the matter, when we must focus our attention on the matter at hand.

Second, God speaks to us about only two kinds of sin: the sin we are in the midst of doing and those sins from the past not yet confessed. The purpose is our repentance. Satan, on the other hand, seldom points out present sin lest we turn from it. He often points out sins that we have already confessed and repented of, simply to make us feel miserable and defeated.

Third, God points out our sin as our Friend. Like a physician whose concern in discovering illness is that we be cured of it, God addresses our sin so that we can forsake it and return to Him. Satan points out our sin to make us either deny it or dwell on it. In either case, he directs us away from the truth and away from God, hiding in either denial or fear.

Fourth, God points out only those behaviors, attitudes, and orientations that are against His will. Satan uses shame. God directs us to things that can and should be changed. Satan points out things that, while possibly embarrassing, are not sin and over which we have no control. While God may say, "You *did* wrong," Satan will say, "You *are* wrong."

Fifth, God directs to the future, toward hope. He reminds us that if we repent, He will forgive (1 John 1:9). He points out that even though some sins have temporal consequences that will never change, He will restore blessings to the penitent, though they may be different from what we threw away. Satan, in the meantime, is the purveyor of despair. "Nothing will ever change," he says. "You will always be like this. Why bother trying?"

Another reason some people reject a connection between sickness and sin is that they refuse to believe in sin or in a God who sovereignly holds us accountable. Many people want to fashion in their own image a God who blesses us and agrees with everything we do, never asking us to change. What God calls sin, they want to deem an "alternative lifestyle."

On the other extreme are those who assume that whenever one is hurting, it is one's own fault. Loud protests against this view are found in both the Book of Job and Jesus' remarks concerning the man born blind. These people, in reaction to the overly permissive views just mentioned, wish so to uphold the holiness of God and humanity's accountability before Him that they go too far in the opposite direction.

These people believe in a stern God. This view could be a projection of their own meanness. It might come from projecting onto God an image of fatherhood derived from unpleasant experiences with their earthly fathers. It might come from an overly strict religious upbringing. It might come from any number of neuroses. In any case, their picture of God is One who punishes us for any slight infraction of the rules.

The balanced statement is found once again in the fifth chapter of James. Speaking about the interrelationship of sickness and sin, James exhorts the elders of the church to anoint the sick person for healing and pray for him, and "*if* he has committed sins, he will be forgiven" (James 5:15, emphasis added).

When someone falls sick or a sickness lingers, it is highly appropriate to ask whether sin is a causal factor. Remembering that sin occurs in what we do and fail to do; that sin is against God, neighbor, and yourself; and that sins include unbalanced diet, gossip, adultery, and bigotry; we should engage in a thorough examination of conscience to compare ourselves against the standard of God's Word. The purpose of this is to indulge in neither self-condemnation nor self-justification, but to discover where we are wrong so that by God's grace we can confess our sins, receive His forgiveness, and change our ways.

This change will lead to greater health in our relationship with God, because the estrangement between us, caused by sin, will be removed when sin is dealt with. This change will often lead, immediately or gradually, to greater emotional and physical health, since our bodies, souls, and spirits all interconnect.

CONFESSING OUR SINS TO ANOTHER PERSON

Because of Jesus' atoning death on the cross, Christians have direct access to the throne of grace through Him (Ephesians 3:12). We can confess our sins to God directly and privately. Yet at times, we can be greatly helped by others in the confession of our sins. The James 5:16 instructs us to confess our sins to one another. There are several good reasons for this.

We confess our sins to others to lead us to humility.

To confess our sins to another person forces us to be humble. It is sometimes easier to confess to God than to another person because of embarrassment. More than once I have refrained from some action I was contemplating because I knew I would be embarrassed later when I confessed it to someone. It was, and remains, an effective deterrent.

We confess our sins to others to remind us of the social nature of sin.

All sin, besides being against God, is against others. Nothing we do leaves others unaffected—thus the folly of those who say that what they do behind closed doors or with a consenting adult is no one's business but their own. Suppose someone is so busy acquiring material goods that he has little time for his family, who need his presence, attention, aid, counsel, or nurture. Or suppose someone on the healing team is hung over. He may go through the motions of praying for the sick on Sunday morning—if he shows up at church at all—but will he hear God clearly, should God direct him in a certain way? Will he be as effective an instrument of God's grace? To confess our sins to another person reminds us how our sins—all of them—affect others. Remember the wise words of John Donne, the seventeenth-century priest and poet: "No man is an Iland, intire of itselfe."[2]

Remember, if we have wronged specific people, we must ask their forgiveness and make amends to them, if possible, unless to do so would harm them further.

We confess our sins to others to keep us from being too hard on ourselves.

Many people are far too hard on themselves because of an overly strict upbringing, a neurotic bent to their psyche, a lack of sound biblical instruction, or the insinuations of Satan, whom Scripture calls the "accuser of our brethren" (Revelation 12:10). They deem something a sin when it may be, at worst, a matter of questionable taste, a breach of etiquette, a lapse in decorum, or failure to observe an arbitrary custom. Or, if the matter *is* a sin, they confess it over and over again, not knowing that Jesus is the perfect sacrificial offering for our sins (1 John 2:1–2). They need to be reminded that to confess a sin to Him means that sin is put as far away from us as the east is from the west, as the psalmist wrote in Psalm 103:12, and that God has forever and truly forgiven us. What a wonderful opportunity there is in confession for someone, wise in insights into human nature and armed with the good news of the gospel, to assure people of their forgiveness and good standing with God!

We confess our sins to others to keep us from being too easy on ourselves.

Sometimes people are not remorseful enough. They fail to see how serious a matter sin is. Sometimes they, by their upbringing, have a convoluted list of sins that emphasizes trivialities or taboos and ignores graver matters. (See Jesus' rebuke of the Pharisees in Matthew 23:23.) I know of a few churches in which a parishioner can be expelled for smoking but not for bigotry. I know some church folk who will go into a tirade if others do not use "inclusive language," but who do not mind sexual relations outside of marriage. Sin is what God's Word says is sin. Often we need someone else to call us back to that standard.

We confess our sins to others to get spiritual guidance.

The word *repent* means much more than sorrow or remorse. It means to change direction or to amend one's life. (See Acts 3:19.) God does not want us to keep stumbling over and over with the same sins; rather, He wants us to become different people. True change takes place, of course, only by the grace of God. The fruit of the Spirit listed in Galatians 5:22–23 is exactly that: characteristics produced by the working of the Spirit within us. Yet, we have our part to play. While only God can grow the fruit, you and I have a gardener's responsibility to tend the plants that produce the fruit. We have our duties in prayer, studying the Bible, being an active member in a church, worship, listening to God's voice, and so on. Other people are helpful in this process of spiritual growth. Our confessor will have a guiding role in our lives.

I do not mean, of course, that such a person should run our lives to get us into servile bondage to him or her. Some in the so-called shepherding/discipleship movement of the 1970s went to excess by literally requiring people to get permission before they remodeled the house, took a new job, moved away, or got engaged. I am referring to someone who can help us in our spiritual growth, keep us within the boundaries of orthodoxy, and help us find the style that is best for us—a person who can answer questions about our spiritual journey and give us wisdom from Scripture and personal experiences of walking with God.

We confess our sins to others so they can pray with us.

Not coincidentally, right after James exhorts us to confess our sins to one another, he reminds us that the "prayer of a righteous man has great power in its effects" (James 5:16). Through prayer God can show us our sins and the way to live a more holy life. Through prayer we can open ourselves to God to receive His power to change.

The scriptural injunction to confess our sins to one another needs to be heeded much more than it is. There are several reasons why it is not:

Pride. We just do not want to admit to others that we have failed or done bad things.

Fear. We are afraid of rejection by those to whom we confess, perhaps because our lifetime experiences have prepared us for condemnation, ridicule, or rejection.

Hypocrisy. The moral failures of a few well-known church leaders have left a bad taste in the mouths of many toward religious leadership in general. As one man asked me, "Why should I confess to hypocrites?"

Prejudice. Some resist confessing their sins to others because of prejudice against the Roman Catholic Church. Confession sounds "Catholic," and some people assume that if something is done by the Roman Catholic Church, it must be wrong. Ironically, in the matter of confessing sins to others, the Roman Catholic Church is far more biblical than many of those churches that proclaim themselves to be Bible-based.

Negative experience. Many who have tried confessing their sins to other people have stopped doing so because for them it was not a particularly helpful experience. In some cases, their confessors were of no help. In other cases, their confessors breached confidentiality. Another way some people have experienced this ministry negatively is through a misuse of church discipline. Scripture tells churches to discipline the flock, but if it is carried out in a non-loving, self-righteous way, we may turn from church discipline altogether[3] (See Matthew 18:15–17; 1 Corinthians 5; 1 Timothy 1:19–20; 5:20.)

It is true that confession of sins to another person can be done in a wrong way. But *when done right,* when done sensitively, discreetly, and biblically, confession to another person can be an occasion of great spiritual help and of spiritual, emotional, and physical healing.

Father Michael Scanlan, former president of the University of Steubenville, Ohio, found that as he took hearing confession seriously, some people were being healed of physical ailments right there in the confessional. Should we be surprised that to confess and forsake one's sins can lead to physical healing, sometimes dramatically and instantaneously?

WHO IS A GOOD CONFESSOR?

We know instinctively that we should not confess our sins indiscriminately. The question is, therefore, to whom should we confess? What do we look for in a good confessor? These criteria can be applied, additionally, to people doing other kinds of ministry, such as pastoral counseling, spiritual direction, inner healing, and so on. We look for:

Godliness

Those to whom we confess our sins should have an active, growing, personal relationship with Jesus Christ as Lord and Savior. They should acknowledge sacred Scripture as the written Word of God and as the final arbiter in matters of faith and morals. Their lifestyles—public and private—should be consistent with profession of this faith. No, we are not to expect perfection from them or anyone else. All of us, even the godliest, will fall short. What we *are* to expect is a high degree of godliness on the part of our confessors, as well as their regular, intentional effort to grow into deeper spiritual maturity. Otherwise, any advice they give would not be "wisdom from above" (James 3:17). As Scripture puts it, there is a way that seems right but whose end is destruction (Proverbs 16:25). We want God's ways.

Good listening

It is important not to butt in too soon with an answer or with advice, but rather to let the person confessing "get it all out." For our confessors to respond too quickly may short-circuit the important purging and cleansing process before it is complete. Listening also needs to be active listening, looking for clues as to underlying patterns, so that these, and not just the surface symptoms, can be addressed.

Discretion

We would obviously be loath to share intimate details with someone likely to spread it around town or throw it up in our faces at a later time. Rather, we want someone who is close-mouthed and will not share with anyone without first securing our permission.

A note of warning, however. While the courts have upheld doctor/patient, lawyer/client, and clergy/penitent confidentiality, such protection does not extend to a layperson's ministry of hearing another's confession. If someone begins to confess a crime to a layperson, therefore, the layperson should immediately warn this person that he might wish, rather, to confess to a priest or minister. A layperson can be compelled to testify in a court case. In some cases, possessing information about a crime and not reporting it makes a lay confessor an "accomplice after the fact."

Empathy

Empathy has been defined as "engaged enough to care, detached enough to guide." An empathetic person truly cares, yet retains objectivity. We would not find helpful someone just going through the motions or playing a role, someone unconcerned about us as an individual. Someone caught up personally in our life, however, might lose objectivity and excuse behavior that needs to change. We want that Pauline ideal of "truth in love" (Ephesians 4:15). We want the response our life warrants, not cold professionalism or sentimental indulgence.

Wisdom

We want a confessor who knows how to apply the truths of the gospel to our situation. We want someone who has personally tasted the degradation of sin and the joys of sins forgiven; someone who knows the ways the devil tempts, the Lord forgives, and the Holy Spirit sanctifies; someone who knows when we are feeling guilty because of actual, true guilt or because of neuroses or the accusations of Satan; and someone who can help us understand when we are experiencing consolation and desolation in their true and counterfeit versions.

Because of the importance of this ministry to people's wholeness, we need to encourage our clergy to become involved or more involved in the ministry of hearing confession. Too often our clergy are so distracted by the administrative details of running a church that they devote insufficient time to pastoring the flock.

We also need to recognize that certain laypeople can fulfill the role of hearing confession, albeit in a nonsacramental way. People with the characteristics of a confessor are present in most churches. In a few they are already at work offering their ministry to burdened people. In most churches, however, they need to be discovered, recruited, trained, deployed, and supervised. It takes work to do this, but the benefit from these people, in their own kind of healing ministry, is well worth the trouble.

Sin and sickness. Repentance and healing. As we realign our actions and attitudes with God's principles, we will be more likely to move back under that shower of divine blessings God has planned for us—blessings, no doubt, evident in good health.

DISCUSSION QUESTIONS

1. How is brokenness inherent in the human condition?

2. How is brokenness the result of sins against God?

3. How is brokenness the result of sins against others?

4. How is brokenness the result of sins against self?

5. How is brokenness the result of spiritual oppression?

6. What is the scriptural authority for confessing sins to God? What are the benefits of it?

7. What is the scriptural authority for confessing sins to others? What are the benefits of it?

8. Assess your own competence as a hearer of confessions.

CHAPTER 6

The Healing of Memories

WE ALL CARRY memories that still cause pain, immature behavior, and physical, emotional, and spiritual sickness. We find ourselves unable to do certain
things, unable to relate to certain groups of people, or unable to
go to certain places because of associations with painful experiences in our past. We find our emotions misshapen by harm
done to us in the past, by things we did wrong in the past. We are
blocked, in certain aspects of our lives, from becoming the happy,
fulfilled persons we want to be and God wants us to be. The healing of memories is a chance to go back and reclaim the past—not
changing it, but changing its influence on our lives. It is a chance
to be released from the shame, guilt, and pain that have hurt us
for years and continue to affect us today.

We have all been exhorted to "get over it." While sometimes
such a "tough love" exhortation is exactly what we need, other
times it is cruel and useless. We would change if we could, but
something is holding us back. I knew a woman, for example, who
simply could not get on a bus. Everyone either teased or ridiculed
her for this. In response, she tried harder and harder, but she
could not get past the first step in the doorway without breaking

out in a cold sweat and feeling faint. In counseling we discovered the reason: she had been assaulted on a bus many years before. Though she was not consciously aware of that event in her past, the mere presence of a bus triggered an emotional crisis. The healing of memories set her free.

The healing of memories is not to be used as an excuse to continue wrong or harmful behavior. On the contrary, when we discover why we do what we do, we are to deal with the causes and become more mature and responsible.

People often ask, "How can you change the past?" We cannot, for example, remove the fact that this woman had been assaulted on a bus. What we can do is remove the present-day harmful consequences of it. As we give over to God any pain, shame, or guilt from past experiences, we find ourselves freer to live happily today.

SCRIPTURAL EXAMPLE

A scriptural example of the healing of memories is found in the life of the apostle Peter. Peter, when he stood beside a charcoal fire, denied Jesus three times (John 18:18–27). After the resurrection Jesus gave Peter three chances to be restored to fellowship with his Lord—beside a charcoal fire (John 21:9–17). Far from being a coincidence, the fact that Jesus encouraged Peter to express his love and that He did it beside a charcoal fire shows His deep insight into human nature.

For Jesus simply to appear to Peter and forgive him might be enough on one level. Relationally, Peter would be back in fellowship with his Lord. Intellectually, Peter would know he was forgiven. But emotionally, Peter might not *feel* forgiven— something that would hinder his future ministry. Additionally, might there not be some vague sense of unworthiness, triggered subconsciously by the sight, smell, or sound of charcoal fires through the years? Jesus, knowing this truth about human nature centuries before it was identified by psychologists, sought to rescue Peter and his future ministry from repeated shame and self-accusation whenever Peter was around a charcoal fire.

CONTEMPORARY EXAMPLES

Let us take a look at some contemporary examples.

I recall meeting a woman at a social function. Quickly I became aware of feelings of anger rising up in me toward her. She had done nothing to make me angry. In fact, she was complimenting me on a talk she once heard me give. It dawned on me what was going on. She was wearing a certain kind of perfume, the kind worn by a woman who, a few years previously, had done me a great deal of harm. Obviously I had not dealt adequately with either the hurts that woman had caused me or my sinful attitudes in response. Both the hurts and my anger had lain dormant subconsciously until triggered by the perfume at the social function. I sought, and received, healing for the hurts the woman had caused me. I confessed to God my sinful attitudes in response to them.

I wonder how many of our irrational fears, prejudices, and bad behaviors are expressive of hurts in our past.

In addition to bad feelings and altered behaviors, sometimes physical illness can be traced to events of the past. I know a man who always came down with physical problems around Christmas. The pains were real. The sicknesses showed up on medical tests. Yet many wondered why they always manifested around the end of December. Eventually we found out. He came from a large family and felt neglected by his parents.

One Christmas as a child he came down with chickenpox. All of a sudden he was the center of attention. Family members went out of their way to make up for events he could not attend. It was his best Christmas ever! Although he did not consciously try to become ill at Christmas, something in his subconscious sent messages to his body that it would be good to be sick, and his body responded accordingly. When we discovered this, we went to work on his lifelong feelings of inadequacy and insecurity. It was a long process of emotional healing for him, but it worked. He now has a happy Christmas each year without becoming ill.

Sometimes the hurts of the past keep us from functioning as we would like. I know a man who, for years in his marriage, found it emotionally difficult to be sexually intimate with his wife. He loved her, and she was good to him. But sometimes even the thought of an embrace was enough to make him tremble. In counseling he was finally able to recollect the painful memories of having been sexually molested as a young boy. Though occurring many years before and in a very different context, those experiences were significantly altering his relationship with his wife.

DISCOVERING THE ROOT OF THE PROBLEM

It is often important to discover the root of the emotional or physical problems we face. Otherwise, despite hard work and the best intentions, we may be trying to rid our lawns of dandelions by mowing off their tops—the visible part may be removed, but the roots are still there. How do we discover those roots? How do we identify those places where we need healing of memories?

First, we list the hurtful experiences from the past that come to mind quickly, memories that still hold considerable pain. We all know the expression, "Someday we'll laugh about this." If, despite the years, we cannot laugh at certain bad experiences of our past, if we cannot recall them without emotional distress, then we need healing of memories. There are events about which we will never laugh, like assault, rape, divorce, or the death of a loved one. The best we can hope for here is to be able to recollect the event without emotional pain. If thinking about them still causes great emotional distress, then we need a healing of memories.

Second, we examine those categories—such as place, time of year, type of person, or kind of event—in which fear or prejudice exists. I knew a woman who could not go into drugstores. Even the thought of it made her anxious. We found it was because she had been in a drugstore once when a woman had a heart attack and died right next to her. Entering a drugstore triggered all the emotions of that event, emotions that had not adequately been dealt with. While she had forgotten why drugstores caused her such a problem, they nevertheless did. We worked backward from the problem to discover the cause and then forward to find the solution.

In terms of types of persons, I counseled a man whose instant, gut-level reaction was to run whenever he saw someone in uniform. The root cause of this was his watching, as a very young boy, a number of movies depicting soldiers butchering civilians. Until he was healed of this memory, his fear was that anyone in a uniform—even a letter carrier—was going to harm him.

Sometimes our fears or prejudices can be secondhand. Everyone knows people who fear or hate certain groups, not because representatives of those groups have done them harm, but because other people have instilled a fear or prejudice about them. If one grows up hating, say, the Irish, because of the bigotry of a family member, those messages need to be discovered and erased from our "memory banks" in order for us to be free.

Third, in order to identify where we need healing of memories, we notice those areas in which there is an inordinate or unrealistic attraction. Many people marry individuals because they remind them of someone else whom they admire. I knew a man who married a woman simply because she looked like the kindly teacher who befriended him in the sixth grade when bullies were picking on him. Even though his wife's personality traits were nothing like those of his kindly teacher, subconsciously he made the comparison based on physical appearance.

Fourth, we look at those areas of "inability" in which the inability is more of an emotional block than simply a lack of skill or interest. I know a man for whom the attempt to work on his car precipitates a severe emotional crisis. It began when, as a boy, he was helping his older brothers and their friends fix an old jalopy in their garage. In his inexperience, he broke a spark plug. The other boys called him names, and he ran into the house, tears streaming down his face. From that day forward, he formed an emotional block to auto repairs. No one would think it odd just because auto repair is not an interest of his. Nor would anyone deem it a problem just because he is not good at mechanical things. But the fact that he gets emotionally distraught when a friend asks him to look under the hood of a car indicates that the healing of memories is needed.

Let us look at another example in which inability to function in a certain way is traceable to emotional distress in one's earlier years. I know a woman, whom I will call Irene, who struck me as brilliant, yet held an unchallenging, low-paying job. When I told her it seemed to me that a woman with her abilities could have a leadership position and a high salary, she responded that she was not good enough for anything like that. She refused to believe it.

Over a period of time, through prayer and counseling, encouragement to recall events in her formative years, and through asking family for insights, we discovered Irene had in junior high school a teacher who disliked her and told her she would probably not amount to much. Somehow the message was internalized. It was as if Irene adopted a script for life written by this teacher. Throughout her life she had been subconsciously acting her part—one who would never amount to much. Not coincidentally, she had been a top student up until that point.

Until we uncovered the incident with her teacher, no amount of pointing out the facts made a difference. Once we discovered the "taped message," as it were, deeply imprinted in her subconscious, we erased it and recorded a message reflective of the facts. Irene gained confidence and fulfilled her God-given potential.

Fifth, we ask others for their input. They may know certain details of our lives that we have forgotten or repressed. They will often be able to point out behaviors we do not see in ourselves.

As for forgotten details, I know one man, whom I will call Sam, who was terribly afraid of dogs. Every time he saw one, his heart started racing. He could not figure out why. He knew of no unpleasant experience with a dog, and he liked all other kinds of animals. Sam knew himself well enough to know it was far more than just preference; it was fear! We prayed together on several occasions to see if God might show us what the root of the problem was, but nothing came to us.

One day Sam called me. "I know the source of the problem," he said. "I asked my aunt if there was an incident in my childhood that might have led to my fear of dogs. 'Oh, yes,' she said. 'When you were three a Great Dane chased your tricycle, knocked you over, and bit you on the leg. You've been afraid of dogs ever since. Don't you remember that?'" With the root problem in hand, we could proceed with inner healing. Dogs are not his favorite pets today, but the fear is broken.

Our friends can also point out behaviors that may have hindered us all of our lives but of which we are unaware. Tim had a certain pattern of behavior in dealing with people. Try as he might, he could not figure it out or get a handle on what was causing it. A job relocation brought Tim into contact with a new group of colleagues, one of whom observed that he had all the behavioral symptoms of an adult child of an alcoholic parent. Instantly the lights went on. He *was* the adult child of an alcoholic parent. The colleague lent him some books on the subject. Now prayers, efforts, and ministry had a specific focus. The enemy, previously elusive, was out in the open, recognized, and more easily defeatable.

Sixth, we can flush to the surface memories—good ones as well as bad ones—by picking a year in our lives and recollecting as much about it as we can. We can make a collage, full of items appertaining to that year. As we construct this collage, we will find all sorts of memories, long forgotten, coming to conscious thought.

Into this collage go photos of ourselves, family, and friends; headlines of significant news stories; songs that were "top of the pops" that we heard many times; images of what our home, neighborhood, school, and church looked like; recollections of what was "in" fashion-wise; pictures of the cars of the era (the advertising pages of old magazines are helpful here); items from diaries, scrapbooks, and old letters we might have saved; any instances of significant events we can remember; and so on. The more the better.

Every time I pick a year in my life to make a collage, three kinds of memories come to me. The first are pleasant memories. Recently I remembered with fondness a trip I took with my grandfather. These memories are for celebrating.

Second are memories of unpleasant things that no longer cause emotional pain when I think about them. These events were not pleasant at the time, but at least they no longer cause emotional distress or negatively affect my life. These memories do not need healing.

Third, however, are memories that, to recollect them even years later, *do* make me upset. When I examine them, it becomes apparent that they control me in some way. These memories are grist for the mill of the healing of memories.

Which year do you start with? It depends. You might want to start with a year known to be generally happy so as to learn how to get in touch with the past by starting with something pleasurable. Or you might wish to focus on a year known to be problematic, so as to get right to the heart of the distress immediately.

The seventh and last way we identify those places where we need healing of memories is by asking God to reveal to us what might be wrong. Through dreams and visions, through words of knowledge, through the "still, small voice" with which God sometimes speaks to us, He can show us not only problem areas in our lives, but also their root causes. (See 1 Kings 19:12; 1 Corinthians 12:8.)

A friend of mine asked God why she was standoffish to a particular uncle of hers. He always seemed friendly to her and everybody liked him, but the block remained. One day while praying, she got a picture of a small girl who looked like herself and a man looking very much like a younger version of her uncle. She saw the man trying to take something away from the child while she tried desperately to hang on to it. Finally, with a mighty tug, he wrested control of it from her. With that she went running off, crying her eyes out. "You know," she told me, "that must have been the incident that triggered the bad feelings I have had for him all my life." After a minute's pause, she added, "How foolish! In the pictures that came to me while praying, I saw what he was trying to take from me: a can of toxic chemicals!"

It is important not to try to gather all the information of painful memories at one time. If we were to spend a concentrated effort accumulating in our conscious thinking all the hurts of our earlier years, we would most likely be so overwhelmed as to become seriously depressed or even suicidal. Rather, we should work on one or two problems from the past at a time, either to their solutions or until it seems wise to leave them and go on to another one.

DEALING WITH UNPLEASANT MEMORIES

Some painful memories are easily dealt with. Others require more attention. Here is a progression of steps that can be followed to minister the healing of memories, starting with the easiest.

1. Allow the problem to be brought to mind.

Often we are affected by an event of the past buried in the subconscious. We fight thinking about it, not wishing to relive the bad experience, feel the shame or pain again, or do the hard work of overcoming it. Yet sometimes simply allowing ourselves to become aware of the bad event is sufficient to break its power over us. Sometimes, however, that is not enough.

2. Talk about it with others.

Sharing an unpleasant memory with a trusted friend, a member of the clergy, a prayer or support group, or a professional counselor will often bring healing. This is one of the reasons for the popularity of groups like Alcoholics Anonymous. We discover we are not alone; others have similar problems. We can share our problems with them without fear or ridicule. In some cases we discover that the problem, when it is out in plain view, is not as enormous as we once thought when we had kept it hidden. Sometimes we discover that others with similar problems have learned to cope well or have been able to find freedom from the damage of the past.

Sometimes this cathartic role can be played by trusted and trustworthy friends. Although they probably will not have had the same hurtful experiences we have, they will accept us lovingly and let us talk things out. The kind of person in whom we confide should share similar characteristics with the person to whom we confess our sins. (Review chapter five for the description of who makes a good confessor.) A number of therapists have told me that at least 50 percent of their clients do not need professional help. They could find considerable healing by talking with a good friend in whom they confide.

There are times when we are just too afraid to share with a friend, or our friends are loving and supportive, but too prone to give immediate advice without letting us get the problem out. In these instances, a therapist or member of the clergy might be most helpful. With their training and experience they will, in many cases, be the affirming presence and listening ear we need. With those memories that hold a great deal of shame and guilt, a counselor or member of the clergy not previously known to them is the best choice.

3. Pray for healing.

Sometimes simply talking it out is sufficient to get a person free. But many times the problem still persists. Thank God we have a rich resource for healing in prayer! Why is prayer so helpful?

First, because in prayer we open the door for the Lord to enter into our problems (Revelation 3:20). So often God, who wishes very much to help us, waits for our request. As I mentioned before, this is because He respects our free will, given to us by

Him in the first place. In addition, if we are not ready to ask for His help, we are probably not able to receive it should it come. James' observation is relevant:

> Ye have not, because ye ask not.
>
> —JAMES 4:2, KJV

Second, prayer is important because God knows us better than we know ourselves. He knows our problems and their sources. In prayer, we let the Master Diagnostician go to work.

Third, prayer is important because God has the power to effect change. I have heard repeated observations about secular therapists being good at finding out the problem, but not as good at solving it. God's power, made available to us as we pray, can transform our memories, removing their harmful effects.

Our praying need not be elaborate or fancy. Sometimes all we need in order to be healed is a simple prayer like this: "Lord Jesus Christ, I am frightened of flying since my friend was killed in a plane crash. Please take this fear away. Amen." Or the prayer may be one of surrender: "Lord, I yield to You these painful and unhappy memories of being beaten by my father. Please cleanse them, and make me whole. In Jesus' name. Amen."

Sometimes, however, we need to pray at some length for the healing to get to the depths of a wounded soul. Dr. Francis MacNutt has popularized the phrase "soaking prayer" to describe how healing prayer sometimes needs to soak in overtime.

In some instances we can minister inner healing through prayer by ourselves. At other times, we need the prayers of others.

Fourth, prayer is important because God is love. Many are reluctant to relive painful memories. Yet as God goes to the root of the problem, He also comforts us. The pain involved in the healing process is much more bearable because He walks the road to wholeness with us.

In prayer, we offer the Lord our hurts, fears, anxieties— whatever seems to be harming us—and ask for His help. It may come instantly or gradually. God might show us the root cause or heal the problem without our ever knowing what started it. He might heal us sovereignly while we remain mostly passive in the process, or He might tell us something we need to do. We should not expect every session of prayer for the healing of memories to be alike. The crucial things to remember are that God wants us made whole, that He is both the source of our blessings and the goal for our lives, and that we need to listen to what He is saying to us every step of the way.

4. Receive Holy Communion.

In Communion, we have what Serapion, a bishop in the early days of the church, called "specific medicine for our souls." As we receive Communion, we lay our burdens, sins, and hurts at the foot of the cross and receive grace to be made whole. While this often comes when we are not thinking about His grace, we discover that when we lay our burdens at the Lord's feet *intentionally*—including the pains and hurts of previous years—and deliberately focus on God's healing grace in the sacrament, more happens, and it happens more often.

Often as a way of focusing on these truths, I picture my burdens inside a large trash bag that, as I kneel down to receive Communion, I leave at the feet of Jesus. Then I picture Jesus extending His hands toward me with a small treasure chest of blessings. While I certainly can have hopes as to what blessings that chest may contain and can even ask Him for blessings I believe I need, it would be inappropriate for me to try to picture the contents. My Lord knows far better than I do which blessings I need and in what order I should receive them. In my picturing, I leave the box closed and let Him open it and show me what is in it if He chooses to.

Yet sometimes these efforts are not enough. Being conscious of the problem, sharing it with others, prayer, and Holy Communion always help, but perhaps not sufficiently to free us from what is hurting us. It is at this point that many give up in frustration or else fall back on the belief that maybe this particular person is not supposed to be healed. I would like to suggest three additional steps. These steps illustrate the fact that we must never isolate the ministry of the healing of memories from other aspects of the healing ministry, or indeed from any aspect of the faith.

5. Forgive others.

Often people block their healing—whether physical or emotional—by clinging to resentment. Early in my ministry of healing I ministered to a man who had been sexually abused as a child. I prayed at some length with him over a period of time but saw no change. Finally I gave up. Several months later he called and said he was healed. Others had ministered to him after I did. One asked him if he had forgiven the person who had molested him. "No," he responded. "I hate him!" He was reminded that our Lord tells us to forgive others and pray for those who persecute us (Matthew 5:44). Indeed, Jesus said that if we do not forgive others, we ourselves will not be forgiven (Matthew 6:15). Forgiving the man who molested him had not been easy, but it had brought healing.

Healing of memories does not excuse bad behavior or attitudes. Inner healing recognizes that even though much of a particular problem may be attributable to the sins of others, any part of it that is due to *our* sins has to be confessed and repented of. This includes any sinful responses or attitudes we allow because we were hurt.

6. Submit to a ministry of deliverance, if needed.

Some emotional problems resist efforts at healing. In some instances, a demonic stranglehold prevents the person from becoming free. Sometimes he or she might have been involved in the occult. This involvement has to be renounced before progress can be made. Sometimes during the course of a traumatic event, the individual was momentarily susceptible to the demonic, perhaps even calling down spiritual forces on those tormenting him. Sometimes a curse has been placed on the individual.

Sometimes Satan chooses to oppress demonically a person who is suffering emotionally. Whatever the reason for, or intensity of, the demonic activity, deliverance prayer could be necessary at some stage in the inner healing process.

7. Seek professional Christian counseling.

Those whose abuse was major and prolonged may need, in addition to prayer, extensive work in counseling with a capable, wise, caring therapist. Often, victims of abuse need a gentle, gradual rebuilding of their lives if deep and lasting change is to occur. These people's whole lives were ordered around a lie, and it takes time to reorder each aspect around the truth.

Although God sometimes graces such a person with dramatic progress, it is wrong to demand such progress of a person when God is not giving it. That would have the effect of revictimizing the victim—shaming him or her for not being whole at a rate that we, and not God, determine.

CHRISTIAN IMAGINING

One vehicle that can help us turn over to God the deep-seated hurts of our lives and receive divine healing is Christian imagining—the experiencing of Christian truths in the imagination. We have already looked at one example of imagining, in laying our burdens at the feet of Jesus while receiving Holy Communion. This is not a required step in the healing process, but for some it is very helpful, *provided we keep it within Christian boundaries.*

God is a God of beauty and of drama. God's truth is so profound that we often need more, but never less, than propositional statements of theology. Jesus often communicated truths not in abstract, philosophical ways, but in story form. His parables were truths easily pictured in the mind's eye. Sometimes, at a youth group retreat, for example, in order to dramatize how Jesus forgives our sins as we confess to Him, I recorded a few pretend gossipy thoughts on a tape recorder. Then I played the tape to the youngsters to let them see how unconfessed sins are "part of the record." After this, I "confessed" to the Lord that my gossip was wrong, that I would try to make amends, and that, by His grace, I would do better the next time. Then, with a tape eraser representing the cleansing and forgiving power of the Lord, I erased the tape. When we played the tape again, it was blank. The sins were gone! This exercise has proven effective in driving the point home to others—and to myself!

The healing of memories is similarly helped by such imaginings. We might sense Jesus standing with us at the time of a tragedy or feel Him hugging and consoling us. Or we could picture ourselves laying the garbage of what was done to us at His feet for disposal. We can grasp His love for us by picturing Him smiling at us or feeling His arm around us, or just sensing the warmth and security of His presence protecting and freeing us.

We must be cautioned, however, that there is a big difference between this Christian imagining of scriptural truths and the kind of visualization popular in secular or New Age self-help programs. For one thing, proper Christian imagining is always based on *specific biblical truths,* never on the invention of "truth" or the thought that one can bring reality into being by simply picturing it or thinking it.

For another thing, we let God be sovereign in the process. Like many others, I encourage a hurting individual to picture walking along a beach on a warm, sunny day. Way down the beach a figure appears who is not recognizable immediately. Eventually, however, it becomes apparent it is Jesus. He comes up to the individual and talks. So far, so good. We may have made it easier for a person for whom Jesus has often seemed far-off and remote to talk with the Lord. I might ask the person I am helping in this exercise, "What are you saying to Jesus, and what is He saying to you?" If God shows me something at the time or gives me a word, I share it, asking the person what it means to him or her. At this point, however, I step out of the way. For me to go further and tell the person what to say or, worse, for me to make up what I would like Jesus to be saying is unwise.

God has given us in His Word a rich history of dreams, visions, and experiences of being caught up into heaven, like Paul's experience described in 2 Corinthians 12. But historically in Christianity this is something *God* does. We can set the stage with beautiful music, worshipful atmosphere, theological reminders, personal witness, or, in this case, by imagining a scene on the beach. To go further is to go beyond how God has led His people through the centuries, to get into the habit of projecting onto God our own thoughts and desires, and to play God in the lives of people.

Also, we are careful in this process to make sure that Jesus—the Jesus of Scripture—is the One we seek. A few in the Christian inner healing movement have said it does not matter whom we picture. What counts is the exercise, the imagining itself. Nothing could be further from the truth! Jesus is the only One who can truly make us whole. He alone has the power, and true wholeness occurs only in relationship to Him. Whatever emotional release may occur in imagining a scene with someone else is paltry compared to the blessings of a deepening relationship with the Lord of the universe. In addition, in picturing or calling out to other spiritual entities, we could be opening ourselves to demonic forces.

Finally, we make sure to check the veracity of any vision, word, or experience against the Scriptures. John reminds us to test the spirits to see if they are from God (1 John 4:1). Thoughts from our subconscious, ideas subtly suggested by others, and impressions given by the evil one may all intermingle with genuine communications from God. Hence, we will never accept anything that comes to us in such an inner healing exercise without making sure that it squares with what God has given us in His written Word.

At the same time, however, we must be careful of going too far in the other direction. There have been a few best-selling books of late that would have Christians deem *any* form of imagining as being New Age. The authors of some of these books belong to a

Christian tradition that is highly rationalistic. Nearly everything in their spirituality is oriented around the intellectual content of the faith. Their tradition offers little or no awareness, much less intentional practicing, of affective, that is, suprarational, learning, mystical prayer, sacramental grace, and rapturous worship.

A closer familiarity with the history of Christian spirituality will teach us the difference between proper, legitimate, time-tested Christian mystical experiences and the New Age, magical, occultic variety.

In his book *Reincarnation*, Mark Albrecht gives a good definition of appropriate mysticism:

> [I]n its classical sense, mysticism may be defined as the seeking of the experience of the presence of God, or union with God and his will. Needless to say, these concepts are quite biblical. So, in that sense we may say that God calls all believers to be mystics. Christianity has a rich heritage of orthodox mysticism and pietism.... [1]

We must be careful that we do not fall off either end of the table, accepting any imagining without careful discrimination or rejecting it in its orthodox Christian form.

There is much from our pasts that continues to affect us negatively today—physically, emotionally, and spiritually. As we bring these hurts before the Lord, we can be set free to be the people we want to be and God wants us to be.

A FEW ADDITIONAL NOTES OF CAUTION

Over the past several years there has been a growing concern that the ministry of inner healing is sometimes misused. We should not be surprised at this. Anything that is good can be twisted. Anything centered in God can be counterfeited. Anything that combines healing with responsibility will be subject to attempts to substitute blaming others for accepting personal accountability. Let me underscore three things to beware of, three cautions we must hold before us, lest the good ministry of inner healing be turned into something that it is not. Please beware of:

1. Victimization

Even secular commentators note how widespread is the invoking of one's being a victim in order to avoid personal responsibility. If I am not happy, it must be the fault of those who raised me. If I do not get ahead in life, it is because other groups in society have conspired to keep people like me oppressed.

Psychologist Erik H. Erikson (1902–1994) argued throughout his life against the prevailing belief—the legacy of Freud's teaching—that the ego is fixed in early childhood. Erikson's belief is that the formation of a person's identity is a lifelong process. If everything has its source in childhood and is somebody else's fault, then trust in one's own power of taking responsibility for oneself may be undermined.

There are several problems, of course, with the cult of the victim. First, it is not always someone else's fault when things do not turn out the way we had hoped. Sometimes our hopes were unrealistic. Sometimes we are our own worst enemy.

Second, a claim of victimization is often selective and self-serving. That is, some who are quick to claim victim status for themselves are just as quick to deny it to others. More than once I have witnessed an argument between a man and woman in which the woman sought to justify her rude behavior by asserting that all men deserved nothing less for the way men treated her in the past. It did not matter that this particular man had done nothing harmful to her. He was a man, so it was right for him to suffer for the sins of his group. Nor was the woman willing to accept the idea that rude behavior directed toward her by a man was equally acceptable if it were payback for all the harmful things women had done over the years to that particular rude man. Once when I pointed out these things to a woman, I was told point-blank that women can only be victims, never victimizers.

Third, the claim of victim status offers no hope. If one's chief self-definition is that of victim, and if one wallows perpetually in the hurt and anger of real or imagined past harm, the focus is backward, not forward. The apostle Paul could acknowledge terrible things that happened to him because he stood for Christ, yet he urged both himself and others to forget what lay in the past to press onward to what lay ahead (Philippians 3:13–14). Not only is Paul's statement God's marching orders to us, but it is also a statement of good news. Things can get better for us if we let go of self-pity and blame.

We must be careful in the ministry of inner healing that, while not trivializing the real and tragic cases of victimization, marginalization, bigotry, and the like, we do not unwittingly encourage the rampant cult of the victim. Rather, we must acknowledge that, yes, terrible things may have happened, but now it is time to forgive, take responsibility for the rest of one's life under the grace and guidance of God, and move on.

2. False memory syndrome

With the explosive growth in the popularity of therapy sessions to "uncover" repressed memories of traumatic events alleged to have happened in childhood, notes of caution have come from many quarters. Although some "uncovered memories" do square with the facts as verified by independent witnesses, there is a growing awareness that some of the "uncovered memories" are not accurate recollections of what happened.

Why is this? One reason has to do with the therapist, or in our case, the minister of inner healing. Some people, in their inexperience, inability, or zeal to help, plant suggestions clumsily or inadvertently in the mind of the client. Such suggestions can work their way into one's subconscious and come out later as "memories." The recent conviction of a worker in a day-care center on charges of child molestation was overturned when the alleged victim later related how certain parts of her testimony about what had happened were suggested to her by a social worker. The alleged victim was not at all sure the things had happened the way her parents and social worker had said, but they, as responsible adults, must be telling the truth, so the youngster testified accordingly.

A second reason for caution has to do with the agenda that various people have. Therapists and ministers of inner healing have issues about which they are concerned, even angry. At times, whether subconsciously or deliberately, they can project their views onto their clients, who then "remember" things about their past. It is being reported that a significant number of clients who uncover "memories" of certain kinds of victimization in their youth are the patients of therapists who themselves were victims. It is true that such therapists would have tremendous compassion and affinity for their clients, and such compassion and affinity would make them more sensitive and capable in the process of recollection. It has also been noted, however, that more than a few therapists use their clients to get back at a class in society by suggesting things to their clients that simply did not happen.

Recently, the retired Roman Catholic archbishop of Davenport, Iowa, was accused by two women of molesting them thirty years earlier. The plaintiffs' "memory" of the events had been recovered during therapy. But not only was the case dropped for lack of evidence, but also the therapist herself became a defendant in lawsuits brought by three other women. The charges, denied by the therapist, were medical malpractice, psychiatric negligence, and fraud.

A third reason for caution is that we are all bombarded daily with various horror stories of this or that person being subjected to this or that brutalization or horrid experience. I wonder how much of this information seeps into our subconscious mind, perhaps to be reworked as dreams, symbols, or "recollections."

I once ministered to a man—let us call him Charlie—who was convinced he had been rescued as a youngster from a terrible fire. No such thing had happened to him. What had happened was that while he was reading at home one evening during his childhood, a television account in the background described a most horrible fire and how someone was rescued by a brave firefighter. We—Charlie's family, Charlie, and I—now theorize that while most of Charlie's attention was on his book, a small portion of it was listening to the background television account, although he himself was not consciously aware he was doing this. Charlie is a sensitive soul, and something deep within him was deeply moved. The news account and his inner emotional response were "filed away" in his memory. Later, as an adult, Charlie was troubled by some difficulties at work, making him especially vulnerable to painful thoughts and feelings rising to the surface. Charlie's concern for his work situation somehow coupled with that fire story and produced in Charlie the belief that he had been rescued from a fire.

The point is, be careful about giving uncritical acceptance to any "hidden memory" that you or someone to whom you minister claims. Maybe the event happened; maybe it did not. While taking the person in ministry seriously, we do not automatically take the details literally.

This is important. Too many therapists or ministers of inner healing have suggested courses of action that *might* be appropriate if the memory were accurate, but would not be appropriate if it were not. If we decide to avoid someone, go public with accusations, or call the police because of a newly discovered "memory," how tragic things might be if we are wrong!

3. The "inner child"

This term has gained considerable popularity, both in Christian inner healing circles and in secular and New Age pop therapies. The belief that there is deep within us an innocent, pure core being, someone who could profitably be listened to for guidance and direction, is contradicted by Scripture. How is this so?

First, we are to listen to Christ and believe and rely only on the truths of His written Word, Scripture. If Jesus wanted us to listen to our inner child, He would have said so. In Matthew

19:13–15, when Jesus commended the little children and told us to be like them, He was telling us to emulate their trust in Him, not to listen to them for guidance and wisdom.

Second, our inner child is not so pure. One need only observe children for a few minutes to see they can be cruel, mean, and self-centered. Historically, theologians have used the term *original sin* to describe the fact that even from the moment of conception, all of us, except for Jesus Himself, are tainted by inherited sin.

Third, if our inner child is so pure, why are we concerned to go back to those moments in our earlier life when serious damage was done to us that affects us today? "In counseling," Leanne Payne rightly reminds us in *Restoring the Christian Soul*, "it is important to realize that the way of the wounded 'inner child' is so often the way of the foolish child...."[2]

The ministry of inner healing is a wonderful ministry when kept within the bounds of biblical revelation. When one transgresses those boundaries, however, serious and harmful difficulties will occur.

DISCUSSION QUESTIONS

1. What is the purpose of "healing of memories"?

2. How is healing of memories different from forgiveness?

3. If you suspect that you may need this type of healing, what should you do?

4. How can you make your imagination available to God?

EXPERIMENT

Block out *at least* twenty minutes of quiet solitude. The purpose of this experiment is to make your imagination available to God. Take at least five minutes for quiet, thoughtful, verbal thanksgiving and praise. Read Isaiah 40 and think about the images God gave Isaiah, and what a joy it must have been for Isaiah to receive these pictures in his mind's eye (imagination). Take at least five minutes to imagine yourself as a person described in verse 31. Record your experiment in your healing notebook.

Chapter 7

Satan, Demons, Temptation, and Oppression

T HE HUMAN MIND and heart raise basic questions about eternal things. Is there a God? If so, what is He like? What is the purpose of human existence? If there is a purpose, what is God's response when we fail to live up to it? Why is there harm and destruction in the world? If God is good and caring, what will He do about such things?

These basic questions are raised by people of every culture and age. The answers given by the various religions and philosophies differ markedly from each other, a point we should remember the next time someone tells us, "All religions teach the same thing." First we will look at a Christian understanding of evil in the world, then contrast it with what some other religions and philosophies have said.

A CHRISTIAN DOCTRINE OF EVIL IN THE WORLD

Christianity affirms an eternal God. In His love, before He created the heavens and earth, God created a variety of other beings—angels, principalities, dominions, powers, and so forth

(Ephesians 6:12). While a majority of angels used their free will to remain loyal to God, a minority, led by their leader, Lucifer, rebelled (Isaiah 14:12–14; Jude 6). These fallen angels, now called demons, and Lucifer, now called the devil (which means "accuser") or Satan (which means "adversary"), seek to spread the rebellion against God and try to inflict harm against God's people. Jesus said Satan was a murderer from the beginning and the father of lies (John 8:44).

We human beings, misusing our free will, succumb at times to Satan's various ploys to entice us to join the rebellion, as illustrated in the tragic fall from grace of our protoparents, Adam and Eve, in Genesis 3:1–6. Adam and Eve's sin had serious consequences for the world, as we saw in chapter one.

Yet this is not just Adam and Eve's story. This is the story of us all. We have inherited from Adam alienation and fallenness. To this "original sin" we add our own. As Scripture reminds us, "All have sinned…" (Romans 3:23).

All this alienation came about because of our rebellion against God and His ways. Amazingly God, because He is love, nevertheless wishes to rescue us from sin and its various consequences.

He started this mission of rescue first by choosing a people to be especially His. Through the revelation of His will via the Law and the prophets, God taught the Jews what was forbidden and what was expected. He told them to have nothing to do with the various abominations the Canaanites practiced, such as divination, sorcery, mediumship, magic, and astrology (Genesis 41:8; Deuteronomy 18:9–14; Isaiah 47:13; Daniel 4:7). These were forbidden and against God's will because they involved the guidance and power of spiritual beings not submitted to God, and because they eventually harmed the people who used them.

The best the people of the Old Testament could do in their battle against Satan was attempt to contain the problem by putting to death anyone following the devil's ways (Exodus 22:18; Leviticus 20:27).

Jesus Christ's birth, ministry, atoning death, and resurrection demonstrated the beginning of God's final assault against Satan, an assault that will continue until our Lord's return to inaugurate the new heaven and new earth (Isaiah 65:17; 2 Peter 3:13; Revelation 21:1). With the coming of God to earth as a human being and the subsequent bestowal of the Holy Spirit on all believers, His power was made more readily available to mankind. Souls could be reclaimed. Satan could be pushed back. Ultimate victory will eventually be won.

On the cross, Jesus destroyed the chief weapon Satan had, that people would suffer the eternal consequences of their sins. Because Jesus took onto Himself the iniquity of us all, as Isaiah wrote in Isaiah 53:6, death for believers, while still painful, now leads not to eternal lostness, but to eternal life with God. As the *Te Deum Laudamus,* an ancient hymn, puts it, Christ has "opened the kingdom of heaven to all believers." As Paul told the Romans:

> The free gift of God is eternal life in Christ Jesus our Lord.
> —ROMANS 6:23

As he told the Corinthians, the sting of death has been removed (1 Corinthians 15:55).

As God's kingly rule on earth expands by His direct work and His work through the Church, these things happen: souls are won for God from the domain of Satan; disease (always directly or indirectly a byproduct of humanity's following Satan's enticements to rebel) is cured; deliverance is obtained from the oppression of the devil; armor is provided to withstand the assaults of the evil one; and offensive weaponry is issued to help us reclaim territory Satan has captured. (See Acts 10:38; Ephesians 6:11–17; 2 Corinthians 10:4.)

Christ continues this work until His glorious return. While His Father has sealed Satan's fate and put some restraints on his activity, Satan is still allowed some measure of freedom. He is still a roaring lion and convincing accuser (1 Peter 5:8; Revelation 12:10).

Why? Why did God not completely remove the (albeit limited) influence Satan has over us? The answer is simple, although not easy to take, especially when we or our loved ones are suffering. A primary reason evil still exists in the world is the sinful misuse of the freedom God has given us. As long as we have this freedom, we will, to various degrees, be agents of Satan's work.

Jesus will deal once and for all with evil at His Second Coming (Revelation 21:1–5). But at that time there will no longer be any chance for people to use free will to turn toward, or away from, God. In order for God to give those alive more time to repent and be saved, Jesus' Second Coming and the final dealing with the existence of evil have been delayed. Peter put it this way:

> The Lord is not slow about his promise as some count slowness, but is forbearing toward you, not wishing that any should perish, but that all should reach repentance.
>
> —2 PETER 3:9

Ultimately, then, the problem with Satan and evil will be solved. In the meantime, we know that Christ's death on the cross has made provision for believers to spend eternity with God in heaven, and Christ's ongoing work today has equipped us with the power necessary to keep Satan at bay when he strikes at us.

Such is the Christian view of the existence—and continued existence—of evil in the world. But what about other views?

OTHER RELIGIONS AND PHILOSOPHIES ON THE SUBJECT OF EVIL

Some religions hold that there is no principle or power of evil at all, that everything that happens is not only approved by God, but also ordained by God. Whatever happens, a convinced Muslim would respond, "Allah wills it."

Thus, while this God may be powerful, is He really good, at

least as we understand goodness? In contrast, Christianity states repeatedly the goodness of God (Mark 10:18; Romans 8:28). It is Satan, not God, who inflicts harm. Although God allows Satan some freedom, He has already made provision for our ultimate triumph over evil in Christ.

Rabbi Harold Kushner, on the other hand, author of *When Bad Things Happen to Good People*, so desires to keep God good that he denies Him much power. To Kushner, God would like to intervene, but His power is limited, so He cannot. Kushner has little or no doctrine of Satan as the cause of evil, nor does he have faith in Christ who redeemed us at Calvary and who will ultimately triumph and right all wrongs. All Kushner can give us is a God who is ultimately not God at all, for how can God not be all-powerful? It is a contradiction.

Another possibility is the beliefs of so-called dualistic religions. They posit two ultimate powers equal in strength, one good, the other evil. These powers alternate in their ruling, with neither triumphing over the other.

But this gives the devil more than his due. Scripture reminds us that only God is eternal; that Satan is a creature, albeit a rebellious one; that his power, though real, is limited; and that God, for all He allows, is still ultimately in control. For all Satan's destructiveness now, "God bats last," and He will eventually right all injustices. There is an omega point to which history is marching.

Some religions, such as Hinduism, see bad events as the resultant punishment for misdeeds done in a previous life. A key belief is that of *karma*—the reward or punishment for our deeds. Thus, it is payment of karmic debt, not the intrusion of Satan that underlies suffering.

While such a religious philosophy is gaining adherents among some spiritually hungry people in the West, it is not a religion of good news. For one reason, in such a religion one has become his or her own Savior, an impossible task if we consider honestly how hard it is to be perfect. (See Psalm 49:7–9.) For another, if someone is suffering to pay off a karmic debt, it would be unloving to help him. It would set him back on his journey. If someone is lying in a ditch, leave him there!

While Jesus came to do many things, chief among them was to be Savior of those who put their trust in Him. In addition, we see Jesus' compassion illustrated in His life and teaching, a compassion that leads us to minister to others. Note that in countries where belief in karma is the dominant view, nearly all the hospitals are built by either Christian missionaries or natives who have been converted or Westernized.

Some people have said, usually in periods of peace and prosperity, that the solution to the problem of evil is found in education. "Ignorance, not evil, is the problem," this philosophy states. "Once people are educated, all will be well, for humanity is fundamentally good." Recall, however, the shrewd comment of President Theodore Roosevelt: "Take an ignorant man who is stealing from a railroad boxcar and give him education, and you may have equipped him to steal the whole railroad."[1]

The naïve optimism prevalent in the first fifteen years of the twentieth century that education would solve all our problems was shattered by the agonizing events of World War I. Why is it that this lesson has to be learned again and again?

Others believe that the ennobling effects of culture will so tame whatever is destructive in us that evil will disappear as culture improves. Thus comes the shock when we see how thin a veneer culture really is, and how puny a dam to hold back the raging torrents of evil working in us and through us. In the TV miniseries *Holocaust*, Frau Weiss, the doctor's wife, expressed amazement that "such things should be happening in Germany!" Naïvely, she did not realize culture may stop someone from spitting on the sidewalk, but it will not stop genocide.

Still others believe that evil does not exist as an objective reality, that it is simply the absence of good. Scott Peck's bestselling book *The People of the Lie* is one of many books in which people discover, often to their surprise, that objective evil does exist. This discovery is often in spite of their educational conditioning. Peck notes in another book, *The Road Less Traveled,* that it is not evil that surprises him, but rather that there is so much good.

WHY IS THE CHRISTIAN ANSWER REJECTED BY MANY, EVEN IN THE CHURCH?

Why is it, then, in spite of clear scriptural teaching and the lack of satisfactory alternative worldviews, that many people, even in the Church, have trouble with the Christian answer to the problem of evil?

First is the argument that the biblical view of Satan and the demonic is nothing more than first-century superstition and ignorance. We would hope, whether as an article of faith or from growing experience, that people would see the Scriptures to be not the groping of people toward theological understanding, but the inspired revelation of truth by God to us. We should be careful to avoid a patronizing attitude of calling an earlier era unsophisticated. Today's urbanized world has generally lost the facility to read weather from the color of the sky, the motion of the trees, and the feel of the soil. Have we similarly lost some of the spiritual discernment known by an earlier age? Is it not possible that we, not first-century Christians, are the ones lacking in spiritual sophistication?

Others claim that people of the first century confused mental illness and epilepsy with demons, that is, what they called demons we now know to call something else. In several places in the Gospels, however, epilepsy and demon possession are distinguished from each other (Matthew 4:24; 8:16; Mark 1:34; Luke 4:40–41; 6:17–19). In marked comparison to the fanciful apocalyptic stories circulating about the devil in the first few centuries B.C. and A.D., the Bible's accounts of the devil are restrained, cautious, and circumspect. In the scriptural accounts, we are not dealing with wild speculations, but rather with their rejection.

Second, our rejection of past paranoia has led to an opposite overreaction. One recalls rituals, sometimes used with malice against problems that were psychological, not demonic. We recall the Salem witch hunts, as much an expression of Puritan insecurity in the face of a rising generation not holding to their elders' views as they were a punishment of actual witches. We have turned off to such extremes.

I would plead, however, that the correct response to an irrational extreme is not a pendulum swing to the opposite irrational extreme! The corrective to seeing Satan everywhere is not to deny his existence anywhere. C. S. Lewis's comment in *The Screwtape Letters* is wise:

> There are two equal and opposite errors into which our race can fall about the devils. One is to disbelieve in their exis-tence. The other is to believe, and to feel an excessive and unhealthy interest in them.[2]

Third, the idea of objective evil power threatens our desire to be in control, so we choose to believe that it does not exist. C. S. Lewis said that Satan's most effective illusion is convincing us that he does not exist, that only the uneducated and unsophisticated would entertain such superstitious beliefs. Some people would rather pay a doctor than go to a healing service, or pay a therapist than go to confession, because payment helps us keep control. Similarly, we feel more control through our efforts to improve humanity than in acknowledging we are caught in a cosmic bat-tle between good and evil, God and Satan. Confessing we need God's help to survive is as humbling as being penitent. Being told by God how to fit into His plans for eventual victory is not as ego-flattering as remolding the world in our own image.

Fourth, many have rejected the biblical view of evil because they have replaced, and have been taught by some theologians to replace, a commitment to biblical truth with a commitment to tolerate any view as long as it is nice and polite. To speak of sin, evil, repentance, and the Lordship of Christ demand too much. It sounds as though it might exclude people.

Allan Bloom commented on this attitude in his 1987 runaway bestseller, *The Closing of the American Mind:*

> They [students, and ultimately most Americans] are unified only in their relativism and in their allegiance to equality. And the two are related in a moral intention. The relativity of truth is not a theoretical insight, but a moral postulate, the condition of a free society, or so they see it.... The danger they have been taught to fear from absolutism is not error, but intolerance. Relativism is necessary to openness, and this is the virtue, the only virtue, which all primary education for more than fifty years has dedicated itself to inculcating. The point is not to correct the mistakes and really be right; rather it is not to think you are right at all.[3]

What Bloom is saying is that many are not on a quest for truth, but a quest for toleration. Language depicting objective good and objective evil, spiritual warfare, Christ defeating Satan, and fallen angels shut out of God's kingdom is offensive language. It is offensive not because it is inaccurate, but because it judges and excludes. Whether it is a correct description of reality is irrelevant. It is opposed because it makes people uncomfortable. The label "fundamentalism" is a convenient term with which to dismiss such views.

But hasn't our refusal to search for truth become a different kind of fundamentalism, a different kind of simplistic thinking? As the Very Reverend Paul Zahl put it:

> Here, perhaps, is a flaw in our church's capacity for pastoral care: for our very charity and riding easy over secondary issues can make us impotent to warn people of the practical, personal dangers that gnosticisms like astrology can

involve. Our vaunted tolerance can render us susceptible to
a damaging nonsense.[4]

In reaction to those Christians who turn away from Scripture's
teaching, other Christians have made deliverance from demons the
major part of their ministry to others, sometimes to the point of
ignoring other kinds of ministry. How do we respond correctly?

First, we need to remember that Christ supplies us with
various kinds of help in combating Satan. Grace helps us
overcome temptation. Defensive armor keeps the arrow stings
of the enemy from harming us (Ephesians 6:11–17). The
ministry of deliverance and exorcism lifts Satan and the demons
from or out of a person (Mark 1:23–26, 34; 3:11; 6:7–13).
Offensive weaponry rolls back Satan from others and society (2
Corinthians 10:4).

Second, we need to keep people from using Satan's activity
as an excuse for all bad behavior. Flip Wilson's humorous
comment, "The devil made me do it," is far too convenient.
While the devil often entices, scarcely does he compel. However
much we may be predisposed to listen to Satan because of our
bad upbringing, debilitating circumstances, or uncontrollable
mood swings, we have the ability to resist. Were this not so,
everyone would have an ironclad excuse to be horrible. And
even when behaviors are produced by possession, the person is
responsible for seeking deliverance.

Third, we need to make sure our ministry is a ministry to
people. While the demonic elements are bound and removed, we
must always deal lovingly with the victims, even if their behavior
is what invited Satan's presence.

Any loud shouting or histrionic displays did not come from
our Lord or His disciples, but from the evil spirits, who were then
bidden to keep silent (Mark 1:23–26, 34; 5:1–13).

Anyone involved in a ministry of deliverance must bear in
mind that the purpose of Jesus' work was to set captives free, not
to harm them emotionally or judge them (Luke 4:18). In setting

117

them free, we set them free unto Jesus. There is no way to release them except unto Christ.

While it is true that overzealous people have often done harm in their immature ministrations against evil, I believe far more damage comes from gentle, polite, overly cautious—and ineffectual—church folk who do nothing. As long as we bear in mind that the direct ministry against Satan is but one aspect of Christian ministry, that the power behind our ministry is God's and not ours, and that our ministry is to model that of Jesus, we will seldom do anyone harm.

Fourth, we need to understand the various ways Satan works on people. A consideration of the rare, but real phenomenon of actual *possession* by demonic spirits is beyond the scope of this study. Much more common are the experiences of Satan's tempting and oppressing God's people. It is to those topics that we will now turn.

TEMPTATION

The most common way Satan seeks to harm us is through temptation to sin. Such temptation marked the beginning of Jesus' public ministry. No doubt Jesus was still basking in the glow of His baptism, the descent of the Holy Spirit upon Him, and the reassuring words from heaven. (See Luke 3:21–22.) No doubt Jesus was eagerly anticipating the important ministry lying just ahead. But first, there was the matter of the temptations in the wilderness.

Some today assert that they could never be tempted in any serious way. They believe that because of the power God makes available to us, they would never give in to Satan. How foolish! A disciple is not above his teacher (Matthew 10:24). If the Lord was tempted, a Christian will be, too. It is true that we have resources available to us. John reminds us that:

> He [Christ] who is in you is greater than he [Satan] who is in the world.
>
> —1 JOHN 4:4

Yet we need to remember that Scripture warns us to be sober and vigilant, because Satan still prowls around like a lion seeking someone to devour (1 Peter 5:8). We should not cower in fear, but neither should we be cocky. Temptation happens to everyone, and that includes us (Matthew 26:41).

Why temptation?

We know that God is not the author of temptation, as James 1:13 tells us, but He must permit it because it does exist. Why does God allow temptation? I believe there are three reasons:

One, to preserve our free will. One of God's great gifts to us is our free will, with which we can make choices. To entice us to choose wrongly, Satan comes with temptations to sin. If we could not be persuaded to sin, how free would we be?

Two, to reveal to us our weaknesses so we can work, with God's help, to grow in Christ. When we are knocked around by various assaults, we see where we are strong and where we are weak. Every one of us has various "besetting sins," those weak spots where we are most vulnerable (Hebrews 12:1, KJV). Satan will naturally try to strike us there. If we ignore the reality of those "Achilles' heels," Satan can blindside us. If we are aware of them, we can be on our guard.

Three, to strengthen us. The successful overcoming of temptation strengthens us. As we are tempted, we get accustomed to the enemy's ways, become more proficient in receiving God's help during times of great need, and learn more about how to defeat Satan. This leads us to victory. As we are tempted, we see that we do not have to accept giving in to sin as inevitable. This leads to greater holiness.

Being tempted and, all too often, giving in might make us very discouraged, were it not for four facts:

1. While God allows the tempter to work on us, He places limits on what Satan can do. This is similar to the limits God placed on Satan's assault of Job (Job 1:12).

2. We are told that we will never be tempted beyond our God-assisted ability to escape (1 Corinthians 10:13). The keyword, however, is "God-assisted."

3. God gives us, in prayer, in Scripture, in the sacraments, and in one another, the help we need to triumph when tempted, provided we make use of these means of grace. These tools are helpful only if we use them.

4. On those occasions when we do give in to temptation, we find the Lord to be a forgiving Friend as we confess those sins (1 John 1:9).

Satan keeps at it

Having tried his utmost to defeat Jesus by tempting Him in the wilderness, the devil departed, but only for a while. He came back again right after Peter's confession that Jesus was the Christ, and again in the Garden. (See Mark 8:29–33; Luke 22:42.) Note several things:

One. *Satan never gives up.* He tried repeatedly to stop Jesus. Never think you will be finished with the devil just because you have resisted him once. He will try again. Be forewarned!

Two. *Satan tries different methods.* It is true that the temptation Satan offered through Peter and the temptation in the Garden of Gethsemane were really the same as the temptation in the wilderness—to win the kingdoms of the world by means other than what God the Father appointed, the redemption of sinners by Jesus' atoning death on the cross. While these three encounters between Jesus and Satan were essentially the same temptation, Satan was too clever to try the same temptation the same way, so he put it in a different cast. In the wilderness, the temptation came from Satan himself; later it came through Peter with his worldly reasoning; and in Gethsemane, it came from within Jesus' own human nature. Jesus' human nature was not fallen, for He was without sin. But He, being fully human, did experience the desire not to suffer: "Father, if thou art willing, remove this cup from me; nevertheless not my will, but thine, be done" (Luke 22:42). In the rest of humanity, however, human nature is fallen. This fallen human nature is given the term "the flesh" in Scripture.

When we recall the threefold renunciation of "the world, the flesh, and the devil" in the historic baptismal liturgy, we should understand that these words are more than poetic; they are the three chief modes through which temptation comes.

Three, Satan's temptations often follow spiritual highs. Billy Graham has stated that his worst battles with temptation come right after a successful evangelistic crusade. As we just noted, Jesus' temptations came right after His baptism, Peter's confession of faith, and His celebration of the Last Supper. I believe temptations come right after times of intense spiritual experience for two reasons: One—Satan delights to be the "skunk at the lawn party." God has just done something wonderful for us or through us. Satan wishes to snatch the victory away. Two—at moments of spiritual triumph we often let our guard down and perhaps even get our pride up. We think we have become so spiritually mature as to be invincible.

Victory

When the things Satan throws at us make us want to scream, we can meditate on the richness of God's grace and boldly proclaim with Paul:

> Thanks be to God, who gives us the victory through our Lord Jesus Christ.
>
> —1 Corinthians 15:57

OPPRESSION

In the spiritual warfare between the forces of darkness and the forces of light, Satan not only keeps up his rebellious opposition to God, but he also seeks to drag the rest of creation down with him. In addition to trying to tempt people to sin, he oppresses us in a variety of ways.

Keeping people in darkness

One of these ways is to keep people's minds dull and eyes blind so they will not respond to the gospel. (See John 9:39–41; Ephesians 4:18–19; Hebrews 5:11.) I was once preaching an evangelistic sermon in a village in the Philippines. It became apparent that nothing was registering in my audience. I started praying silently while preaching, asking God to show me what the problem was. I felt in my spirit there was a strong presence of evil there, actively keeping people from hearing.

I stopped my sermon and went over to several believing Christians, Filipino and American, who understood spiritual warfare, and I asked them to take authority in the name of Jesus to bind whatever forces of Satan were loose. Then I resumed preaching. I could sense a change almost immediately. Most people became very receptive. Several remained behind after the service to profess faith in Christ as Lord and Savior.

We later discovered that a group of occultists had put a spell on what we were trying to do in that service. The spell had reality and power, but, of course, God's power, *when utilized,* is more powerful. Our taking authority over the magic spell and our prayers for the people in the congregation did not force people to faith. But our prayers and binding of evil powers made it possible for them to hear the gospel and exercise their wills unfettered by the bondage caused by magic spells and evil spirits.

Not all such resistance to the gospel is caused by the direct operation of evil spirits. Sometimes resistance is due to human pride and the refusal to bend one's will to God. Sometimes the listener cannot figure out what the preacher is trying to say! But on many other occasions, the problem is demonic oppression.

Blocking worship

This oppression can also occur during worship. Since our "bounden duty" as well as our joy is to worship God in spirit and truth, as Jesus said in John 4:23, Satan will seek to make worship dull and uninteresting, or else encourage the enthusiasm to be human-generated emotionalism rather than a Holy Spirit–directed fervor. Good worship should do three things: glorify God, edify Christians, and evangelize nonbelievers. Dull or out-of-control worship will do none of these.

One Friday night, during team "prep time" of prayer before our healing service, it was apparent that our prayers were "not reaching the ceiling." Often, these prep times are special moments of drawing close to God and to each other—wonderful preparation for the ministries we would be leading in the service. But not this night. Finally, Mary, a wise, experienced layperson on the team, stated the problem: "There's an oppressing spirit here." With that, we took authority and bound it in the name of Jesus. Our word of command was something like this: "You spirit of oppression, we bind you in the name of Jesus and command you to leave this place at once. You go to Jesus for your future fate, harming no one on the way." Immediately our time of worship became rich and full.

Once again, let it be said that demonic oppression is not the only reason for dull worship. There are times that we rush to church, getting there at the last minute. We are just not ready to be still before God. Other times, like Martha of Bethany, we are distracted by many things. Or we are just plain tired. Sometimes we would rather go through the motions of religious activity than have a true encounter with God. Satanic oppression must not be a catchall diagnosis to excuse our faults. But on many occasions, the problem is demonic oppression.

Believers and accusations

A third occasion of oppression is in the area of accusations. Satan is "the accuser of our brethren" (Revelation 12:10). He tries to convince God of our unworthiness—not a difficult thing to do, since our sins make us unworthy indeed! But our Savior Jesus Christ's twofold ministry of atonement and advocacy is more than adequate.

Through His atonement Christ took the guilt of our sins onto Himself, suffering in our stead (Mark 10:45; 2 Corinthians

5:21; 1 Peter 2:24). When the Father looks at us, He sees Jesus' righteousness covering us like a cloak, and He pronounces us sinless in Him (Romans 6:23; 1 Corinthians 1:30; 6:11; Ephesians 1:7). And Jesus is our advocate before the Father, so when Satan gives his half-truths ("They are sinners"), Jesus responds with the whole truth, which sets us free ("They are sinners, but redeemed by My blood").

Since Satan cannot convince God of the lostness of those who believe in His Son, he will try to accuse us directly. If he cannot get us to deny our sins, he will try to get us to wallow in them. Just as bad as pride is humiliation. Sometimes, of course, the inability to feel forgiven once we have been forgiven is due to other factors, such as hormonal or body chemical imbalance, psychological difficulties, and so on. But we must never rule out satanic accusation as a contributing, if not primary, cause. The remedy is to tell Satan to get lost, for once we have confessed our sins and repented, those sins are forgiven in Jesus.

Satan will also try to stir up accusations between or among believers. I never cease to be amazed at how churches can split or Christians can become estranged over the most inconsequential matters. Such disruption keeps us from our tasks, gives a terrible witness to nonbelievers, and is disobedient to Scripture (Ephesians 4:1–4). Once again, Satan's behind-the-scenes influence does not excuse sinful human behavior. But it should help us see that we are not wrestling against people, but against "spiritual hosts of wickedness in the heavenly places" and to be on our guard against such satanic tricks (Ephesians 6:12). So, Christians, do not gang up against each other. Gang up together against the devil while you discuss your disagreements as brothers and sisters. As Benjamin Franklin said during the war of American independence, "We must all hang together, or assuredly we shall all hang separately."[5]

Sometimes churches seem prone to constant bickering over many generations about the same matters. I know of one church that, three times in one century, had a major division over music.

Another always seems to fight over property. Many other churches try regularly to fire their clergy. Even though the details change and the people involved are different, there are surprising similarities to each problem the churches have. I believe that just as there are guardian angels protecting each church, there are also attending evil spirits that cause disruption in special areas. (For example, see Revelation 2:8, 12, 18.) They work behind the scenes periodically to influence people to act sinfully in particular ways.

Once, a pastor of a church with recurring difficulties called me in for help. He knew about spiritual warfare and knew we had to work together to bind the spirits of division and rancor that were harming his church. Now, of course, this was only the first step. It would not take away the need for individuals to repent, ask for forgiveness, and forgive others. It would not take away the need for individuals to vow to settle their differences in the love of Jesus. But we seriously doubted that any of these things could ever happen if we did not address the spiritual problem first, and that was, in fact, the key. It is like a house fire being fueled by a gas leak. Until the gas is shut off, putting out the fire is difficult, if not impossible.

The devil's role in illness

A fourth kind of satanic oppression is through illness. Not all, or even the majority of, illness is directly caused by Satan. We may, by being sinfully anxious, raise our blood pressure or bring on ulcers. (See Philippians 4:6; 1 Peter 5:7.) We may be the victims of the malevolent words or deeds of others, and develop fears and insecurities. We may have been taught a distorted view of God and fail, as a result, to enter into a relationship with Him. Our bodies wear out, due to the aging process that became part of the human experience at the Fall. (See Genesis 2:1–7; 3:19; James 1:1–5.) The devil is lurking in the background here, but satanic oppression is not the direct cause in any of these events.

Some illness, however, *is* directly the devil's doing. Jesus said that the woman who was all bent over was bound by Satan (Luke

125

13:10–17). This is not a poetic or symbolic way of speaking. Nor can we patronize Jesus by saying He spoke this way as an accommodation to, or participation in, the ignorance of His time. Jesus was always quick to correct people who had a wrong or distorted view of things. He loved people, but He never met them halfway when it came to truth. Plus, there are many places where Scripture distinguishes illness, including epilepsy, from demon possession.

Several years ago a woman, I will call her Kellie, was referred to me. She had been suffering from recurrent epileptic seizures for many years. She did not lack for medical care, but her doctors were unable to help her in any significant way. The discernment of the priest who spoke with her initially was that her epilepsy was demonic in origin. I concurred.

In the course of one of our public healing services, I prayed and laid hands on Kellie's head, quietly commanding the evil spirit to depart in Jesus' name. She started to go into an epileptic seizure immediately. The ushers at our service helped her to a chair and attended to her. After the service, she said to me, "That was most unusual! My seizures always come at a certain time each month, never at any other time. But this one was not according to schedule. And at the end of the seizure it felt as though something got up and left me! Am I healed?"

Unless I am "100 percent certain" God is telling me that some one is healed, I do not say yes. Even then, I refer the person to a physician for medical verification. Otherwise there is the potential for much harm. I simply told Kellie that we should praise God for whatever He had just done, ask Him to continue to work, and wait to see if the seizures returned. That was October 1982—we are still waiting! Here was a case of an oppressing evil spirit manifesting itself by directly causing an illness. Discernment is needed to know which illnesses are caused by our sin, by disease, by repressed memories of sins against us, by bad diet, by evil spirits, or by any one of a number of causes.

Oppression in general

A fifth occasion of satanic oppression is the "little nastinesses" Satan throws in our paths. Years ago, I was part of a team helping out at a large healing service conducted on Tuesday evenings. Until we learned about satanic harassment, we were amazed at the "coincidence" of how minor disasters always seemed to strike us in the hours right before the service. If anyone's child was going to fall down a flight of stairs, if anyone's baby was going to get diarrhea, if anyone's car was to die, if anyone's mother was to call with bad news, if anyone's teenager was going to act horribly, or if anyone's tooth filling was to fall out, it was right before the Tuesday evening healing service! People from other healing teams have shared similar experiences.

The answer is to pray protection over yourself and your loved ones regularly, but especially on those days when you join in ministry. When we started doing this before our Tuesday evening healing services, the number of these little "nastinesses" diminished significantly.

I learned later that praying protection for ourselves *after* the services was important as well. An individual or healing team that has just concluded a time of ministry is especially vulnerable for two reasons:

First, we are spiritually drained. This means that without prayer we will be much more likely to think and act in an all-too-human way. We will do or say things that we regret, we will get into arguments with loved ones, and so on. We will be "running on empty." It also means that any additional ministry we attempt will likely fail, for we will not be ministering in the power of the Holy Spirit but in our own strength. We will, furthermore, be vulnerable to Satan's actions on us, without, as it were, the divine shields of protection in place. Note how Jesus frequently went off for periods of quiet fellowship with His Father after times of ministry (Luke 9:18). His human nature was drained, as His statement in Luke 8:46 in reference to the woman with the issue of blood indicates. He needed, as it were, to be "tanked up" again.

That is to say, His human nature needed to be replenished by the Holy Spirit.

Second, we have angered Satan. He has failed in his attempt to deflect us from ministering God's blessings. In his anger, he tries to harm us or inflict us with physical, emotional, or spiritual distress. He does this to get us to stop ministering in the future ("It's not worth the pain to minister to others," we might conclude), to discredit us and God's work in the eyes of others ("They claim to be God's instruments, but look at them!" others might say), or just to get his little revenge.

I saw an example of this when I was ministering healing in a city in the Philippines. Assisting a team of Americans were several devout people from a local church and from the missionary hospital, including a surgeon at the hospital. We had concluded the healing service and spent a few moments praising God for the many healing and conversions to Christ that had occurred during the service. We also took a few minutes to ask the Lord to replenish us in the Holy Spirit and to protect us from what the devil might try to do. As we were leaving the church, a jeep full of people drove up. They explained that they were late because they had had a flat tire. They wondered if they could be prayed for anyway.

Most of us on the team were so tired from having ministered virtually all day that we begged off further ministry. (By the way, although our hearts may go out to people in need, there are times when saying, "No, I just cannot" is the best response to give, as long as you explain that you are so drained you just have nothing to give.)

The surgeon felt he was still able to minister. We left him to pray briefly with these latecomers and went off to supper. About ten minutes later, we heard a terrible squeal of tires and saw people running in the direction of the church. There was the doctor sprawled in the road. A few of the people he had prayed for had been wonderfully and instantly healed as he prayed for them. After praying for the last of them, the doctor started walking toward the little restaurant to join the rest of the team. In his spiritual euphoria, he forgot his need to pray again for a refilling of the Holy Spirit and protection from the forces of darkness.

Thanks be to God, his injuries were slight, and he was able to join us for the service the next day. But the lesson of the need to pray protection after we minister was firmly grafted onto our minds.

Some might say that his experience was just a coincidence, and maybe it was. Yet the large number of these "coincidences" happening to people who do not pray God's protection before or after they minister leads many to believe they are much more than that.

While we do not pretend to know all the reasons for satanic harassment, we do know it is real, and the protection of God, while not preventing everything bad from happening, makes a big difference when we ask for it.

How Do You Know the Problem Is Satanic in Origin?

Earlier in this chapter, I mentioned a priest's discernment that the epilepsy Kellie suffered was demonic in origin. This question needs to be raised: how can we tell the origin of something that might variously be caused by a biochemical disorder, spiritual disobedience, emotional woundedness in childhood, improper diet, evil spirits, or any number of other causes? In one sense, we cannot always tell. The root cause or causes of various physical, emotional, and spiritual illnesses are, on many occasions, too complicated or elusive for exact diagnosis. Sometimes this does not matter. As we apply various remedies, the problem often clears up, even though we may never know which remedy was the one that actually affected the cure.

On other occasions, correctly discovering the root cause is essential. An automatic snap diagnosis of demonic activity may harm people. Sometimes the harm comes by giving people excuses for their behavior ("I cannot help myself; Satan has a grip on me"). Sometimes the harm comes by deflecting people from the work they need to do in inner healing or in confession. Sometimes the harm is done by forcing something heroic and dramatic, like an exorcism, when the problem is of less severity. As a physician friend pointed out to me, "You do not schedule brain surgery before they've tried aspirin!"

A second reason for discovering the root cause is the hysteria sometimes associated with the ministry of deliverance. Done by well-meaning but spiritually unbalanced "healers," the ministry of deliverance has frequently frightened people into thinking they are thoroughly and utterly possessed of Satan, when that is not the case. Compare this to the fright in a person who is told, incorrectly and in an offhand manner, that she has cancer. There is no need for screaming or jumping up and down. Such antics do not frighten Satan. They may, however, leave people emotionally frightened or spiritually wounded.

Sometimes the harm comes from keeping appropriate medical or psychiatric treatment away. There is a similarity between schizophrenia and demonic possession in several ways: potential for lack of contact with reality, hearing voices or seeing things that are not there, and profound withdrawal. While on some occasions, schizophrenia is the symptom and demonic activity is the root cause, sometimes schizophrenia is not demonic in origin. To continue to "exorcise" nonexistent demons, while keeping counseling and medicine away, harms the patient twice: by keeping away appropriate treatment, and possibly by scaring the patient.

An interesting study was done among Christian psychiatrists regarding appropriate approaches to the severely mentally disturbed. Questionnaires were mailed to the 260 psychiatrists and psychiatry residents who, at the time of the study, were members of the Christian Medical and Dental Association (CMDA). They were asked to estimate which of three possible interventions— Bible and prayer, insight psychotherapy, and psychotropic medications—would be most effective on seven psychological or psychiatric diagnoses. Their general conclusion, while not ruling out the helpfulness of prayer, was that pharmacotherapy, or medicine, is the best way of the three to treat schizophrenia and mania, and that Bible study and prayer are more effective than the other two for the diagnoses of alcoholism, sociopathy, suicidal intent, and grief reaction.[6]

I am happy to receive such wisdom from people who are both mental health experts and practicing, biblical Christians. Too often, Christians have arrogantly dismissed everything in the realm of psychiatry or psychotropic medicines due to frequent encounters with psychiatrists hostile to both Christianity and the ministry of deliverance. I have met open-minded, sincere psychiatrists, on the other hand, who are not at all hostile to religion, but who have been turned off to the healing ministry because of the harm done by amateurish practitioners.

When I am confronted with a situation in which a diagnosis of demonic activity is possible, I do two things. First, I make sure that the more regular approaches have been tried and found wanting. Has the person had a thorough physical examination lately? Does he or she eat a balanced diet? Has he or she made a good, thorough confession recently? Has someone been working with him or her about inner healing issues? Is the person under the care of a psychologist or psychiatrist? What is the person's spiritual life like? Except in extreme cases, I will not begin an in-depth ministry of deliverance until we have covered these bases.

Second, having tried to rule out demonic activity, if possible, I proceed only if there seem to be positive reasons to do so. What do I look for?

I ask about occultic involvement, whether done innocently or as a deliberate rebellion against God. (See Appendix 5 for a partial list of occultic practices.) Next, I ask if there are close relatives who are practicing occultists. I ask if the person has called upon Satan, evil powers, or spiritual powers other than God and the holy angels, either for assistance, to minister healing to another person, to render harm to another person, or to cause something to happen. I ask if the person has knowledge of any curses having been placed on him or her. I ask the person if he believes there are demons; if so, I ask, "What are they like? How do they act? What are their names?" Sometimes I will address the demons quietly: "I command any demons who are present to reveal yourselves. In the name of Jesus, tell me your names." There is no need for screaming. It does not frighten the demons; it may frighten the person we are trying to help.

While this approach is biblical, it is not foolproof. (See Mark 5:9.) Some demons play tricks or hide and reveal themselves only after repeated commands. Other times, a responding "voice" may not be demonic, but an indicator of a deep psychological disturbance. In general, though, if done gently, this approach can yield helpful information.

I then look to see if there are unusual spiritual distractions, or "blockings," that may indicate Satan at work. I look especially for an unusual inability to confess or praise God. I do not mean by this the boredom or distraction in worship that happens even to the most devout. I mean the inability to take on one's lips the name of Jesus or offer aloud statements of praise.

Let me give you an example. Several years ago I was conducting a healing service in the Chapel of St. Andrew's Seminary in Quezon City, the Philippines. During the service, I noticed two students leering at me and making a mockery of the event. When they came up for prayer, I felt a strong sense of evil and foreboding. I asked them both to repeat after me, "Jesus is Lord." Neither could utter the phrase. My prayer partner was the Most Reverend Manuel Lumpias, then-Presiding Bishop of the Philippine Episcopal Church. Together, we commanded the evil spirits in Jesus' name to depart. We continued to do this for about ten minutes. Finally both students blurted out, "Jesus is Lord." With that they fell to the floor, physically and spiritually exhausted.

We learned later, that in the years prior to seminary, they had both participated in several occultic healing services in their native villages. They had done this not out of intentional rebellion against God, but because loved ones were ill and none of the Christian clergy in their area believed in Jesus' power to heal the sick today. The lack of belief in the healing ministry on the part of their clergy was expressive of theological liberalism that denied basic truths of the gospel and was centered on a political agenda. No wonder these students were both driven to occultists, and no wonder they were ignorant of the dangers!

These six steps I take in ascertaining whether a person's problem is due, in whole or part, to demonic presence have kept me from making snap, often erroneous, judgments. Although they have proven helpful, they are not foolproof. For that reason, as well as the need not to alarm or frighten unnecessarily, we must be especially careful in how we proceed.

I will leave to the more specialized manuals on spiritual warfare a discussion of full-blown exorcism and focus instead on ministering deliverance. What is the difference between the two? Chiefly, one of degree. An exorcism may be called for in someone *possessed* by the devil or by a greater number of evil spirits, by particularly tough ones, or both. Deliverance is for someone *oppressed* by evil spirits, particularly a small number. An exorcism needs far more serious prayer preparation before, and prayer covering during, the time of ministry; deliverance, while not a trivial matter, needs relatively less. In extreme situations, any Christian may be called on to conduct an exorcism, though this ministry is usually best left to those specially called, thoroughly trained, and carefully prepared for it. A deliverance prayer can be offered by most Christians.

While these distinctions are not to be seen as technical or foolproof, I hope they provide a working definition between the more "entry level" and the advanced kinds of spiritual warfare.

MINISTERING DELIVERANCE

Following are the steps to a deliverance session.

Preparation

Unless the situation warrants immediate action, deliverance is best scheduled in advance to allow proper preparation on the part of those who will be ministering. Whenever possible, deliverance should be conducted by two or three people. Their preparation should be bathed in prayer, especially prayer for protection by the blood of Christ and by the holy angels. They should confess any unconfessed sins and remind themselves of the forgiveness that is theirs by faith in Christ. The reason: sometimes Satan plants thoughts of unworthiness in our minds or speaks to us audibly during the deliverance session about our sin.

His speech, as usual, is full of half-truths. True, we committed those sins. But if we can say, "My sins have been confessed and washed away by the blood of Jesus," we can successfully parry the accusations of Satan and continue our ministry undistracted. Sometimes preparation for deliverance ministry includes fasting. We may also want to have others in prayer and fasting for us at the appointed hour of ministry.

Preliminary to actual ministry

Unless it is an emergency, we should spend some time talking with the person needing deliverance. We have already talked with him or her enough to conclude that the ministry of deliverance may be warranted. Now we are talking for other reasons.

First, to offer reassurance. A person about to undergo deliverance ministry is most likely frightened. Many have seen the movie *The Exorcist* or heard stories, real or exaggerated, about the wild things that happen during this kind of ministry. Our job is to calm them and assure them that, while some frightening things may happen during the time of ministry, we are not interested in histrionics. We might tell them a little bit about what usually happens during a deliverance ministry session.

Second, to elicit their active participation. In most instances, people are not to be passive in ministry, but an active part of the team. It is, after all, their life, not ours, and it would be inappropriate for them to become dependent. We can help them take responsibility for their spiritual walk right now by getting them, as much as is possible, to pray aloud with us. Sooner or later they will have to renounce any occultic involvement and (re)dedicate their life to Jesus, so why not get them on board now?

The time of ministry

Our words are a simple command to Satan and the evil spirits to depart in the name of Jesus. As believers in the Lord Jesus Christ, we have authority in His name to cast out evil spirits (Matthew 10:1). Once again, we do not have to shout, because neither Satan nor the evil spirits are deaf, nor are they frightened by such nonsense. What does frighten them is the name of Jesus. This holy name is not magic. When the seven sons of Sceva tried to use it apart from the acknowledgment of Jesus as Lord and Savior, an evil spirit drove them out of the house naked and wounded (Acts 19:13–16). The name of Jesus is a reminder to Satan that Jesus defeated Satan's chief weapon, death, on the cross, and that Jesus' blood makes atonement for sin, defeating the eternal lostness people suffer because of sin.

Be careful of magic. Even done with a veneer of Christian language, the use of magic to cast out evil spirits is trying to defeat the devil by using the devil's tools. I have seen harm done by using incantations; by calling down undefined "spiritual powers"; by attempting to overpower Satan with one's own spiritual strength or "soul power"; and by the use of a cross or picture of Jesus, not as an adjunct to calling on the Lord's name, but as a magic amulet, however Christian-looking. Some black Pentecostal groups, especially those with strong ties to the Caribbean, make use of enemas. Popular in the 1970s, though thankfully less so now, was the practice of asking people to retch out the demons into a paper bag. While any of these less-than-Christian approaches may yield some results (some demons may actually leave), others may enter, invited in some cases by the very approaches used to scare the others away. I often pray quietly, "I command any evil spirits present to depart in the name of Jesus. You will depart, going to Jesus for your future fate, harming no one on the way."

Sometimes there is a noticeable response—sometimes tears; sometimes deep groanings or sighing; sometimes, though not often, flailing of arms or rolling of eyes. Occasionally evil spirits will speak. Because they are spiritual beings, they may possess information about one of the ministry team or about anything at all that is correct. The beginner in this ministry may be confused by this. "How did this demon know my mother's maiden name?" Having said this, however, note that only God is all-knowing. Sometimes the demon may remind us of a sin we committed. This is why a good confession beforehand is helpful. Sometimes the demon will try to play on our sympathies. One addressed me in a sad, childlike voice, "I never wanted to oppress this person in the first place."

The purpose of any of this communication, of course, is to deflect us from our sole purpose: getting the person free in the name of Jesus. That someone would know Mom's maiden name is interesting but irrelevant. "Be gone, in Jesus' name!" That we committed such-and-such a sin is none of the demon's business. We confessed that to Jesus anyway. "Be gone, in Jesus' name!" That some poor little demon may or may not have joined in his fellows' oppressing of a person is not our concern. "Be gone, in Jesus' name!" In no case are we to enter into a discussion with any evil spirits. We ignore what they are saying and keep repeating the command for them to leave, in Jesus' name.

Often, however, there is no outward manifestation of anything.

How do we know when the task is complete and it is time to stop? Once again, while there is no foolproof answer, here are some things I look for:

First, is my discernment telling me the task has been accomplished? This discernment grows with experience. Second, does the person to whom we have been ministering now sense a release from bondage, a new freedom within, a removal of whatever he or she sensed was wrong? Third, is the person now able to do things he or she was demonically prevented from doing before (for example, praising the name of Jesus or confessing that He is Lord)?

Sometimes nothing seems to have changed. There are two possible reasons: first, we were not wise enough or prayed up enough. We attempted to do it in our own strength. Do not be discouraged. Even Jesus' disciples had to go back to school when they failed at first at deliverance (Matthew 17:19–21). Take stock of what you may have done wrong, ask God for forgiveness and wisdom, do more reading on the subject, and do better next time. In the meantime, find someone wiser and more experienced to help the person you failed to help. Second, we may need to consider whether the diagnosis of demonic oppression or possession was correct.

Aftercare for the person set free

After the time of deliverance ministry is over, it is important that "aftercare" happens. Immediately after any evil spirits have departed, we need to pray with the person a prayer of (re)commitment to Jesus as Lord and Savior and to be filled with the Holy Spirit. We need to teach them how to pray, worship, and study Scripture. It is not enough for the evil to depart. The good now has to enter in. The reason for this is threefold.

First, for protection. Jesus said that when an unclean spirit leaves a place, unless that space is filled, the evil spirit will return and reoccupy the empty place, accompanied this time by several other spirits (Matthew 12:43–45).

Second, for fulfillment of spiritual desires. In many cases, people got involved in occultic/New Age practices because they were spiritually hungry, and either did not know the gospel or, if they did, did not want to pay the price of following Jesus. If we do not point out the dangers of false spiritual choices, which lead to the need for deliverance, and if we do not introduce them to the only One who can satisfy their spiritual longings, they might go back to occultic/New Age practices.

Third, and most importantly, for wholeness. Only Jesus saves. Even if the person is protected somehow from the return of the evil spirits, and even if the person feels satisfied and fulfilled in life, if he or she does not know Jesus as Lord and Savior, his or her future destiny will be lostness, not eternal life in heaven. What is the point of being set free from "diseases," whether physical, emotional, or spiritual, only to lose your soul. (See Luke 12:20.)

Aftercare includes other aspects of the healing ministry, too. Seldom does deliverance stand alone. Sometimes there needs to be confession for all manner of sins committed during one's bondage. Sometimes I encourage a person to pray, "Lord, I do not know what percentage of this was my fault, but whatever amount was, I ask Your forgiveness. I also ask Your cleansing for everything unclean within me and Your power to help me change. In Jesus' name. Amen."

Sometimes a person needs inner healing. Often bad things happened to them while they were in spiritual bondage. They may have been targeted for ridicule by others because they acted in unusual ways. They may have been emotionally hurt by the demons themselves. We may have been emotionally distressed simply because there is much emotional wounding in society. Whatever the reason, I have never seen anyone set free from demonic presence through a ministry of deliverance who did not also need some degree of inner healing.

Aftercare for the ministry team

Remember, the team needs aftercare as well. Spiritual warfare, even of a moderate variety, leaves one drained spiritually and tired physically. Remember to put some time into prayer, asking God to replenish you. Additionally, pray for protection. God has used you to roll back Satan, even if just a bit. Satan may try to strike back, to punish you and scare you off from future ministry against him. Pray for protection, and there will be far less likelihood of anything bad happening. Positively, spend some time enjoying fellowship with the Lord, for whom you were an instrument of ministry and healing.

DISCUSSION QUESTIONS

1. What does the Fall of Adam and Eve (original sin) mean to you?

2. What does the Fall have to do with brokenness, healing, and wholeness?

3. What do you believe the Scriptures mean when referring to the devil, demons, and other evil spiritual beings in the world?

4. Satan's favorite weapon is the lie. Discuss Satan's lies in
    a. the temptations of Jesus.
    b. our own temptations.
    c. "besetting sins" or compulsive and addictive behavior.

5. What is meant by *spiritual warfare*? How important is it in your life?

6. Why is it important to obtain protection before ministering healing? And afterward?

EXPERIMENT

Block out *at least* twenty minutes of quiet solitude. The purpose of this experiment is to expose some lies of Satan and to put on some armor. Take at least five minutes in quiet, thoughtful, verbal thanksgiving and praise. Read Ephesians 4:17–24. Assume a comfortable posture. Relax. Ask God to bring to your mind those things that hinder your effectiveness in prayer and healing. Record these in your healing notebook.

CHAPTER 8

Christian Healing and the New Age Movement

O
NE OF THE current challenges to Christianity in general, and to Christian healing in particular, is that collection of philosophies and spiritualities given the name "the New Age movement." There is nothing new about the New Age movement, except for the packaging. Many of its beliefs and practices repeat the Baalism against which the Old Testament prophets spoke and the gnosticism against which such Church Fathers as Irenaeus had to contend.

Although it is beyond the scope of this book to describe in detail the origins and beliefs of the New Age movement, I will list briefly some of its central beliefs in order to illustrate its infiltration into the Church's ministry of healing.

NEW AGE BELIEFS

Monism

This is the belief that all is one. This does not mean a close connectedness, such as the fellowship we enjoy in our personal relationships with God. Rather, *monism* means "a oneness of *essence.*" That is, monists believe there is no difference at all between "creator" and the various objects of creation, except for an illusory, outward appearance. To a monist, the problem of the universe is not one of sin, but of separateness. The parts of the One have become separated, and the goal is to get everything back together. This is one element behind many forms of witchcraft. Opposites—good and evil, male and female—must be reunited if there is to be a restoration to Oneness.

God as force

Most New Age groups see "god" as impersonal force, energy, or consciousness. Recall "the force" from the *Star Wars* movies. There can be no personal relationship with this power. One learns instead how to gain access to it. New Age leaders do not help people come to know the transcendent-yet-personal God, who has a will for their lives. Rather a leader, who may be called magician, witch, adept, wizard, shaman, or guru, seeks to instruct people in gaining and using divine power for their own purposes, whatever they may be.

We are God

The old humanistic challenge to Christianity asserted that no matter how noble or worthy we are, we are essentially naked apes, the present end product of an impersonal time-plus-chance evolutionary process. The New Age movement teaches that we are all gods in disguise, emanations from the once-whole One. Werner Erhard, founder of est, the Mastery Foundation, and Forum, put it this way, "You are God in your universe."[1] The Maharishi Mahesh Yogi, founder of Transcendental Meditation, said, "Be still and know that *you* are God."[2] New Age leaders tell us that we can trust our "inner light" as infallible and that we need no authority—not the Bible, the Church, or other people—to tell us what to do or believe.

The Christ Spirit vs. Jesus the Christ

While the old theological liberalism saw Jesus as a human being with a particularly well-developed God-consciousness, but not as God made flesh, New Age spirituality sees Jesus as a manifestation of God, but not uniquely so. Rather, Jesus of Nazareth was only one of a number of ascended masters who possessed "the Christ Spirit" in a special way. The founders of all the religions of the world possessed this Christ Spirit. Thus, say New Agers, all the religions of the world teach essentially the same thing, and dogmas and doctrinal distinctions are irrelevant. Nearly all cults use the words *God, Jesus, Christ, the Spirit,* and so on, but with different meanings attached. Therefore, do not ask, "Do you believe in Jesus?" Instead ask, "What do you believe about Jesus?" For that reason, Christians must know the Scriptures, the creeds, and, as much as possible, the doctrinal controversies in which the post-apostolic Church was embroiled. Otherwise, we may get caught up in a group or by a teaching that sounds good but is subtly, dangerously wrong.

Salvation through knowledge

According to New Age teaching, it is not our sins, but the ignorance of our essential goodness and oneness with the entire universe that keeps us from being who and what we are meant to be. In order to grow and develop—and find healing—we need to break through this ignorance. There are, depending on which New Age group we explore, various ways to do this. Some include meditation techniques that involve emptying oneself, hearing the wisdom of spirit guides speaking through channels, learning to hear and trust the guidance of one's inner voice, accepting the insights of humanistic psychology, participating in consciousness-raising techniques such as sensory deprivation or mind-expanding drugs, or by experiencing such occult practices as astrology, palmistry, or séances. The purpose, in any case, is to gain wisdom presently secret or hidden. The word *occult* literally means "hidden" or "secret." The reference is to esoteric, deeper truths known only by the specially enlightened elite.

Biblical Christianity, by contrast, is far more democratic. It can be understood by scholars and nonscholars, the brilliant and the simple, adults and even children. In combating a form of gnosticism, Paul taught that the fullness of the Godhead dwelt bodily in Christ, and that in Christ we have come to spiritual fullness (Colossians 2:9–10). There is nothing else to get from God, except His grace to live more fully into our discipleship. There is no special teaching about doctrine or morality reserved only for the elite, the specially educated, those who have experienced certain special revelations, or those who, through their pain, have come to a different revelation of God. The basics of Christian doctrine and morality are clearly written in Scripture. The problem is not gaining more information or enjoying exhilarating experiences. The problem is surrendering our minds and wills to believe and obey what God has taught.

Reincarnation

This is the belief that souls will keep coming back endlessly until they are enlightened enough to escape into the core of the One. Connected with this is the belief in *karma*, a Sanskrit word meaning "the result of our deeds." That is, whatever happens to us in this life is determined by our behavior in previous lives. Through "past life regression" we can learn about previous lives so as not to make the same mistakes. Through gaining knowledge of our "true essence" we may escape the cycle of endless incarnations and meld into the One.

Some Bible passages that clearly rule out reincarnation are 2 Samuel 12:23; 14:14; Psalm 78:39; Luke 23:39–43; Acts 17:31; 2 Corinthians 5:1, 4–8; 6:2; Galatians 2:16; 3:10–13; Ephesians 2:8–9; Philippians 1:23; Hebrews 9:27; 10:12–14; Revelation 20:11–15.

While we must be careful not to label as "New Age" anything that differs from our own opinions or that bears superficial resemblance to New Age teaching, we must be on our guard that these beliefs do not work their way into the practice of Christian healing. The reasons are twofold: First, because one of the ways disciples of Christ honor Him is by believing what He taught, especially in the face of philosophies that contradict. Second, because wrong belief leads to bad consequences. While we seek to obey God *because He is God,* we soon discover that His commands are good for us and that anything to the contrary is sooner or later harmful. As Jesus said, it is the truth that sets us free (John 8:32).

AREAS TO WATCH

Here are some areas in which we have to be careful that the ministry of Christian healing not be poisoned by New Age beliefs:

An uncritical acceptance of psychology

Psychology is a broad discipline with many branches. Some of these branches are compatible with the teachings of Christ, some are friendly but contain points that contradict, and others are hostile and contemptuous. As we welcome the many positive benefits psychology can bring to troubled people, we must be aware of the dangers. We must be aware of the presuppositions of a particular school of psychology or a particular practitioner of psychology.

Is the revealed truth of the Christian faith believed in or merely tolerated, or even seen as part of a person's problem?

Is the basis for counseling the Christian view of man: created in the image of God, but fallen through sin, in need of a Savior, faith in whom leads to forgiveness, whole only when in relationship with God in Christ? Or is man seen as "come of age," able to be made whole apart from a saving relationship with God in Christ?

Is sin seen as a departure from God's will with serious consequences or as another form of neurosis, foisted on people by religion or parents, to be dismissed as a false and harmful idea?

Christians need not cave in before the supposed authority of psychology anymore than we should before any other human authority. God has revealed to us in Scripture the true nature of people and what we need to be whole. We hold these tenets not because "it is our religion," but because we believe they are true. Thus, any counselor who has a different set of presuppositions must be seen as (perhaps) sincere, but possibly ineffectual or even harmful. This is not because we are jealous of others in the helping professions—we need all the help we can get—but because we know that only what lines up with reality will ultimately help people.

Closely related to this is the area of self-image. Much has been written on this, from scholarly treatises to mass-market paperbacks, and many in the Church assume the best we can do for someone is help him or her overcome a bad self-image. But sometimes bad self-image and some of the guilt feelings we have stem from *real moral guilt* before God and humanity. *False guilt* (and religion, sad to say, is sometimes to blame for some of this in people) needs to be exposed for the falsehood that it is. True guilt will never go away, however, until it is confessed to God with full purpose of amendment of life, with promise to make whatever restitution is called for, and with the willingness to ask the forgiveness of others.

Pumping up a person with a sense of "You're OK" is like building a house on a shaky foundation. It may make a person feel confident for a while, but it masks the deeper issues, problems that will once again come crashing to the surface. I have seen guilty people go to therapy session after therapy session in which others are blamed for problems, biblical morality is denied, and belief in sin dismissed as foolish. They continue to go to expensive therapy and are no better for it, condemned to a modern equivalent of Lady MacBeth's endless hand washing—always washing, but never getting clean. Thank God for Christian counseling, though be warned that a psychologist who is a Christian does not necessarily practice "Christian psychology," in which those insights of psychology compatible with Christian understanding of mankind, our problems, and our hopes can be used to set people truly free.

Our true image emerges only in Christ. As we are related to Him, we have the tarnish of our fallenness removed and take on a new nature. I once heard a black evangelist describe how his conversion to Christ changed his self-esteem. Although he hated the put-downs of white racists, he believed inwardly much of what they said. Not long after he came to Christ, he read in 1 Peter 2:9 the description of who a person is in Christ. The next day, when a bigot taunted him, he turned and said, "Don't you know whom you are talking to? I am a member of the royal priesthood, the holy nation. I am one of God's own, and Jesus dwells within me!" Not only did the bigot turn and flee, but also his own inferiority complex.

A transformation like the evangelist's does not usually happen that quickly. Often a person's sense of worthlessness comes from a whole life of emotional deprivation or abuse. Sharing the good news of God's unconditional love is a necessary first step in a person's healing, but it is seldom enough. Anyone with a rotten self-image needs more than *knowing about* God's love; he needs to *feel* it and feel it over a period of time. This often happens as he is loved unconditionally by another human being. As such human love is given, he can begin to understand and experience the infinitely more powerful love of God, which alone can bring the root transformation of self-esteem.

Positive prayer as a way to coerce God

Confidence that God can do wonderful things is important in opening us up to receive those blessings. Jesus was stopped in His desire to bless His hometown people because of their unbelief (Matthew 13:58). James tells us that one of the reasons we lack certain things God wants to give us is that we do not ask in faith (James 4:2).

The Church too often wears a false humility before God, assuming that God seldom wishes to bless us. We take Jesus' statement in John 10:10 that He came to give us a life of new and special quality and substitute stoic resignation as our fate. We put aside Jesus' many examples of healing the sick and instead counsel sick people to cope with their pain. Certainly the Church needs a lot of teaching if we are going to exercise positive, believing faith.

A perversion of positive faith has arisen in the so-called positive confession movement. In this brand of teaching, Christians are taught to make a "faith statement" about something they desire, believing that God is then obligated to grant whatever they have prayed for. In another form of this, we are encouraged to visualize ourselves as we want to be, which is almost always successful, in a position of influence and power, and with accompanying material possessions. By visualizing this, confessing it verbally to ourselves and others, and banishing as faithless doubt any thought to the contrary, our desires will come true. (For an excellent discussion of the positive confession movement, see the chapter "The Prosperity Gospel" in Charles E. Hummel's book *Fire in the Fireplace: Charismatic Renewal in the Nineties*.)

There are several problems for the Christian in this way of thinking.

First and foremost, where is God in such a scheme? If we have determined what is right for us and then tell God to go do it, we no longer seek God's desire for our lives and instead see Him as a celestial waiter.

I thank God that on many occasions He did *not* give me what I so earnestly desired. Although His answer was often different from what I wanted, it was always better. We have to be careful, further, that in the process of forming mental pictures of what we want, we are not unwittingly reaching out to spiritual entities not submitted to God.

Second, the desires so often "claimed" in prayers of positive confession are self-indulgent. I have seldom heard such emotional investment in prayers for peace, justice, the poor, or one's enemies. Nor have I heard prayers such as Solomon spoke, when he turned down the opportunity to pray for his own prosperity and asked instead for wisdom to rule wisely (1 Kings 3:7–12).

Third, this system of thought leaves little room for suffering or walking in the way of the cross. While I agree that the Church is often resigned to illness, not grasping the words or actions of Jesus, still we are told in the Gospels that there will be suffering, ridicule, and persecution for bearing His name. We have the examples of Jesus who had nowhere to lay His head, and of Paul who was beaten, shipwrecked, and jailed (Matthew 8:20; 2 Corinthians 11:23–28). Paul reminds us that it is sometimes amid famine, peril, persecution, nakedness, and the sword that we conquer, not by their removal (Romans 8:35–37).

The "gospel" of the positive confession movement is a severe, punishing gospel. As long as everything is working according to plan, we seem to be worthy practitioners of this message. But when things go wrong, when a prayer is not answered, when we are not rolling in material blessings or enjoying perfect health, the implication is we allowed doubt to creep in or that we are harboring major unconfessed sin.

To suggest that to someone who is suffering is as insensitive as the comments of Job's friends, who said that if Job were sick and remained sick, it had to be his fault (Job 4:7–9; 8:3–7; 11:3–6, 13–20). Sometimes, to be sure, we do not receive God's blessings because we have done something wrong or because of unbelief or sin (Mark 2:10–11; John 5:14). But as the account of Job shows, this is not always true. Positive-confession teaching ill equips us for times of hardship, nor does it kindly dispose us to Christians who are suffering. One man told me, "They deserve to suffer, because if they had practiced positive confession, they'd be on easy street now."

Fourth, the "technique" of gaining what we want through praying "the right way" is an exercise in magic. Magic, or sorcery, is the attempt to get a desired result by reciting certain words or following certain procedures. The words or procedures are paramount, not God. Our ability to use them, not the grace of God, determines the results.

A few in the positive confession movement even say that nonbelievers can get what they want because the laws of positive confession work for anybody who performs them correctly. I

149

wonder if they ever read about the sons of Sceva in Acts 19:13–16, who tried an exorcism "by the Jesus whom Paul preaches," only to have the evil spirits turn on them for such foolishness. Prayer is not the manipulation of God through technique, but a relationship of love.

Fifth, it perverts the meaning of faith. While "the faith" is a body of truths or doctrines, *faith* is always *faith in* someone or something. In positive confession teaching, faith is not faith in God, no matter how much proponents say it is. If God is so unwise, unloving, or unable to be trusted with the needs of my life that I have to tell Him exactly what to do, how can I say I have faith in Him? Dr. Charles Farah, a Pentecostal pastor from Tulsa, Oklahoma, rightly calls this attitude presumption. If everything hinges on the correct wording of my faith statement with no doubts on my part, then the faith has to be *in me*—in my ability to phrase that confession correctly and keep myself from doubt.

Faith, correctly, is the confident trust in God who has proven trustworthy and who can be trusted with my needs because He is love. While God delights to have us tell Him what our needs are as we perceive them—what loving parent does not let a child prattle on with his or her wish list?—we can rest secure in His wise love. We trust Him, who has in store for those who love Him things beyond our desires, much less our deserving. This, and not some presumptuous foot-stomping or magical manipulation, is the ultimate faith statement.

Sixth, by denying the reality of lingering symptoms, we have stepped over the line into Christian Science. Christian Science is not just another denomination that happens to stress healing. It is a religious philosophy that denies the reality of material things. In Christian Science, one's body cannot be sick because the body is illusory. The problem is in *thinking* oneself to be sick. "Healing" in Christian Science is bringing a person to believe in the non-reality of the problem. The statement "I am healed, but the symptoms don't know it yet" is illustrative of this philosophy.

Too many operations have been called off, too much medicine has been thrown away, and too many people have been harmed by the belief that if we just say the right words everything is healed immediately, no matter what the symptoms indicate. A person is not healed until the symptoms are healed! It is much better to say, "I believe Jesus is healing me right now. I do not know how quickly or slowly He will do this, so until the symptoms clear up, I will continue to pray and take my medicine."

Healing through magic

In the laudable growth of the restoration of healing in the Church, we have to be careful that we do not slip into a form of healing that is occult-like. We have to be on our guard in three areas especially.

First, we in the Church have to be on our guard in terms of diagnosis. We find two methods of diagnosis in Scripture: observation/testing/conversation, and a word of knowledge.

As for the former, Jesus or the apostles often saw what the problem was, or else the sick person or a loved one told them. Expanding this into current medical practice, we have the intake interview and the evidence yielded by various diagnostic tools such as taking one's temperature or blood pressure, or taking an x-ray or CT scan. In sessions of healing or counseling, the persons seeking prayer will tell us what they believe the problem to be. The person ministering healing or doing counseling will ask questions to garner further information. Problems in a person's life will often point directly to certain root causes.

The word of knowledge, as we will see in chapter ten, is one of the gifts of the Holy Spirit referred to in 1 Corinthians 12:8. It means a supernatural bestowal of information by God directly to a person. Someone in a healing ministry will often pray with an individual and get a strong impression that something is wrong instead of or in addition to what the sick person spoke of. In some cases, the sick person knows about the problem and is surprised when the one praying says, "Can we pray for your gallbladder problem, too?" In other cases, the sick person does not know he has a problem in that area. Many times, the people being prayed for are amazed and thankful when their physicians not only confirm a problem in that area, but also express gladness that it was discovered when it was.

In occult healing, other means of diagnosis are employed, such as spirit guides speaking through "channels," séances, or psychometry (which is holding an object owned by a person to receive impressions or thoughts). Olga Worrell, a well-known occult healer in Baltimore, received words from her dead husband in "the spirit world." Others try to discern illness by becoming sensitive to energy waves emanating from a body. What is wrong with these practices?

All occultic practices are condemned in Scripture. (See Leviticus 19:31; 20:6, 27; Deuteronomy 18:9–14.) Followers of Jesus do not wish to participate in anything God rules out, even if we do not always understand why He rules it out.

Also, the power source behind them is satanic. While some occultic practices may look harmless, Christians know that their power source is the devil. Paul tells us that objects people sacrifice to idols are sacrificed, however unknowingly, to demons (1 Corinthians 10:20). Paul also tells us in 2 Corinthians 11:14 that Satan can masquerade as an angel of light, until someone has been involved with forbidden practices long enough to get hooked, harmed, or both. I have spoken to dozens of clergy of many denominations who have told me of the problems that eventually befell parishioners who got involved in occult-based healing services. This has been my experience, too. Problems such as deep, lasting depression, onset of compulsivity in particular sins, indifference to God in those once keen for Him, and, in a few cases, a series of bizarre accidents have been observed in those who have made use of healers not following God's ways. Lengthy sessions of deliverance or exorcism have often been necessary.

Second, we in the Church have to be on our guard regarding the means of cure. Christian healing is based on prayers for healing to God who cures. While the whole tenor of Scripture indicates that God is on the side of health—indeed, we do not find Jesus ever refusing anyone who comes to Him for healing—God retains sovereignty over the outcome. God may heal with no appeal made to Him by anyone. God may heal directly in response to prayer. God may choose to make use of material objects by which grace, blessing, and healing are conveyed. In Scripture and Church tradition, we read of blessed prayer cloths and holy oil (Acts 19:11–12; James 5:14). God may use Communion, holy water, or any number of objects. The historical term in the Church for these things is *sacramentals*. One contemporary Pentecostal minister of healing has called them "delivery systems." In addition, the laying on of hands is frequently a part of healing—indeed, of many different acts of blessing.

The most crucial thing to remember when ministering to the sick is that the Lord likes to heal in a variety of ways. On one occasion, Jesus put His fingers in someone's ears; another time He placed mud on someone's eyes; on other occasions He issued a command to walk, rebuked a fever, and simply stated that someone back home was no longer ill.

The reason for this variation in manner of healing is so that *the focus will be kept on God.* Since we are never certain as to which way God will choose to heal or the time frame in which He will accomplish it, our focus is kept on Him. There is no "technique of healing."

In various New Age healings, cure is effected by invoking spiritual powers or readjusting the flow of energy either from outside or from within. Whether this involves energy emanating from therapeutic touch, cooking up a potion of herbs, rubbing crystals over an infected area, or invoking spiritual entities by chanting, the central focus is off the God of Scripture and onto a procedure or ritual.

One might ask why, if our Lord likes to heal in a variety of ways, are these New Age ways ruled out? While God does use a number of ways, He has ruled out many others. We are not limiting God. He is limiting us. Anyone wishing to perform a Christian ministry of healing will make use of the diversity God allows, while turning from those things He does not. Also, we can corrupt even the means God does use to heal if we focus on them for the healing and not on Him.

Healing can be done through New Age practice. Caring for and tending to another person has salutary effects. The placebo effect can be at work. And one can get in touch, whether deliberately or unwittingly, with demonic powers that initially may bless (though eventually will harm).

But such New Age techniques of healing miss the point. More than our receiving a healing, God wants us *whole.* Healing, whether physical or emotional, is only part of it—and not the most important part. What God wants for us and what we so desperately need, whether we recognize it or not, is a vital and growing relationship between Him and ourselves. Like the rich young ruler, we may be graced with wonderful things but miss the Kingdom of God. What is the point of going to hell healthy? (See Matthew 5:29–30.) We certainly can have both, both the Healer and the healing, as long as we remind ourselves regularly of the correct order of priority:

> Seek ye *first* the kingdom of God, and his righteousness;
> and [then] all these things shall be added unto you.
> —MATTHEW 6:33, KJV, EMPHASIS ADDED

Third, we in the Church have to be on our guard against occult healing in terms of morality. By focusing on techniques, we ignore the strong moral component to Christian healing. If someone is suffering the physical complications of a life filled with anxiety, repressed anger, or bitterness, and those attempting to help do not deal with the underlying causes of the illness, they are not helping the individual be more whole. They may just be removing one symptom only to see another pop up at a later date in a different part of the body. While, as we have said, not all physical or emotional sickness is based on one's own sin, some of it is. And all spiritual sickness, to a greater or lesser degree, involves sin.

In light of all of this, what should be said about medical science? Because God is a God of order, our discoveries hold true on a regular basis, even though our Newtonian-Cartesian belief in immutable "laws of nature" is being revised. Because God told us to subdue creation, we have a mandate for scientific exploration, however watchful we must be against polluting and despoiling (Genesis 1:28). Medical science is legitimate. But it too must be careful, lest it sees a medical cure as all-important, the diagnosis of symptoms (and not root causes) as sufficient, and science as God.

Uncritical acceptance that anything unusual is a gift of the Holy Spirit

So many in the Church are starving for direct contact with God or for miraculous manifestation of God that when something out of the ordinary comes, they sometimes accept it uncritically.

Occultic clairvoyance may be confused with a word of knowledge, clairaudience with the "still, small voice" of God, or words of "spirit guides" channeled through mediums as words of prophecy. Yet, while not being duped by such spiritual counterfeits (a false path at best, dangerous at worst), neither do we want to go to the opposite extreme and say that the gifts of the Holy Spirit were only for the purpose of getting the Church going and that any purported gift of God via special knowledge is satanic.

How can we make use of the gifts of the Holy Spirit while not falling victim to Satan's masquerade?

- By placing ourselves under the protection of God and His holy angels (Psalm 91:1, 11; Hebrews 1:14).

- By asking God to remove any supernatural ability to know, sense, hear, or speak that is not of Him and to take firm control of any that is of Him.

- By testing any word spoken to us directly, or given to us by another, against the written Word of God. Since God is not a God of confusion, as Paul writes in 1 Corinthians 14:33, anything said by God now will not contradict the revelation He has already given us in Scripture. Be especially careful to note what is being said about the nature of God; the virgin birth; the divinity, sinless life, and bodily resurrection of Jesus Christ; the uniqueness of Jesus; the forgiveness of sin only by faith in Jesus' atonement on the cross; and the moral and ethical commandments of Scripture. As John said, "Test the spirits" (1 John 4:1). Does the purported message square with Scripture, and does it lead to holiness, obedience, love, and service?

- By examining the lifestyles of those who purport to speak for God. While we have heavenly treasure in earthen vessels (2 Corinthians 4:7) and will always experience a gap between what we are and what we ought to be, those who speak for God should be a representation of His message in their lives. I remember giving a sermon on gentleness that changed several lives on the same day I got into an argument with a colleague. While we do not want to push this point too far, the life of the purported vehicle of communication must still ring true.

- By consulting the wisdom of the faithful over the centuries. As we read through the history of the Church, we are reminded that we are not the first generation of believers to confront this issue. Throughout the centuries, Christians have had to discern the difference between the authentic movement of the Spirit, merely human experiences, and various spiritual counterfeits of the enemy. Many such Christians have written about their efforts in discernment. Their writings are extremely helpful to guide us as we similarly have to discern. We ignore such sacred tradition at our peril.[3]

WHY THIS PROBLEM OF NEW AGE INFILTRATION?

A cook can serve tainted meat and do great harm, no matter how sincerely the food was prepared or how tasty it was to the palate. Similarly, New Age teaching can be served up with the best of intent and still wreak havoc in the body of Christ. But why? Why should some in the Church be so vulnerable to such aberrant teaching?

Spiritual hunger

Many people have gotten involved in dubious or even dangerous groups because their own churches have left them spiritually starving. Many have gone to occultic healing services because their churches neglect, or even refuse to have, services of Christian healing. Many accept New Age mysticism because their churches overemphasize doctrine or community service, to the neglect of spiritual experience.

Itching ears

Scripture tells us there will be times when people will find the regular, solid teaching of the faith boring after a while and will run after whatever is new and exciting (2 Timothy 4:3).

Laziness

Many Christians fail to do the hard work of Scripture study, opting instead for grabbing a few verses out of context or reading magazine articles. Lacking a grounding in the truths of the faith, such people can be seduced easily by something that sounds spiritual even though it is not from God. More desirable is the example of the Jews of Berea, who, upon hearing Paul proclaim the gospel, "[examined] the scriptures daily to see if these things were so" (Acts 17:11).

Misapplied tolerance

Jesus, who exhibited and commanded love of people, insisted at the same time that error be refuted and the truth be communicated (Mark 12:24; John 8:32). He showed that error enslaves and truth liberates. That is something we understand in all other areas of life. We do not want dentists to drill our gums but our teeth, and only the ones with cavities. We want banks to have our accounts correct. But when it comes to the truths that Jesus taught, we confuse loving people with believing that their opinions, however contradictory to God's revelation, are just as good as any other opinions. We confuse acceptance of people with acceptance of opinion. As a result, the very people we are trying to love eat tainted meat, not wholesome spiritual food.

Self-indulgence

New Age spirituality is morally easy. With the loving and moral personal God of the Bible reduced to impersonal force, and with cure of sickness seen as the redirection of energy rather than being related in some way to lifestyle, New Age teaching offers spirituality without accountability, religion without repentance, blessings without discipleship. A student who learns various ways to acquire secret wisdom, manipulate energy, or even cast spells learns to be in charge. For those used to being the captain of their ship and the master of their soul, being in control is far more palatable than submitting to God. Ramtha, a 35,000-year-old warrior "channeled" by J. Z. Knight, is said to teach no right or wrong, just individual reality.[4]

Power

Church history is replete with examples, from medieval popes to present-day TV preachers, of misuse of religion as a way to gain power. To a Christian tired of being run-down while a secular neighbor prospers, to a salesperson pressured to produce, or to a grievously ill person desperate for healing, the possibility of making reality happen through visualization, positive confession, or channeling energy is an alluring temptation.

Satan

As always, Satan offers wisdom (of a sort) and power to those who will fall in with him. Masquerading as an angel of light, he seduces people to turn away from God, whether through outright rejection or through compromise.

As the movements of renewal struggle to restore sound scriptural theology and recover neglected ministries, such as healing, may God grant us the ability to be both gentle and firm. May He help us hold fast to what is good and make it more widely *available,* and may He show us how to root New Age errors out of the Church.

DISCUSSION QUESTIONS

1. Review each of the five New Age beliefs described, and reflect whether you have heard it, in some form, in the context of your Christian community.

2. How would you go about selecting or recommending a psychotherapist?

3. Consider the usual prayers in your prayer fellowships (church, prayer group). Can you detect the development of techniques, formulas, or protocols? If so, analyze them in the light of this chapter.

4. Define "occult practices."

5. What do you understand to be the dangers of occult practices?

6. Can spiritual healing originate outside the Church? Why or why not?

CHAPTER 9

The Sacraments As
Vehicles of Healing

CHRISTIANITY IS INCARNATIONAL. It is based on the truth that God, who is Spirit, became flesh in Jesus of Nazareth. Christians should have no trouble understanding, therefore, that God can use physical objects as vehicles for conveying various blessings, including healing. The sacraments are some of those vehicles.

Although in the early centuries of the Church a variety of rites and ceremonies were considered sacraments, the number was fixed in the eleventh century at seven. Certain Christian groups today observe all seven. Other Christian groups count only baptism and Holy Communion as sacraments. Still, other Christian groups observe these two, but call them ordinances. A few Christian groups do not observe even baptism and Communion. For the purpose of this study, I will look at the seven historic sacraments.

Throughout the centuries there have been unbalanced views of the sacraments as the Church went to one extreme or the other in her understanding of them. I would like to examine three ways in which the Church has fallen, or can fall today, into imbalance.

The first imbalance is in treating the physical elements of a sacrament either as magic objects or as mere symbols. In the former case, the physical elements of a sacrament—water in baptism, bread and wine in Communion, oil in unction—are seen as possessing such power that personal faith in God is unnecessary. In the Middle Ages, for example, some people would bury a consecrated host from Communion in their fields to ensure a good harvest and ward off natural disaster. Personal faith in God was not as important to them as the presence of the sacramental bread.

On the other hand, and in reaction to this, some see the sacraments as mere symbols, simply visual aids to belief. Many Protestants today would say that this was a much-needed theological correction by the leaders of the Reformation. But this understanding of the Reformation is historically incorrect. While some in the Reformation viewed sacraments as symbols, they were very much in the minority. Rather, it was the Enlightenment era 150 years later that championed this view. The Enlightenment denied any belief in the supernatural, reducing Christianity to merely ethical moralism. While most evangelical Protestant churches today have turned their backs on most of the teachings of the Enlightenment and embrace the virgin birth of Christ, the incarnation, His bodily resurrection, and so on, they have not similarly restored the dominant Reformation view of the sacraments.

Even in calling the sacraments symbols, moreover, people forget there are two kinds of symbols: *mere symbols* and *participatory symbols*. A *mere symbol* is one that stands for something else, nothing more. A flag, for example, is a mere symbol, because it stands for a country. In no way is it that country. A *participatory symbol* both stands for something and, to various degrees, is the thing it symbolizes. A dollar bill stands for one dollar's worth of the credit of the United States, but it can also be spent for a dollar's worth of goods. If we are to use the word *symbol* to describe a sacrament, it is this kind of symbol we should mean. A sacrament points to something beyond itself, yet it also participates in it in a way that a mental tool cannot.

A second imbalance is between the objective and subjective parts of a sacrament—that is, between the objective reality of what a sacrament is and does, and our subjective, or personal, appropriation of God's grace through our faith.

If too much emphasis is placed on the objective reality of the sacrament, it may replace God as the object of our faith. If too much emphasis is placed on the necessity of our faith, on the other hand, we make our weak grasp of God more important than His strong grasp of us. Then, when our faith is shaky, we will deny ourselves blessings in the sacraments when we need them most.

After Jesus rose from the dead, two of His disciples met Him on the road to Emmaus, although they did not recognize Him (Luke 24:13–35.) They later described how their hearts burned within them during that journey. Although part of this inward glow was because they were discussing the Word of God, part of it was because the Lord was with them though they did not know it. This demonstrates the objective reality of what happens when Christ is present, even when we have no knowledge of His presence. In a similar way, the sacraments are a real blessing, even when knowledge or faith is not present.

The third imbalance has to do with how we know God. Scripture tells us to love God with our minds (Mark 12:30). Christianity involves assent to doctrinal revelation. Without this, faith quickly degenerates into subjective experiences and sentimental feelings.

Knowing God through our minds is not the only way to know or experience God. People can encounter God in more mystical ways such as by observing a sunset, in worship, in an encounter with a holy person, or even in being "caught up to the third heaven," like the apostle Paul in 2 Corinthians 12:1–4. People can encounter God deep within their spirits while they are asleep or in a coma. This is not to say that *any* religious experience is an encounter with God. John tells us in 1 John 4:1 to test the spirits to see if they are from God, and God's test is a doctrinal one. It is safe to say, however, that God comes to us in ways besides pondering the truths of doctrine in our minds. One of these ways is through the sacraments.

United Methodist leader Dr. Ross Whetstone has pointed out that Protestantism is the religious expression of the print culture. Protestantism was shaped by the rise of literacy, the explosion of books, and the availability of the Scriptures made possible by the invention of movable type in the century preceding the Reformation. As a result, Protestantism has put so great an emphasis on knowing God through the mind that it has sometimes neglected, or even denied, knowing God in other ways. When we consider the superstition rampant in Christianity in late medieval Europe, we can understand this. It is, however, an imbalance.

What is needed, as always, is balance. Scriptural revelation always judges personal experience, but personal experience helps us understand scriptural revelation in ways that go beyond, but never contradict, what we know in our minds. Or, put another way, God heals as the forms and elements of the sacraments serve as object lessons of scriptural truth and to help our faith grow, but God also uses the sacraments in and of themselves, which is a great blessing, when our minds are tired, weak, or distracted.

THREE OBJECTIONS TO THE SACRAMENTS

Objections are raised to belief in the sacraments. Let me list and respond to some of these objections.

Objection 1: The sacraments are just "dead religion."

We have all witnessed spiritually lifeless administration of sacraments. But is that the fault of the sacraments, I would ask, or the fault of those leading and participating in the service? Nonsacramental worship can be "dead religion," too. So can a Bible study. The important thing is for those involved to see

163

what the sacraments can be. Many bear witness to tremendous blessings God mediated to them through the sacraments. Later in this chapter I will quote from the book *And Their Eyes Were Opened: Encountering Jesus in the Sacraments* by Michael Scanlan and Ann Therese Shields.[1] The authors, a Roman Catholic priest/retired university president and a nun, give a wealth of practical help to those wishing the sacraments to be what they are supposed to be—life-changing encounters with Jesus.

As for the sacraments being "dead," remember that God is in the resurrection business, not the funeral business. If something is wrong, God wants to change it. If it is dead, God wants to make it alive again.

Objection 2: Traditionalism is an enemy of the gospel, and the sacraments are traditional.

There are two answers to this objection. First, the Lord Jesus was not opposed to traditions. He told His followers to repeat the Lord's Prayer. He instituted the Lord's Supper to be observed until His return. Our Lord's objection to tradition was when it was used to deny God's truth (Mark 7:11–13).

Second, there is a difference between *tradition* and *traditionalism*. Church historian Jaroslav Pelikan has noted that tradition is the living faith of the dead, while traditionalism is the dead faith of the living. That is, tradition is the goodly and godly heritage passed on from previous generations to those alive today, while traditionalism is people today going through religious forms either with no faith or as an attempt to keep faith at a distance. Periodically, churches revise their forms of worship. Different forms of worship can express various aspects of the truth inherent in a sacrament. Different ways of worship minister to people with different preferences in worship style, or with different personality types.[2]

It is helpful to see a sacrament as wine and the forms as the wineskin. As the power of God in the sacrament comes to us as new wine, the wineskins—the outward forms—may often need to be changed. It would be incorrect, however, to denigrate the sacraments as being old wineskins worthy only of being thrown out. Many churches of all types are realizing the truth that the sacraments are important and central to the faith. Many churches, which until recently had observed Communion infrequently and as a mere symbol, are now observing it more often and as something far greater than a mere visual aid to faith.

Objection 3: The sacraments look Catholic.

I hope God's people will see this for the unbiblical prejudice that it is. Christians of all persuasions are learning from each other. Just as many Roman Catholics are learning to study the Bible as evangelical Protestants do and are expressing the spiritual gifts as Pentecostals do, non-Catholic Christians can rejoice in a fuller participation in the sacraments.

Let us now take a look at the sacraments and see how they relate to Christian healing.

BAPTISM

As for baptism, Scanlan and Shields write:

> In Baptism, an adult, or a child through his parents, by the power of the Spirit, rejects the kingdom of darkness as having any authority to rule his life. He accepts the kingdom of light and is consecrated and dedicated to the Lord. The sacrament empowers the individual to live and move in the victory of Jesus Christ, won for him on the cross. The community welcomes the person and pledges responsibility to incorporate him lovingly and supportively into the body of Jesus Christ.[3]

The Jews learned the need for formal incorporation into the community of faith when God instructed them to circumcise their sons on the eighth day after birth. The early Christian church saw baptism as the New Covenant fulfillment of the Old Covenant rite of circumcision. Although most of the baptisms described in the New Testament are of adults—they were the first generation to hear and respond to the gospel, just as Abraham was the first Jew—there is ample evidence for acknowledging baptism as something also right and proper for the children of believing parents. Infant baptism is much more than a little ceremony to celebrate the addition of a baby to the family. It is the time when the church incorporates a child into the covenant community of faith. When the Philippian jailer put his faith in Christ, not only he, but his whole household was baptized (Acts 16:33). Similarly, when Lydia, a seller of purple goods, came to faith in Christ, she was baptized with her household (Acts 16:15). We have copies of services for baptism from the late second century in which, after the adult converts were baptized, children and infants had their turn. Far from arguing for this practice as if it were some innovation or perversion of the original order, that liturgy simply states that this is what is to be done. From this, most scholars have inferred that baptism was administered to the children and infants of believers from the earliest days of the Church.

To be thus brought into covenant relationship with God is the greatest healing possible. While anyone baptized as an infant has to go on to embrace Christ as Lord and Savior in a mature adult commitment, infant or believer baptism signals the removal of an individual from the kingdom of darkness into God's kingdom of light.

Let me illustrate with the story of some friends of mine, Bishop Philip Zampino and his wife, Jean. Their infant son, Mark, was having a tough time sleeping at night. It seemed that something was severely aggitating him. They had been waiting for a convenient time to have Mark baptized, but after prayer the Lord revealed to them that they should not postpone Mark's baptism. They went ahead in obedience, and immediately after Mark was baptized, he began sleeping through the night. This was one of many experiences the Lord used to show the Zampinos that, as Christian believers, they had not only the privilege of bringing their children out of the world of darkness and into the covenant of faith, but also the duty to do so.

Most liturgies of baptism include a prayer of renunciation of Satan and his forces. Some churches include a prayer of exorcism, that any evil powers oppressing or possessing the person being baptized will be driven away by Christ. This was especially important in the early centuries of the Church when many had been involved in occult practices before they came to Christ. With the rise of the New Age movement and Satanism in our day, these prayers in the baptismal service once again take on urgency.

HOLY COMMUNION

The service of Holy Communion is also called the Eucharist, divine Liturgy, the Mass, or the Lord's Supper. After Jesus rose from the dead, the spiritual eyes of two of His disciples were opened as He "broke bread" with them (Luke 24:30–31). This was the Lord's way of reminding them that although He was soon to ascend back to heaven, they would continue to encounter Him as they repeated the Lord's Supper. In Acts 2:42, we read that one of the marks of the ongoing life of the Church was the breaking of bread, another way of describing a service of Holy Communion. Along with fellowship, prayer, and lessons based on the teachings of the apostles, Communion was to be a regular occurrence in the life of the Church. This is why, from her earliest days, Communion was the Church's Sunday service of worship.

Commenting on Communion, Scanlan and Shields observe:

> In the Eucharist, we can expect to be healed each time we receive—healed physically, spiritually, and empowered to deal with those relationships and situations of that day, with Jesus' wisdom, love, and strength. We are given those gifts in his body and blood.... Finally, through the Eucharist, we are drawn into deeper personal union with him who is Lord of our lives.[4]

The apostolic and postapostolic Church recognized Communion as a means of healing. When anyone was ill, deacons would bring the consecrated elements to the sick person's home directly from the Sunday Eucharistic celebration. They would continue this until he or she recovered. People were encouraged to see that receiving Communion was not only good for them spiritually, but was also a way to be blessed and healed physically. Father Ted Dobson in his book *Say But the Word* writes:

> In the earliest Christian days, the Eucharist was seen as a sacrament of healing and transformation, a rite that brought wholeness to the people who celebrated it. For example, St. Augustine in his greatest book, *The City of God*, as well as in his last book, *Revisions*, witnessed to the healing he had seen in his own church as a result of people receiving Eucharist.[5]

When the elements are consecrated, or made holy and set apart as vehicles through which God blesses, feeds, and heals His people, we are reminded that Jesus Christ offered Himself on Calvary to forgive our sins and open up other blessings to believers. The historic words of the Anglican liturgy bring home this point forcefully: "...Through faith in His blood we...have remission of our sins *and all other benefits of his passion*" (emphasis added).

One of these benefits is healing. Barbara Shlemon Ryan noted in a leaflet entitled "The Healing Power of the Eucharist":

> Each time we attend the [Eucharistic] celebration...we are at a healing service. As we approach the altar, we pray, "Lord, I am not worthy to receive You, but only say the word and I shall be healed." This is a prayer of confidence in the power of Jesus Christ to transform our physical, emotional, and spiritual needs. If we truly believe that Jesus is present in the consecrated bread, then we should expect to obtain wholeness as we accept His body into ourselves.

Over the years I have seen many people healed as they receive Communion. While sometimes they were using Communion as a time to plead with God for their needs, in some cases people were not asking God for anything. Several people told me later they were thinking of what they were going to do after church was over! God had used Communion sovereignly as a vehicle for healing people who needed it, even when they were not paying particular attention.

It is important, therefore, to see the objective nature of Holy Communion. Until recently, in many Protestant circles Communion, though deemed important, was celebrated infrequently. Simple reminders of Jesus' work on the cross, after all, can be given in lots of ways besides the Lord's Supper. But when one starts to discover, or rediscover, the forgotten truth that receiving Communion is, in and of itself, important and beneficial, one will desire such feeding far more regularly. In Roman Catholic circles, until the liturgical renewal that accompanied Vatican II, Roman Catholics went to mass weekly, or more often, but seldom received Communion. The focus, as with Protestants, was on hearing the events of Calvary, but not receiving those benefits sacramentally. Now it is much less likely for a Roman Catholic to go to mass and not receive Communion.

In the closing prayer, blessing, and dismissal of a Communion service, we ask God to equip us to go into the world to be His blessing to others. This reminds us that while our relationship with God must be personal, it is never private. We are to take His Word, His love, and His healing to this broken and hurting world.[6]

CONFIRMATION

Just as infant baptism is the Christian equivalent of infant circumcision, Confirmation is the equivalent of the Jewish Bar Mitzvah. If in infant baptism others made promises to God on our behalf, in Confirmation we take these promises on for ourselves. We ask

Jesus Christ to be our Lord and Savior, and we ask the Holy Spirit to empower us to be obedient, effective disciples of the Lord. As Scanlan and Shields put it:

> In Confirmation, we accept responsibility to live in the body of Christ, and to support it by those gifts God has given us. The Church confirms that those gifts are truly of the Spirit and empowers and calls us to use them for service. We are now witnesses of God's love and power in our lives. We can testify to it through our ministries, and the community of the Church pledges to support our growth.[7]

There is a connection, as we have seen, between sin and sickness, obedience and wholeness. As the Holy Spirit strengthens us to obey, we find our lives more whole and, frequently, less sick. With the tremendous needs all around us, God wants His disciples to go forth to minister in a variety of ways, including healing. Confirmation is a time for this strengthening and equipping. We read in Acts 19:1–7 how the laying on of hands by Paul was the occasion for the Holy Spirit to fall on a group of people who then spoke in tongues and prophesied.

While Confirmation for some people is little more than a church-joining ceremony, for many it is that special time of commitment and empowerment God intends it to be. Let me share the story of one such service of confirmation I was privileged to witness.

During the middle 1970s, one of my tasks as a staff member of St. Timothy's Episcopal Church, Catonsville, Maryland, was to prepare adults for confirmation. One year I had an exceptional class of approximately sixty people. During the classes I stressed not only various events of Church history and various church customs, but also especially the centrality of dedicating one's life to Christ as Lord and Savior and receiving the empowerment of the Holy Spirit for discipleship and service. Just about everyone in the class was looking forward to the service as an opportunity for public witness to their commitment to Christ and as a time to be strengthened by the Holy Spirit.

The bishop who was to do the confirming was the Right Reverend William Cox, a most godly man who knows the Lord and the power of the Holy Spirit. In fact, Bishop Cox has a nationally respected ministry in leading healing missions.

That service was a powerful witness to the reality of the Holy Spirit. Nearly everyone confirmed was "slain in the Spirit." (See Appendix 1.) Several spoke in tongues for the first time, a few received visions, and others prophesied. A number were healed physically or emotionally. It became apparent afterward that many had been given various gifts of the Holy Spirit for ministry, including gifts of healing.

A number of people who had been to confirmations many times before commented on how unusual the service was that evening. While the service may have been different, it was not abnormal. Although some may not have seen this kind of service before, what we witnessed that evening was the norm, the way confirmation is supposed to be. When individuals are making a conscious commitment to Christ and seeking the Spirit's power, and when the one presiding knows firsthand the centrality of these truths, results will follow.

Notice the tie-ins to healing. First, profession of faith in Christ as Lord and Savior brings the greatest healing of all—reconciliation with God. Second, physical and emotional healing may take place. Third, some receive one or more of the healing gifts of the Holy Spirit. Fourth, others receive different gifts that, while not specifically healing gifts, assist the ministry of healing.

Roman Catholic scholars Kilian McDonnell, OSB, and George Montague, SM, have published an exhaustive study of the writings of Christian authors in the first several centuries after the apostolic era.[8] The evidence is overwhelming that baptism in the Holy Spirit was integral to, and expected at, services of Christian initiation. If we are to be faithful to the beliefs and practices of the primitive

Church, we must view baptism in the Spirit not as belonging to the private piety of those so inclined, but as normative in the life of the Church and necessary for each Christian.

PENANCE

This sacrament is popularly called *confession* but is now often called *reconciliation*.

We have already seen in chapter five the connection between confession of sin and healing. Confessing our sins, as with anything else, can be either a mechanical ritual to satisfy an obligation or make us feel good, or a life-giving reality to help move us toward holy living and selfless love of others.

Father Scanlan told me once that in the early years of his priesthood, hearing confession had become, as for many priests, a duty to endure. Some coming to confession rattled off a list of relatively trivial sins while avoiding more serious root attitudes. However, many others would present themselves for confession with the desire to do serious business with God. He noticed that in some cases, such people were healed physically, either right there in the confessional or shortly after making their confessions. These experiences helped him see both the reality of the ministry of healing and the riches offered in the sacrament of reconciliation when done seriously.

As the word *reconciliation* implies, the focus is not solely unburdening oneself from guilt, but also reestablishing the fellowship with God and others that has been broken through sin.

Another step toward healing is the assurance of pardon as we confess our sins, for God is indeed faithful and just and cleanses us (1 John 1:9). As our consciences are cleared from guilt, we know that, in spite of our imperfections, God wishes to use us in service to others. As Scanlan and Shields put it:

> In Penance, we now know that to be holy is first to desire
> and experience forgiveness. The sacrament is a life-giving

experience, not an act of condescension on the part of God. In God's healing presence, with the gifts given the confessor and penitent, we can discern the root of a sin, know that it can be destroyed, and know that the pain can be healed by his power.[9]

HOLY MATRIMONY

Because so many weddings we attend are really secular weddings held in a church building for social reasons, we may lose sight of what matrimony is intended to be. In a Christian marriage God binds two people together in Him in a special covenant. The Protestant reformer John Calvin, while rejecting much of late medieval Roman Catholic sacramental theology, numbered matrimony as a sacrament along with baptism and Communion.

As two people become one in Christ, God pours out His grace that their love may heal any emotional wounds brought to the marriage. Hurts and insecurities are ministered to, and each person becomes more whole. As this happens, they become a sign to the world of the transforming and healing power of Christ.

I thank God that He has given my wife and me to each other as companions, fellow servants, and ministers to each other's hurts.

Scanlan and Shields state:

> In matrimony, God anoints two people to be the sign, the tangible witness of the way he loves and is united to his church. Two people make public their desire to lay down their lives for one another in love, to so be for the other that their love can encourage and support and be a sign of hope to the whole body. Their covenant, made public by the sacrament, is to become a reflection of God's covenant of love with his people. The sacrament so empowers them to give their lives to one another that they are made one. That physical and spiritual union is a concrete sign of God's desire to be one with his people.[10]

UNCTION OR ANOINTING WITH OIL

James 5:14 states, "Is any among you sick? Let him call for the elders of the church, and let them ... [anoint] him with oil." We do not, of course, want to limit God to working healing only in this way. I recall a woman once asking me to anoint her for healing. When I told her that I left my anointing oil at home, she replied, "Never mind. I'll be ministered to another time." Although I tried to assure her that God could heal without the oil and that we could pray for healing nevertheless, she said she would rather wait until I had my oil with me. She had confused *one* way of healing with the *only* way of healing.

On the other hand, while God can use a variety of means to heal, we should never rule any of them out. On another occasion a man told me, "You can pray for my healing, but do not anoint me with oil. I am not into that sort of thing." My response to the man was that while there is nothing magical about the oil, the statement in James 5 *is a command*: if you are sick, call for the elders to anoint you. If he was not willing to submit to that, he was placing a roadblock in God's way, and perhaps that refusal was blocking his healing. He responded that he never thought of it in that way before, and he consented to my anointing him. He was healed immediately! God wanted him to be healed through the agency of anointing to teach him that in order to seek God's blessings, one cannot tell God how to go about His work.

Listen to the expectancy in Scanlan and Shields' description of coming to this sacrament:

> In the Anointing of the Sick, we can experience in our need the most loving thing God desires to do for us. We *expect* that to happen to us and to those for whom we gather to pray as they receive the sacrament. We expect to see the sick restored to health ... we expect to see those [so] called [to] approach death with joy and total confidence.[11]

Recall how at the beginning of this chapter we discussed both objective and subjective elements of a sacrament. Sometimes we depend too much on the personal faith of those ministering and need to remember the other side—the objective nature of a sacrament. A good example of God at work in the sacraments apart from individual worthiness came in the Church in the fourth century during a time of persecution of the Church in northern Africa. Some Church leaders caved in under persecution. Many in the Church wondered if the sacraments performed by these weak leaders were valid. If their leaders were that weak, how could God use them? As the Church sought the mind of the Lord on this, God showed them that the unworthiness of the minister does not hinder the efficacy of the sacrament. This belief has been part of the Church's faith ever since, and rightly so. No one is worthy enough to minister the sacraments, teach the Scriptures, or lead the flock. If spiritual blessings depend on the worthiness of the leaders, no one in the Church could receive much of anything. God wishes us to know that His promises in the sacraments are not dependent on men's foibles but on God's faithfulness.

Let me illustrate this in regard to anointing. Often at a healing mission I tell people that while I will be happy to anoint them for healing, I would like them to ask the clergy of their home churches to anoint them as well. When people respond that their clergy have never done this or even make fun of the idea of anointing, I respond that they should *insist* on it. Some have called or written to tell me that they received a healing not when I prayed for them, but when the leaders of their own church anointed them! In several cases, the clergy did this primarily to get their parishioners off their backs and were as surprised as anyone when it actually worked! God honored the sacrament regardless of the faith of those ministering it. In some cases this was the occasion for those ministers to come to believe in the power of God to heal.

ORDINATION

This is the setting apart and empowering of individuals that God has raised up for ministry. Scripture uses the terms *bishops, elders,* and *deacons.* This includes clergy known today as *ministers, pastors,* and *priests.* We see in Scripture that from the earliest days of the Church, individuals were specially empowered with spiritual gifts (Romans 12; 1 Corinthians 12; Ephesians 4). Individuals were raised up to the office of bishop, elder, and deacon (1 Timothy 3; Titus 1). It is not a case of spiritually gifted people *or* ordained clergy, but both spiritually gifted people *and* ordained clergy. Both are scriptural. As Scanlan and Shields say regarding ordination:

> In Holy Orders, a person is called into a special order within the body of Christ. It is a uniquely holy position, for he is called by the community which has supported his gifts and life...to call forth adoration and praise. As that person has grown, the members of the Christian community recognize that they can place special confidence and trust in him, [and are] hereafter responsible for what [they have] nurtured, called forth, and confirmed. He who accepts that call is empowered by the sacrament to lay down his life for God's own.[12]

The sacrament of ordination relates to healing in at least four ways:

1. As we have already seen, clergy are ministers of healing by virtue of office. James 5:14 does not say to call for those elders who also possess spiritual gifts of healing, but simply to *call for the elders.* They have a sacramental ministry of healing by virtue of their office.

2. The ordained leadership of a Christian community possesses a disciplinary role. Bishops and priests hear sacramental confession and have the power to retain or remit people in their sins (John 20:22). The purpose of

church discipline is always restoration of an offending individual to the community and to godly living (Matthew 18:15–20). While we are not to obey spiritual leaders who ask us to believe something that contradicts the clear teaching of Scripture, on all other occasions God calls us to submit to His authorities (Hebrews 13:17). On several occasions, my submission to authority has led me to renounce certain sins I might not otherwise have renounced. To repeat, there is a connection between sin and sickness.

3. The ordained leadership has a pastoral role to the flock. As the leaders bring us comfort and counsel, we come into greater wholeness.

4. Ephesians 4:11–12 includes in the definition of the role of the pastor/teacher the equipping of the saints for the work of ministry. It is their task to help identify those being raised up by God to minister healing, to train them, and to deploy and supervise them for this ministry.

Yes, the sacraments have often been ministered wrongly or experienced as ineffectual. But that can be said about everything else in the life of the Church. Our task is to ask God to restore lively sacramental life in the Church and to work toward that restoration. God's provision for our wholeness through the sacraments is great, and so is our need. As Scanlan and Shields remind us, "The sacraments promise the gift of grace we seek, healing, nourishing, cleansing, freeing, consecrating, blessing, empowering us to accept His reign in our lives, and deepen our covenant with Him and His people."[13]

DISCUSSION QUESTIONS

1. How does the Enlightenment complement Christianity?

2. How does the Enlightenment undermine Christianity?

3. Think of an example of God touching you or someone else by means of (a) intellect, (b) emotions, (c) imagination, (d) memories, or (e) will.

4. Which of the above are purely rational? Which are nonrational?

5. If God speaks to us through all five of these aspects of our being, in how many ways have you been neglecting to look for Him?

6. For each of the sacraments discussed in this chapter, answer two questions:

   a. What symbolism is involved?

   b. In what ways can the symbol legitimately be the thing it symbolizes?

EXPERIMENT

In anticipation of a celebration of the Eucharist, read about the early Passovers in the Old Testament (Exodus 12:1–28; Leviticus 23:4–8; 2 Chronicles 35:10–19; Ezra 6:16–22). Ask God to enable you to participate with Old Testament believers in a Passover. Anticipating another Eucharist, read about the Last Supper (Luke 22:7–30). Ask God to enable you to participate in that meal. Anticipating still another, read about the Marriage Feast of the Lamb (Revelation 19:1–9). Ask God to enable you to participate even now in that meal. Reflect on the Passover and the Marriage Feast of the Lamb during the liturgy, while partaking of Communion, and afterward.

CHAPTER 10

Ministering Healing Using the Spiritual Gifts

I N ORDER TO help us minister healing effectively, God has given the Church various spiritual gifts. These gifts are mentioned in several places in the New Testament, usually with an encouragement to use them:

> Having gifts that differ according to the grace given to us, let us use them.
>
> —ROMANS 12:6

> To each is given the manifestation of the Spirit for the common good.
>
> —1 CORINTHIANS 12:7

> When he ascended on high he led a host of captives, and he gave gifts to men...to equip the saints for the work of ministry, for building up the body of Christ.
>
> —EPHESIANS 4:8, 12

> As each has received a gift, employ it for one another, as good stewards of God's varied grace.
>
> —1 PETER 4:10

179

What is a spiritual gift? Dr. C. Peter Wagner of Fuller Theological Seminary, author of *Your Spiritual Gifts Can Help Your Church Grow*, starts each definition of a gift with these words, "The gift of _____ is that special ability that God gives to certain members of the body of Christ to . . ." We certainly need God's help if we are to render effective service to others and glorify His holy name.

It is often pointed out that between the two chapters on the gifts of the Spirit in 1 Corinthians is a chapter on love. From this, some conclude that the Corinthian Christians needed to be reminded to exercise the gifts of the Spirit in love, lest they become a "noisy gong or a clanging cymbal" (1 Corinthians 13:1). That conclusion is not only correct, but also as much needed today as it was then. We have all seen people with great ministry ability hurt the people they were trying to help by ministering in an insensitive, unloving manner. We have also seen people use spiritual gifts to gain improper control over others. Anyone who wants to use the spiritual gifts must use them in love.

Yet the reverse is also true. The chapter on love is given in the context of spiritual gifts. Love is much more than sentimental feelings, noble intentions, or words of pity. Love includes helping a person in need. Love is practical, not just sentimental. So while the love chapter tells us how to use the gifts, the gifts chapters tell us how to love. I find it no coincidence that in each of the major lists of spiritual gifts in Scripture there is also a statement about love (Romans 12; 1 Corinthians 12–14; Ephesians 4; 1 Peter 4). To give God's love, we must use God's gifts.

HOW DO WE RECEIVE THE GIFTS?

If the spiritual gifts are important for effective, practical, loving ministry, how do we come by them? I believe there are two ways:

First, we can offer the abilities and talents we have had all our lives to God for Him to correct and use.

When I was five years old, I climbed onto the piano bench and played the first several notes of the song my grandmother had just played. My parents and grandparents concluded that I had musical talent, so piano and, later, organ lessons were arranged. At age sixteen I started assisting on the organ in a church with a venerable men and boys choir. At age twenty, my commitment to Jesus Christ deepened significantly. I consciously laid my music at the feet of the Lord, that He might correct anything that was wrong and use my ability as He saw fit to His honor and glory. After church the next Sunday, several people remarked how differently I had played that day. They could not explain what they meant. I had not played more accurately, nor were the stop registrations different. But all seemed to agree with the statement one person made, that I played "more worshipfully." By asking God to be in control of my music, I believe He was more able to use it for His purposes.

We have many abilities or talents that have been with us all our lives. We call them natural abilities, although, of course, they come from God. As we offer them to God for correction and control, we find that He will use them more directly for His purposes.

The second way we acquire spiritual gifts is by a direct, sudden intervention of God, either in response to a request or as a sovereign act.

Let me illustrate this with the experience of a friend of mine. Bertha, let's call her, is a fine woman and a deeply committed Christian. She lacks the ability, however, to read people or situations. One day while praying with someone, she had a profound insight into that person's problems. We knew it had to have come from God! Far from being an isolated incident, this ability continued. Soon we were marveling at how well Bertha could detect root problems in people's lives. God had given her a spiritual gift—in this case, the gift called the word of wisdom.

As long as our motives are to serve others and glorify God, it is not wrong to ask for spiritual gifts. In fact, when a Christian realizes the call of God to minister in His name, he or she should ask God for the tools to do that job better. We might ask God in this way, "Dear God, I know You want me to serve Your people effectively. I know that I can bear no fruit in ministry without Your grace. I ask You to give me those gifts that You want me to have so I may fulfill that ministry to which You call me. Please keep me from using these gifts to my own glory or in a manner that harms others. In Jesus' name. Amen."

OBJECTIONS TO THE GIFTS

Some people warn that involvement with spiritual gifts is a risky business. Given the encouragement in the New Testament to use the gifts and the evidence that they can help people and glorify God, why do they oppose their use? I have found three reasons.

The first objection comes observing their misuse. People see someone getting proud and self-important. Or they see someone using spiritual gifts in a harmful way. It is abusive to go up to someone and bowl them over with, "God has given me a word for you. If you are wise, you will listen to what I have to say."

In addition, they see the gifts used in such a way that other blessings of God are ignored. They see someone paying more attention to a word God has given him than he does to Scripture. They see someone refuse medical treatment because she demands a miraculous and instantaneous healing.

The proper response to this objection is to say that just because some people treat the gifts incorrectly is no reason to stop using them. Anything good can be misused.

A second objection to the spiritual gifts is the belief that they were only an interim measure, to be used only to get the Church established. We looked at this objection briefly in chapter three. Let us now consider it more fully.

Scripture does not place a time limit on the use of the spiritual gifts. Mark 16:17–18 says:

These signs will accompany those who believe: in my name they will cast out demons; they will speak in new tongues…they will lay their hands on the sick, and they will recover.

Nothing suggests that this promise is only for a period of time.

Verse 8 of 1 Corinthians 13 states that prophecies will pass away and tongues will cease, but verse 10 explains that the imperfect will pass away "when the perfect comes." It is obvious that this cannot refer to the establishment of the Church, for the Church is far from perfect. Nor can it mean the final writing of Scripture, for, although Scripture is perfect, we know from Church history that the use of the spiritual gifts continued as a major part of the Church for a long time afterward. Many commentators see the phrase "when the perfect comes" to mean "when *the perfect one* comes," the Lord's Second Coming. So, yes, the gifts will cease, but not until they have no further purpose, when Jesus returns.

The purpose of the gifts is to bring God's powerful love to particular situations, not just to expand the Church. While it often happens that people who are miraculously healed then become disciples of Jesus, the Lord's motive in healing, according to the Gospel writers, is primarily compassion, not evangelism (Matthew 14:14). The prophetic word given by Agabus in Acts 11:28 that there would be a famine gave Christians time to plan a course of action to respond. The usefulness of this divine warning had nothing to do with how well the Church was established. The writer of Hebrews reminds us that Jesus Christ is the same yesterday and today and forever (Hebrews 13:8). We should not be surprised, therefore, that His love for us continues to be expressed through the spiritual gifts.

While it might make a convenient theory to say that the gifts of the Spirit died out after the Church got going and are, therefore, not available to us today, the fact is they did not die out! It is true that they *died down,* but that was because the Church became a religious establishment, not because the gifts had no further purpose. As we read Church history, we discover that whenever faith flourishes, such supernatural occurrences again become widespread.

A third objection to the spiritual gifts is really more an objection to the theology and culture that have grown up around them than to the gifts themselves. That is to say, many are put off by the "packaging" in which they see the gifts expressed. This is the same problem some people have with the sacraments.

Many who champion the spiritual gifts teach that a Christian must have a distinct post-conversion experience of grace called the baptism of the Holy Spirit. They believe that the evidence of this having taken place is the ability to speak in tongues, and they point to several places in the Book of Acts where tongues evidenced the reception of the Holy Spirit and/or conversion to Christ.

Without getting into the whole issue of this particular theological viewpoint, let me point out that I have known many people who have been used greatly in spiritual gifts who would claim neither a distinct experience called the baptism in the Holy Spirit nor the ability ever to have spoken in tongues. Certainly Billy Graham has the gift of evangelism ministered in the power of the Holy Spirit. Yet he has stated several times that he has never spoken in tongues. Many Scripture scholars would say that what we see before us in Acts is a *description* of what happened on some occasions, not a *prescription* of what should in every case.

In any event, it boils down to this: we should not reject the use of the spiritual gifts just because we do not necessarily accept a Pentecostal understanding of the baptism of the Holy Spirit. Christians with a variety of understandings of this subject are today making use of the spiritual gifts, with good results.

As for culture, many who stress spiritual gifts also express their Christian faith in a particular cultural style. Sadly, many who do not like that style turn off to the spiritual gifts as well. In other words, if the only context in which someone sees the spiritual gifts being used is a loud, demonstrative worship service with contemporary music, guitars, and synthesizer, dislike of loudness and those instruments might put him off to the spiritual gifts as well.

Please note, the cultural expression of Charismatic Renewal is incidental to the reality of the spiritual gifts. I have seen the spiritual gifts used in a variety of worship settings, from Pentecostal tent meeting, to formal Presbyterian worship, to Roman Catholic High Mass! What is necessary for the gifts to be manifested is an openness to the Holy Spirit's working, not a particular style of worship. As a Southern Baptist pastor told me, "I can have the riches of Pentecost without turning Pentecostal."

HOW DO WE KNOW WE HAVE A PARTICULAR GIFT?

One way is obvious. Something significant happens as we minister. That is to say, we teach and people learn; we sense that we know some piece of information that we have not studied or been told, and, behold, we are correct. Or we try to straighten out an organizational mess, and things start flowing smoothly. Or we pray with people for healing and they are healed. In short, we know we have the gift because the results are obvious.

Another way is when others point out to us that we have a gift. Many times, Emma Parent was told she made her guests feel especially welcome. A few out-of-town speakers our Institute brought in for conferences told me they had never been made to feel so much at home as when they stayed with Emma and her husband, Nelson. Emma had not previously thought she had the "gift of hospitality" mentioned in 1 Peter 4:9, but she most certainly did.

Another way of discovery comes as we sense interest in a particular area of service. Often God will awaken an interest as a way of readying us for a gift He wishes to give us. God raises the interest and slowly gifts us, testing our faithfulness and calling us progressively higher to greater usefulness (Luke 19:16–17).

But just because we are interested in a particular ministry or sense we have a particular spiritual gift does not automatically mean we are called to that manner of service. I remember Tim, who thought he was gifted with the word of knowledge. In times of prayer with other members of a healing team, Tim would say regularly, "I believe God is telling me this or that" about a particular person on the team. Almost invariably Tim had it wrong. Though Tim was sincere, Tim was sincerely mistaken. Because Tim was gentle in his approach and because he was among friends who understood the sometimes trial-and-error approach of discovering and using the spiritual gifts, no harm was done. But after several months of expressing what he thought were words from the Lord, Tim was finally persuaded that while God was gifting him in several things, the word of knowledge was not one of them!

THE GIFTS AND HEALING

Of the various spiritual gifts mentioned in Scripture, which come into play in the ministry of healing? In some ways they all do, although some more particularly so.

Gifts of healings

The Bible does not speak of "a gift of healing" but of "gifts of healings" (1 Corinthians 12:28, NAS). It is a double plural. There is a variety of gifts in the ministry of healing, and few persons, including those specially used in a healing ministry, seem to possess them all. We find that some have a particularly effective ministry to certain individuals, to children, for example, but not to everyone. Some exercise an effective healing ministry to people with emotional distress, but not to people with physical problems. A person may have particular success in praying for asthma, but not for cancer. This does not mean that we should refuse to minister to those outside our area of chief effectiveness. If it seems, however, that God is using a particular person with great success in some aspects of the ministry of healing, we may want that person to pray for those whose problems fall into that area of ministry.

The word of knowledge

This is the gift of knowing a piece of information we have not learned or been told (1 Corinthians 12:8). It is something God tells us directly.

The value of this gift is twofold. One, sometimes we do not know what particular problem is bothering an individual. Or if we do, we do not know its root cause. I recall counseling a man who seemed to be distressed, but he was not able to articulate what was troubling him. When I asked God silently to show me what the problem was, He revealed to me that the man was afraid his wife was being unfaithful. I asked the man gently if he was afraid his wife was having an affair. "Yes!" he blurted out. He was relieved that the concern was finally out on the table. Now we could focus on the problem.

Sometimes it is important to know what the problem is, but not always. Sometimes it is sufficient to pray, "Lord, we lift Harry to Your throne of grace. You know what the need is."

A second value of this gift is in demonstrating that God actually intervenes in lives today. Several years ago in St. Louis I was asked to pray for the sick in conjunction with a midweek service of Holy Communion. About twenty-five people were present. As they remained at the altar rail after receiving Communion, I anointed each one with oil and prayed a brief prayer over each bowed head. Almost without thinking, I prayed a sentence like, "Lord, please take away that anxiety," or "May her mother be healed of her gout," or "May that decision about the job be resolved."

After the service was over, they all waited to speak to me. One woman put it this way: "You do not know us or our problems. Yet as we discuss this among ourselves, we find that you prayed for specific problems in our lives and were correct every time. How did this happen?" I took that as an occasion to share not only about the spiritual gifts, but also about the reality, power, and presence of God in the world today. One woman later commented to me privately, "My belief in God has always been fairly shallow. What happened today made me see that the things talked about in the Bible are real."

The word of wisdom

"Wisdom" is the specific application of truth to given situations (1 Corinthians 12:8). How often does someone know God's truth but not how it applies to specific life situations?

Sometimes this gift manifests itself in a regular, matter-of-course way. Some people are known for being wise. Whenever we face a dilemma or have to make a decision, they naturally share a wise piece of guidance with us. They have this gift and are known for it.

Sometimes, however, this gift manifests itself in someone who does not have much wisdom, except on those occasions when God grants it. I mentioned Bertha earlier, the woman who lacks common sense, except when ministering to people. I recall another situation in which a man on a healing team shared a helpful insight with a woman who had come for prayer. After she left our healing station, I asked Charlie how he knew what to tell her. "It had to be the Lord," Charlie replied. "I did not know what I was saying until it came out. I felt as though God was giving me something to say. It certainly wasn't me!"

Prophecy

This means *forth*telling God's word in a particular situation (1 Corinthians 12:10). Prophecy is sometimes confused with "good preaching," or preaching the gospel as it relates to the sins of society, or *fore*telling the future. Although a word of prophecy may involve all of these, the more precise definition of prophecy is God giving a specific word to a person or group via an individual.

The word may come spontaneously at the time it is to be spoken, or God may give it ahead of time. It may be a word of comfort to those who are troubled, such as when God spoke about Israel in Isaiah 40:1. Other times it may be denunciation of sin, such as the Lord's rebuke of Israel in Amos 5:18–27. On far fewer occasions, where it must be confirmed by other means of knowing God's will, it is a word of direction or guidance.

Let me give you an example of prophecy. I was the guest preacher one Sunday at a charismatic church. They had and still have an extensive ministry to the poor in their community. They seemed to be generous, giving folk. During a time in the worship service when the congregation was invited to speak any words the Lord was giving them, a visitor stood and said, "My children, you say that you love Me, but you are holding back. You must honor the poor in your midst. Do not reject them, for they are loved by Me."

Later I asked the woman who had given the prophecy why she said what she did. She told me she was mystified by those words. Surely if any church needed to hear that word, it was not *this* congregation. But she felt it was a prophetic word given to her by God, and she had to speak it.

I asked the pastor of the church what he thought. He told me it was right on target! Although the parishioners were involved in ministry to the poor, their attitude was one of charity, not love. The church ministered to the poor, but saw them as *them* and did not want *them* to be present for worship on Sundays. The prophetic word was God's way of saying that a change of attitude was sorely needed.

Since some of our physical and emotional sickness and much of our spiritual sickness are related to sin, a chastening word from God calling us to more righteous behavior relates to the ministry of healing. Additionally, as some of our emotional sickness and, therefore, some of our physical sickness can be traced to thoughts and feelings of worthlessness, a prophetic word of comfort relates to the ministry of healing.

It is imperative that any word claiming to be a word from God square with Scripture. God does not contradict Himself and will not give any word today that contradicts what He has given us once for all in the Bible.

It is also important to take seriously those prophetic words discerned to be authentic. Many churches tape-record that portion of the service during which people bring forth prophetic words. Should a message given during worship be discerned as truly coming from God, it is published in the next Sunday's bulletin and the congregation encouraged to pay heed. The church leadership tries to discern what God would have the congregation do next, especially if several messages indicate a common theme.

Not every church is this responsible, however. I know one church that counts the number of different prophetic words it receives on Sunday but never seems to heed them. God does not send us words as toys or trophies, but as tools—vehicles to bring us into greater conformity to God's will.

Speaking in tongues

Speaking in tongues is speaking a language we have not learned (1 Corinthians 12:10). Sometimes it is a known language, though not one known to the speaker. In his book *Nine O'Clock in the Morning,* Canon Dennis Bennett told how he tried in vain to minister to a man in the hospital. The man in the bed and Canon Bennett were unable to communicate because of a language barrier. Finally Canon Bennett started to pray over the man using the gift of tongues. While he did not know what he was saying, the man in the bed did. Later Canon Bennett discovered that he had been speaking a dialect of Spanish and that the words he spoke were a distinct blessing to the sick man.[1]

The application to ministry should be obvious. Sometimes the barrier of human speech blocking effective ministry may be overcome through the gift of tongues. Such an experience, like the word of knowledge, demonstrates the reality of God.

A second way in which the gift of tongues is a blessing is as a personal prayer language. Scripture tells us that we do not always know how we should pray, so the Spirit helps us pray with sighs and groans too deep for words (Romans 8:26). I often have a burden to pray for someone or something. Using my "prayer language," speaking in tongues as I pray, I feel the burden lift. I know God is providing the words. I may not know what I am saying, but God does.

Sometimes when I pray in this way I get a picture of or a thought about someone. On occasion I will be asked later, "Were you praying for me at such-and-such a time?" "Why, yes," I will respond. "But I was praying in tongues, so I do not know what I was praying for. Will you tell me?" Often they will, but more than once I have been told, "Oh, that's OK. I would just as soon not have you know. The problem is resolved. I am grateful you prayed for me. I am also grateful God did not tell you what the problem was!"

Mercy

This means giving mercy, comfort, or compassion in a way far beyond what all Christians would normally give (Romans 12:8). This gift has great application to the ministry of healing. Sometimes what a person needs in order to be healed of emotional wounds is to receive genuine, deep love. At other times, as a person feels the mercy of another, he is able to share, perhaps for the first time, what his problems are. Once these are out in the open, other forms of ministry can help bring solutions. This gift can also enhance other forms of ministry. Confessing our sins, for example, works so much better when the confessor ministers in a merciful way. Most people find it far easier to deal with their sins with one who is understanding, not condemnatory.

Discernment of spirits

This is the gift of being able to know whether a person's underlying motive or the underlying power that controls a person is godly, human, or satanic (Hebrews 5:14; 1 John 4:1).

I recall praying with one man who was depressed. Depression can come from any number of root causes: seasonal adjustment disorder, hormonal problems, guilt over sins, hurt from being sinned against, false guilt feelings from Satan, or an overly strict upbringing. My attempts at ministering to him had been unsuccessful, and I was feeling frustrated.

A team member felt she was discerning a presence of evil hovering around the depressed person. She asked the man if he had been involved in occult practices. He responded that over the years he had been. For a while they had satisfied him, but eventually he stopped praying to God and attending church, and now he was feeling that the powers he had been calling on were turning against him. We led him in a prayer of renunciation of this involvement, and within an hour the depression had lifted. It was not that *he* was evil, but that his involvement in the things of darkness, forbidden by God, had opened him up to evil spirits. The gift of discernment led my team member to know this.

Other gifts

Other spiritual gifts may not be as obviously related to the ministry of healing, but they do assist it. Consider how crucial to a large and active church-based healing team is a person with a gift for keeping things straight. Who but someone with administrative gifts (1 Corinthians 12:28) can keep track of the various requests for ministry, the team members who have the gifts needed for a particular person's need, and ensuring such ministry gets carried out? I know of one healing team in which one of the most valuable members is a person who never herself prays directly for the sick but simply keeps track of those who do.

USING THE GIFTS IN MINISTRY

Let me give you an illustration of how spiritual gifts other than gifts of healing can come together in ministry.

Several years ago, I was part of a four-person healing team at public services of healing. Ruth, John, and Ida were the other team members. A man came to our prayer station. Even as he walked toward us, Ruth sensed that this man, though appearing outwardly to be in fine shape, was hurting deeply. Ruth reached out her hands toward him and radiated the love and mercy of God. This enabled the man, whom I will call Ed, to relax a bit and trust what we were doing.

Despite this, however, he was still unable to state his need. After a few moments of watching him struggle, John said, "You are afraid your company will force you into retirement and you will not be able to provide for your family, aren't you?" Ed responded that this was indeed his concern, and he was glad John had said it because he knew he could not. The four of us prayed that God would help him in his circumstances. We prayed in addition that, whatever else happened, he would receive an emotional healing for the feelings of inadequacy and shame he was feeling and that he would draw closer to God.

Then Ida, usually a quiet person, piped up, "I believe there are a few things you could be doing right now to help the situation and yourself." Ed listened to her suggestions and responded, "I've never thought of those things, but I believe you're right."

In that brief time of ministry several spiritual gifts came into play. First was the gift of discernment, as God showed Ed's inner state to Ruth. Then came the gift of mercy as she offered God's comfort to someone in pain. John then manifested the gift of knowledge as he received supernatural revelation as to the nature of Ed's concern. Finally, Ida exhibited the gift of wisdom as she applied truths to a specific situation. No one was specifically used in a gift of healing *per se,* although the whole ministry taken together was therapeutic.

It is important to remember that using the various spiritual gifts requires both an empowering of the Spirit and a careful process of development. I have profited over the years from the phrase *fire in the fireplace.* It is from the book of the same title by Dr. Charles E. Hummel. I apply that phrase to the spiritual gifts in this way: if the various operations of the Holy Spirit, particularly the more spectacular ones, can be likened to a fire, and the careful, steady process of education, training and supervision to a fireplace, then the fire and the fireplace need each other.

We have all seen the harm done when one of these exists without the other. Fire outside the fireplace—the power and gifts of the Holy Spirit without proper safeguards—can become wildfire. It may be exciting and dramatic, but it can also burn down the house. As Victor Borge used to say, "My parents yelled at me for building a fire in the living room, probably because we did not have a fireplace in the living room." When the spiritual gifts are not used wisely, people are not warmed by the ministry of others, but fried to a crisp.

On the other hand, a beautiful fireplace may be aesthetically pleasing, but with no fire burning in it, we are left cold and dark. Many churches that attempt to do ministry without seeking the empowerment of the Spirit and His gifts may have impressive programs and leaders with academic qualifications, but they leave people unhelped. We need to ask such churches the tough question of whether they see themselves as spiritual bodies or merely secular organizations with a religious veneer. I know one priest, a fine man not as yet converted to Christ, who had the integrity to leave church work when he noticed that his people were no better for being members of a church than a similar number of unchurched people. Only after he was converted and filled with the Holy Spirit did he return to parish work. Now he sees lives being transformed on a regular basis. As Martin Luther wrote in his hymn "A Mighty Fortress Is Our God," "Did we in our own strength confide, Our striving would be losing."

Simply put, we need *both* the fire of the Spirit and the fireplace of education, training, and supervision in ministry. This dual approach characterized Paul's guidance of his young protégé, Timothy. Paul told him:

> Rekindle the gift of God that is within you through the
> laying on of my hands; for God…[gave us]a spirit of
> power…
>
> —2 TIMOTHY 1:6–7

But he also told him:

> Do your best to present yourself to God as one approved, a
> workman who has no need to be ashamed, rightly handling
> the word of truth.
>
> —2 TIMOTHY 2:15

Rekindle the fire; be trained.

As for the fire, we pray and have others pray with us that God will empower us for service. We note that even Jesus did not begin His ministry until His human nature was filled with the Spirit at His baptism in the Jordan River. We ask God to give us the spiritual gifts He wants us to have, ruling none out. We remind ourselves that we cannot accomplish anything of lasting value by our own strength; otherwise we may grow luscious foliage, but not bear fruit. Before we minister, we ask for divine protection, empowerment, and guidance. After we minister, we ask for a refilling of the Holy Spirit and God's protection.

As for the fireplace, we read about wise, proper use of whatever gifts we have been given. We recall that, not only have others in centuries gone by been used in the spiritual gifts, but also they left behind wise words of caution, warning, and guidance—words we neglect at our peril. We learn from those already ministering in an effective, balanced way. We submit ourselves to one another and to the leadership of our churches. We ask God to give us an attitude of humility, for the gifts are exactly that—gifts. They are not merit badges or accomplishments, nor are they rewards for being spiritually mature. The reason that no one person has all the gifts of the Spirit listed in 1 Corinthians 12:29–30 is so that we will have to depend on one another as we depend on God.

As we minister, we need to remember that we have this heavenly treasure in earthen vessels (2 Corinthians 4:7). As my friend Tim learned, a person does not always have the gifts he thinks he has. First Corinthians 13:12 tells us we know only in part. However much God may use us, we are still fallible creatures. This is why spiritual direction, supervision in ministry, and accountability to others are so vitally important.

It is also why we need to be gentle. Using the gifts in an overly self-assured, high-powered way is wrong for several reasons. First, it scares people. People are so busy looking for a way to escape someone ministering in this manner that they are not able to receive his or her ministry. Second, such a ministry is often done in human power rather than in the power of the Holy Spirit. Third, it often wrongly establishes superiority on the part of the one ministering and dependence on the part of the one receiving such "ministry." One is not taught to listen to the Holy Spirit for oneself, but to keep going back to a person claiming a superior ability to hear God speak or minister God's blessings. Fourth, we might be wrong. The Bible tells us, as we just saw, that we know only in part. If we are proven wrong after having asserted that we know exactly what God is saying, people might be turned off to the subject of the spiritual gifts in particular, or even to God Himself.

God can use any Christian who is open to Him in any gift at any time. While it seems that God *tends* to use certain people in certain gifts, we should not limit Him. We should never become too dependent on one or two people with particular gifts, therefore, but rather stay open to God, who surprises us with what He will do through each member of the team.

Similarly, we need to avoid seeing the spiritual gifts as our permanent possessions. God can cease to use us in particular gifts and start using us in others. Bishop Michael Baughen once said that as rector of a church in the English Midlands, his great gift was writing contemporary-style songs of praise, but when he became rector of All Souls Church, Langham Place, London, his music-writing pen dried up and he wrote no more songs.

Instead, he noticed that his ability to teach and preach increased significantly. Then, when he became bishop of Chester, God started using him in gifts more applicable to the office of bishop.

When we think of the gifts as our permanent possessions, we are in danger of being closed to God's future plans for us. In addition, we become proud, forgetting that the gifts are talents on loan from God.

As we realize that God has much work for His people to do and that we cannot do it without His empowering grace, we will see how important the spiritual gifts are for the work of ministry. We will understand that the spiritual gifts far transcend any particular theology of the Holy Spirit or cultural manifestation regarding them. We will know that the gifts are not just for some people, but for all members of the Church to enable us to do the work God has given us, for the betterment of His people, and for the glory of His name.

DISCUSSION QUESTIONS

1. Distinguish between natural talents and spiritual gifts.

2. What part do spiritual gifts play in the body of Christ?

3. What is the significance of the double plural "gifts of healings"?

4. How do other spiritual gifts assist in healing?

5. Would it be appropriate to pray for a particular gift to assist your ministry in a particular situation? Discuss.

6. Name and describe three major objections to spiritual gifts.

7. What do you think 1 Corinthians 13:8–10 means by "when the perfect comes"?

EXPERIMENT

If you have not already done so, find out what your spiritual gifts are. List them in your notebook, and do what is necessary to release them for ministry. Keep an accurate account of what you do and of what happens.

discern emotional needs,

How to Introduce a Healing Ministry Into Your Church

T HE POINT OF studying Christian healing, of course, is so that you will, by God's grace, be able to minister to the sick in a sane, balanced, and effective way. A hungry person, after all, does not want to learn about good cuisine; he wants to eat! We wish, similarly, to provide a vehicle whereby people may receive God's healing blessings. We wish to do this in such a way as to minimize the risk of causing disharmony and division. God calls us to dwell together in unity and to be at peace with one another (Psalm 133:1; Mark 9:50; Romans 12:18; Ephesians 4:3). It would be tragically ironic to introduce healing into a church in such a way as to put the church into dis-ease. C. Peter Wagner underscored this in a humorous way when he entitled his book *How to Have a Healing Ministry Without Making Your Church Sick.*

Whenever a healing ministry is introduced in a church—or whenever any significant change is attempted—at least three different kinds of people emerge. You need to be aware of this and try to understand the thoughts, needs, and motives of these persons and respond to them wisely; otherwise your healing ministry may never get going. In some cases disaster can ensue!

The first kind of person might be called *the enthusiast*. Enthusiasts will want you to move the congregation into the ministry of healing at a rapid rate, whether the congregation is ready or not. It is easy to be susceptible to enthusiasts; they seem to be our biggest supporters. They agree with what we are trying to do, and they bring us encouragement and confidence when we are having doubts. But they can be harmful. Sometimes the enthusiasts scare away those who would have embraced Christian healing had they been brought on board at a more gradual pace. Sometimes the enthusiasts cause us to skip necessary steps in the planning or educational processes or to ignore issues in which prudent caution and regular supervision are needed.

How do you make use of the enthusiasm of these people while preventing the damage they can do? Channel their zeal into worthwhile projects. Keep them from occupying center stage in your endeavors, lest the ministry of healing be identified with them too closely in the minds of the congregation. If they are at all open and teachable, point out the need and reason for practicing patience and gentleness.

If these individuals are not tractable regarding their enthusiasm, or if they show any other personality traits that could be harmful or disruptive to others, they need to be helped pastorally to discover the reasons for their behavior. They should then pray about and work on both the behavior and the root causes behind it. Such reactions indicate underlying problems of either a spiritual or emotional nature or both.

The second kind of person might be called *the honest doubter*. Honest doubters are open-minded people who often become supporters of the ministry of healing, *once they are convinced*. The idea of God's healing the sick in response to prayer is new to them. It sounds odd, quite possibly unscientific, even superstitious. It brings to mind those faith-healing ministries that have gone wrong and brought hurt and division. The honest doubter does not want anything for his church that is crazy or harmful.

Answer the questions of the honest doubter as best you can. Genuinely thank the honest doubters for their concerns about what might go wrong. They may well be bringing godly wisdom. Encourage them to pray that only God's will be done.

The third kind of person is *the blocker.* Blockers may raise the same objections as honest doubters. The difference is, while honest doubters will come on board once their objections are answered and their fears allayed, blockers do not want answers or assurance. They do not want this change, or often any change, to take place. Sometimes it is insecurity that makes them cling to the past instead of to God. Sometimes they wish to maintain a tight control over what they regard as their personal fiefdom—their church. Sometimes they know instinctively that if God is at work healing, He will confront them in a way that will demand commitment. On occasion blockers are "enemy agents," sent by the evil one to inhibit and prevent ministry.

Blockers may try devious ways to impede the ministry of healing, such as spreading malicious gossip or heightening fears that this is something bizarre. Perhaps, more subtly, they will raise concerns about people being hurt or turned off, or that the congregation is not "ready" for this kind of ministry. Any pastor who is not careful could become so susceptible to the fear of people being hurt or offended that he would have nothing further to do with healing. When that happens, people will be hurt all the more, for they will miss out on a ministry that helps at the deepest levels of need. The pastor should listen lovingly to the concerns of the blockers, but not let them drag the healing ministry to a halt. Our marching orders for ministry come from what God tells us to do, *not* from those who are resistant to Him, no matter how important they seem to be or how much they pledge.

HOW TO PROCEED

How should the clergy and lay leadership prepare their church for a ministry of healing? Here are six areas of direction.

Study

<u>There needs first to be a well-thought-through period of education.</u> The leadership would do well to plan a program of education lasting several months before embarking on a healing ministry. To those already convinced about healing, this may sound like a long time, but the rest of the church needs to be brought on board at the rate they can absorb this new information, especially if Christian healing seems radically different from what they have hitherto been taught.

Remember that the worldview of many in the Church is this-worldly and rationalistic. No matter how otherwise pious and devout, no matter how decent and moral, no matter how dedicated and active, many people simply do not believe that God intervenes directly in people's lives, nor do they believe they have any evidence from their own experiences that He does. They have lived their lives with such a view for so long that it will take a while for them to think otherwise.[1]

Let me illustrate how something that seems perfectly normal to one person may seem to another foreign to the point of being ridiculous. Several years ago on a ministry trip abroad, I spent some time in rural Kenya. Let us suppose I was speaking to a group of people in a remote tribal village about my years growing up outside of Boston. What if I spoke to them about blizzards? How could these people, living in the tropics, possibly understand a three-day storm of bitter cold, howling winds, and an accumulation of a white substance measuring twenty-five inches deep that lay on the ground for months afterward? A few people might believe me, especially if I had otherwise proven myself to them to be a believable person. But many others might think I was speaking in myths—where the general point of the story is true but the details are not to be taken literally. Others might think I was trying to deceive them to gain money or power. Still others might think I had taken leave of my senses. In their frame of reference, how could accounts of a New England blizzard possibly be true?

In the same manner, how can church members who have been taught all their lives to believe that God does not intervene directly to change things come to believe that healings take place in answer to prayer? Thus, we have to educate people—carefully, thoroughly, patiently. Lest the concept of healing look bizarre and foreign, we need to place it into the context of what people already know and accept. We do this in three ways.

First, we show how much the four Gospels deal with healing and how healing both signifies and effects the inbreaking of the kingdom of God. We compare healing with the Resurrection: If God indeed raised Jesus Christ from the dead, such events as healing in response to prayer are eminently possible.

Second, we encourage people to tell their own stories of times when God did something extraordinary in their lives in response to prayer. Every church has people with stories to tell. Let me illustrate with two examples:

The first is about healing. I was filling in one Sunday for a priest who was ill. At the eight o'clock service I preached on healing and on how God still heals today. After the service an elderly woman said to me in hushed tones, "I was dramatically healed once! It was thirty years ago when Agnes Sanford prayed for me." I asked her why we were whispering. She said, "No one here would believe me."

Three more women spoke to me after the service telling me how they were healed in dramatic, noticeable, lasting ways. Each thought she was the only one in the church who had had such an experience and that everyone else would laugh.

If only we could get people to tell their stories to each other! They would discover they were not alone and that, far from being ashamed for believing what the Scriptures teach about healing, they could share this good news with others confidently.

My second story builds on the first. One day I was conducting a midweek noon Eucharist and preached on how some people today, as in Bible times, have been blessed to receive visitations from angels. I told those gathered that while this is not something that happens to everyone, these events sometimes happen today. After the service, while the dozen or so people were greeting each other, one woman shared that she had once seen an angel. A few others then shared their experiences, appreciative that they could tell someone else for the first time. It was a blessing for them to be able to do so and a blessing for the others to hear the accounts.

Many people have stories to tell. They need to tell them. Others need to hear them. When our stories are told in a gentle, humble manner, others are freed to tell their stories and to believe that God is working today in the lives of people like themselves. Thus they are encouraged to ask God for His help. Parishioners see that healings occur in churches like theirs, to people like themselves, in situations that are not bizarre. Sharing our stories "legitimizes" healing for many people.

One man put it to me this way: "I never believed in all this stuff until it happened to my friend Jim. I do not trust those frauds on TV, but I do trust Jim. He's convinced me this stuff about healing is for real."

Ask people to share their stories of healing before the congregation on Sunday, in a sharing group, or on a special occasion. Or have them write out their stories and place them in the church newsletter or bulletin.

Ask the pastor of a nearby church if he has a parishioner who has a story to tell, and borrow that person. Make use of the testimonies of healing in Christian magazines. *Sharing* magazine of the Order of St. Luke is a good resource. It is devoted solely to Christian healing.

Three words of caution, however.

First, make sure that the people who share are ones who will add to the credibility of healing, not detract from it, and will keep the focus of their testimonies on God, not themselves or others. If a person rubs people the wrong way or is thought to be a fanatic or religious crackpot, his testimony of healing, however genuine, might have the opposite effect, alienating people from the ministry of healing.

Second, make sure that the testimonies of healing are not all of the dramatic, instantaneous variety. God heals in a variety of ways. We may keep people from receiving all God has in store for them if we are, in effect, encouraging them to believe He works only one way.

Third, set healing in a context by showing that your denomination believes in healing. Now, not everything one's church believes or has believed is true, of course. Churches err. But when a church's statement of faith and traditions are illustrative of biblical truth, we can make use of them to show it is OK for people in their denomination to believe in healing.

It would be humorous if it were not so sad that some people do not care whether or not something is in the Bible as long as it is Methodist (or Baptist or Episcopalian). But until they come to trust the Scriptures as the primary authority for belief and practice, we can certainly remove roadblocks by showing how the healing ministry we want to introduce is part of our denomination's belief. We might call this the "kosher factor"—healing is "kosher" in our church.

Episcopalians, for example, can point to the service of healing in *The Book of Common Prayer* and the reference to it in the Catechism. They can refer to the detailed and highly favorable report on Christian healing issued by the 1964 General Convention and subsequent statements since. They can point to the powerful healing ministries of Bishop William Cox in the United States and Bishop Morris Maddocks in England. People of other denominations can, to various degrees, do the same from the statements of faith, orders of services, denominational reports, and statements of leaders of their churches. Confronted with all of this, no one whose concern is fidelity to the denominational heritage can oppose Christian healing. In fact, denominational loyalists, to be consistent, should *insist* that their churches have ministries of healing.

Thus, by placing healing in the context of what we already believe, we can make it much easier to introduce an intentional ministry of healing into a congregation. The local church has various means at its disposal for educating its people about healing.

Sermons

In the course of the year, and especially during the time when the ministry of healing is being introduced, several sermons should be devoted to aspects of Christian healing. In addition to the pastor's teaching, other voices should be heard. Why devote several sermons to this one subject? The answer is, frankly, that we have to make up for years of no, or sometimes bad, preaching on the subject. In addition, a sermon is supposed to move people to action. It will take more than one sermon to move people to avail themselves of the ministry of healing and to seek God expectantly in prayer for His intervention.

The church newsletter

We have already seen that carefully selected testimonies of healing given by respected people in the congregation can have a salutary effect. A major article on Christian healing should appear in the newsletter from time to time. With permission, articles from Christian magazines can be reprinted. (Please be sure to secure permission. It is ironic that in the attempt to make their church more attuned to the blessings of God, some should violate the fundamental commandment not to steal!) Once again, this is not to be seen as a one-time event, but an ongoing educational process.

Adult education classes

Christian education is for people of all ages. Many churches have adult education hours before, after, or between Sunday services. Many churches have a weeknight forum or study group. A segment of several weeks can be devoted to Christian healing. Participants can read and discuss books. They can listen to video or audiotapes. In your study materials do not neglect the scriptural accounts of healing performed in the Old Testament, by our Lord, and by the early Christians. (A list of these appears in Appendix 3.)

Speakers

An outside speaker can be brought in for a weekend healing mission. I have done several of these a year for over twenty years. A three-day healing mission might look something like this:

Friday evening: Covered-dish supper followed by a general, introductory overview of Christian healing. The nature of this program usually draws a good percentage of the committed members of the congregation.

Saturday: Further teaching on various aspects of Christian healing. This session generally draws only those truly committed to Christian healing, especially those who will likely form the parish healing team.

Saturday evening: Either a healing service open to the public with members of the parish healing team assisting (even if this is their very first time praying for the sick) or an informal gathering in a parishioner's home to discuss practical ways of implementing or enhancing a church-based healing ministry. This may be the better choice if it seems to be too soon for a public healing service or if the perceived need is to develop a strategy. If this is your choice for Saturday evening, it is important to have present both those who would like to be part of the ministry of healing and those in positions of authority, leadership, and decision-making.

Sunday morning: A simple, basic message on healing as the sermon. While this may be anticlimactic for those who have participated fully in the weekend, it is important to get the rest of the congregation on board, many of whom were not at any sessions of the weekend's mission. You may wish to have a carefully selected testimony of healing given. Sometimes it is appropriate for people to be invited to the front for healing prayer.

I have been asked why I recommend a weekend-long special emphasis on healing. The answer is this: we put special emphasis from time to time on different aspects of our faith. There are times, for example, when we place special emphasis on stewardship. We do not think good stewardship is less important on other occasions, of course, but we do call special attention to this aspect of Christian discipleship from time to time. Similarly, many churches have a time in the course of the year when special emphasis is put on Christian education, social responsibility, foreign missions, or repentance. So too with healing. But, just as with these other aspects of the faith, highlighting healing on particular occasions does not mean to imply it is not part of the regular, ongoing life of the church.

The example of the clergy and others who believe in healing

If the clergy have taught about healing but respond to someone's illness with sympathy and the telephone number of a specialist, not with an offer to pray for healing, they are saying by their actions that Christian healing is not something to believe in. If, however, the clergy respond to sickness with immediate, believing prayer, and perhaps also anointing with oil, they are saying that they truly believe healing works. I observed one church that came to believe in and experience God's healing through prayer because of the regular, gentle ministry of an elderly assistant pastor who visited people at home and in the hospital, sharing scriptural truths and his personal experience of healing, praying with them for God to intervene.

In the sixfold manner described above, a regular, systematic, ongoing method of education about healing will answer questions, defuse objections, raise hope, and give careful instruction about the ministry of healing you are anticipating.

SERVICES OF HEALING

In addition to the ministry of healing conducted in the context of visits to people in the hospital or in their homes, public services of healing are ways in which our Lord's healing is made available to His people. Here are three different times at which you may wish to have such services:

Daytime—midweek

Have prayers for healing, the laying on of hands, and anointing of individuals in the context of a daytime midweek Communion service. The advantage of this kind of service is that it makes the healing ministry available to those, especially the elderly, who cannot come out at night. The disadvantage is its inaccessibility to those at work or in school. We need, therefore, to provide healing prayer at other times as well.

Evening—midweek or Sunday

There are two ways to have evening services:

One, a program, or service, where healing ministry is available but is not the main focus of the evening. Many churches have midweek or Sunday evening services of prayer and praise, adult Bible studies, or fellowship. Healing prayers and anointing can be made available in the course of the evening's event or after the event for those who wish to stay.

Two, a service of healing *per se,* in which the whole service is oriented around healing, with hymns, Scripture readings, personal testimonies, teaching, and prayers on the theme of healing. Prayers for individuals with laying on of hands and anointing with oil could be placed after the sermon, right after Communion is received, or after the final blessing/dismissal. There are advantages to each of these three approaches:

After the sermon. If the sermon is an encouragement to faith in the God who expresses His inexhaustible love through healing, among other ways, having healing prayers directly after the sermon gives people an opportunity to respond while their motivation is high.

After receiving Communion. In the early centuries of the Church, Communion was seen as a sacrament of healing. In the course of preparing to receive Communion, we have confessed our sins, often necessary to remove a blockage to healing, focused on our Lord's self-giving love in dying for our sins, and knelt in humility and anticipation. In receiving Communion, we receive Him into our lives in a special way and receive His grace. To proceed directly from receiving Communion to receiving healing prayer adds to, and in many cases completes, the process of healing.

After the service is over. An advantage here is that the team can take more time with individuals. Although God can, and often does, heal in response to a one-sentence prayer, sometimes it is more helpful to have "soaking prayer," prayer that soaks in gently over a longer period of time. Sometimes words of counsel from the team members, a time of sharing or asking for guidance, or a period of confessing of sin is needed. Sometimes the person we are praying for loses composure and needs time to regain it. Sometimes the therapeutic value of spending time with people who obviously need our loving presence is most helpful. By delaying the time of prayer until after the service is over, the tendency to rush is lessened. Those who need to leave can do so without embarrassment.

I have made use of each of the three times of offering healing ministry in an evening service and find that each has its advantages. The healing team should both discern prayerfully and monitor carefully to see which seems to be best at a given time.

Sunday morning

There is much to be said for having healing available every Sunday in conjunction with the services of worship. Theologically, it demonstrates the truth that the God we worship cares and wishes to meet us at our points of need. We would deem it foolish if a salesperson spent time articulating the various virtues of a given product only to fail to offer us the chance to buy. Yet in many churches, while the hymns, readings, sermon, and prayers all speak of how God cares for us today, there is no direct opportunity for people to be brought to the throne of grace to receive the expression of such divine care.

Some object that because God knows a person's needs, such direct ministry is unnecessary. I tell them that God similarly knows our need for enlightening and motivation to do His will, yet we still preach sermons. If we truly grasp how much God cares for hurting people and how much time Jesus spent ministering to them, if we understand how much healing has historically been a part of the Church, then we will find a Sunday service that lacks prayers for healing just as odd as we would a Sunday service that lacks prayer, Scripture, a sermon, or a collection!

Practically, Sunday morning is the time when the largest number of our congregation is present. We appreciate physicians or government agencies that offer Saturday or evening hours. Should we not make the richness of God similarly accessible, especially when not everyone is convinced that healing works? In other words, parishioners who are "open but not yet convinced" might avail themselves of the ministry if it were offered on Sunday while they are already at church, but might not come to a midweek healing service. We have to start where they are; otherwise we may not get any further with them.

The question again arises as to where prayers for healing should be placed. As with a midweek service, there are three possibilities: after the sermon, after receiving Communion, and after the service.

After the sermon. Some churches offer a litany of healing and a time of general prayer for categories of illnesses said for the congregation en masse, with pauses so individuals can add their own personal needs, silently or aloud.

Some churches deploy several teams of healing ministries in different locations around the church. People who want prayer would go to a team, state their concern in one or two sentences, and receive a brief prayer and anointing. The whole operation lasts no more than a minute per person. If a person needs counseling, confession, inner healing, guidance, etc., he can be asked to meet with the team for further ministry after the service or to make an appointment for later.

Other churches ask the congregation to break into groups of four or five right where they are in the pews. People then share their needs briefly and pray with and for one another. Some might object that this forces people to talk with each other, get involved in the hurts of others, and engage in ministry themselves rather than leave it to the clergy and a few designated lay people. To this objection I say, "Yes! Absolutely!" Whatever one's style or preference of spirituality, Christianity is not a spectator sport, nor is it individualistic, sealed off from the lives and problems of others, nor is it done by a designated few for my benefit without my having to get involved. While it may take some time to learn how to be a ministering community, the march toward that goal must not stop.

After Communion. The healing team receives Communion first, then proceeds directly to a side chapel, to an out-of-the-way section of the main church, or, as a last resort, to a special prayer room somewhere in the church building. Individuals desiring ministry would go there right after receiving Communion. Those awaiting their turn for ministry would sit nearby ready to go to the next available ministry team, yet remaining enough distance away from the team to afford privacy and respect to the person to whom ministry is currently being directed. Done this way, there is no break between receiving Communion and receiving healing prayer, or prayerfully awaiting it. The service of worship continues and concludes while the healing ministry proceeds in its location.

After the service is over. The ministry begins right after the service is over. As others are either shaking hands at the door or proceeding to fellowship hour, those desiring prayer move to the front of the church. They remain in prayer near, but not too near, where the ministry is taking place, awaiting their turn. Churches with altar rails will find their use an advantage here.

STYLE

In most cases, the style of healing services should be in the style of your church. Sometimes what turns people off to the ministry of healing is not healing itself, but the style in which it is expressed or the atmosphere that surrounds it. If, for example, in a church whose worship style is gentle and quiet, a healing service is conducted in the style of an energetic revival meeting, the people of that church will have an additional stumbling block to overcome in their acceptance of healing. If they see that healing can be ministered in a gentle, quiet style, however, this roadblock is removed.

Part of the problem comes from the fact that often those most interested in establishing a ministry of healing have seen it only in churches of a very different style. It is natural to assume in those cases that this is the only way healing ministry can be conducted. In assuming this, however, style is confused with substance—an easy thing to do. In order to prevent this from happening, we need to do four things.

First, be on your guard against imposing a foreign pattern onto your congregation. This is not to say that God may not be leading your church to move into different patterns of worship. But doing that while introducing the healing ministry throws too much change at people at once and leads them to link healing with the other changes. If they do not like the other changes, they will assume it is the fault of the healing ministry and reject it along with the other changes.

Second, remember that basic truths can be expressed in different ways. Recall how different the apostles were in personality—the blue-collar, rough-and-tumble Peter; the intellectual yet emotional Paul; the mystical John—yet how united they were in the faith and in commitment to Jesus. Try to imagine a "Peter kind of healing service," or a "Paul kind," or a "John kind." I am sure they would look very different yet be equally effective.

Third, try to find a church similar to your own in style that has an effective healing ministry. Although you will not want to copy everything they do, chances are you will find that their experience and their way of prayer, worship, and seeking God's blessings are a good model.

Fourth, keep listening to the Holy Spirit to guide you. God knows what He wants for your church, and He will lead you into a format and style that are right for you. Remember, though, to keep listening. God will not keep things static. Our Friday night service in Malden took several different shapes over the years.

SUPERVISION

Leaders, you heighten significantly the chances of the acceptance of a healing ministry if you exercise careful supervision. Although you are not to be "controlling," you are responsible for supervising what goes on.

Start by supervising the process of introducing the healing ministry to the congregation. It has been my experience that the way in which change is introduced has as much to do with its ultimate acceptance as the particular change itself. It is one thing for a minister to say, in effect, "We are going to have a healing ministry here. It is what God wants. So there!" It is an altogether different thing to say, "I would very much like to have a ministry of healing at our church. After a period of teaching about it, I would like a six-month experiment. During that time we will watch carefully how it goes. If you have any questions, I will answer them as best I can. I would like your input and feedback. Then, after the experiment is over, let us stop and evaluate to see whether we should continue and, if so, with what changes." Only the most negative, controlling, or fearful person would oppose an honest and humble request like that.

In addition to the supervision by the pastor and lay leaders, it is wise to ask for a critique by an outsider experienced in the ministry of healing. He or she can bring both the wisdom that comes from experience and the different perspective of an outsider.

As you introduce the ministry of healing, remember the scriptural admonition not to despise the day of small beginnings (Zechariah 4:10). You are, or should be, building for the long term. It is better to build slowly and have something that lasts than to build quickly and see your work crumble and God's people alienated from the ministry of healing. In our admiration for the great, well-known ministers of healing, we often forget that many of them spent years in quiet obscurity, with little fanfare and with few people presenting themselves for prayer. Only after some long periods of testing and learning did these ministries grow.

But "slow and careful" does not mean "not at all." This ministry is too important to let our fears and cautions keep us from acting. Yet, God's people must always remember the scriptural truth that "he who believes will not be in haste" (Isaiah 28:16).

You also need to exercise careful supervision of those who will compose the healing team. We will look at that more thoroughly in the next chapter.

DISCUSSION QUESTIONS

1. Describe the good and bad aspects of each of the three kinds of people who surface when a healing ministry is proposed in a local church.

2. How can effective study of the subject of Christian healing occur?

3. What are the essential ingredients in beginning services of healing in a local church?

EXPERIMENT

Since this is necessarily a corporate function, and since the experiment will have a profound effect, one way or the other, begin where you are with as many others as are willing toward a ministry of healing in your church. Include a prayer for wisdom every time you pray. Using this book, start moving cautiously and prayerfully from where you are to where God leads you. This experiment is the most important one. Record every step in your healing notebook.

CHAPTER 12

The Selection, Training, and Supervision of the Healing Team

LTHOUGH IT IS true that God can use any believer to pray for the sick, as written in Mark 16:17–18, much of the ministry of healing in a congregation will be conducted by the healing team. While divine call and Spirit empowerment are essential for ministry, so are careful training and supervision. The Lord Jesus spent three years carefully training His closest followers for the work they would do after He ascended to heaven. Paul told Timothy to study to show himself approved as a worker for God (2 Timothy 2:15). The parish healing team is a group of people like the apostles and Timothy who receive in-depth training and supervision, in this case for the ministry of praying for the sick.

It is not a good idea to ask for volunteers for this ministry, because sometimes the wrong people step forward. Rather, we approach people we believe would make good ministers of healing and pray with them to see if they also perceive a call.

QUALITIES

Here are the qualities I look for in a minister of healing (or, indeed, in anyone who ministers to others):

Spiritual life

Healing is not just the elimination of a physical or emotional problem. Healing is *wholeness*, and it comes as one grows into fuller stature in Christ. To help others come to that, the minister of healing needs to have a living, dynamic relationship with God in Christ. In addition, he or she should be working actively toward spiritual maturity.

Love of people

Many medical professionals believe that patients recover more quickly when they have doctors who are genuinely concerned for them as people. Anyone seeking prayer can soon tell whether or not ministry is being done out of genuine love and concern. (See what Jesus said about that in John 10:7–15.)

Ability to take direction

The pastor or healing team leader will sometimes ask a team member to minister or not to minister to a particular individual, or to do or not to do something as he or she ministers. There is not always time to give an explanation. On other occasions, because of issues of confidentiality, an explanation cannot be given. At those times the team member must simply follow direction without argument. While no one is to follow an order involving something illegal, immoral, or heretical, of course, on all other occasions the minister of healing is simply to obey. (See Hebrews 13:17.)

Healthy emotional life

While we never outgrow our need for further emotional and spiritual healing—we are all, to use Henri Nouwen's phrase, "wounded healers"—a certain degree of emotional health is necessary in order to minister to others. If a person's need for succor is too high, the focus of his ministry will be his own needs, not the needs of others. If a person is ministering primarily to shore up a weak self-esteem, to look important to others, or to gain favor with God, it is unlikely that he will offer the kind of ministry a hurting person needs. In fact, real harm can happen. Thus, we seek only those who have a generally healthy emotional life and self-image.

Teachability

We all have much to learn. Those people who are good candidates for membership on the team are the ones who can be corrected without getting hurt or angry. It is understandable for beginners in the ministry to make lots of mistakes. It is not acceptable for them to continue making the same mistakes because they refuse to be taught or corrected.

A desire to improve as a minister of healing

While the word *professionalism* carries some connotations inappropriate for Christian ministry, still, those involved are to take seriously the importance of being the best ministers of healing they can be. Just as physicians, teachers, and musicians, to name just a few, should keep working to improve, so should those ministering healing. We want on our team the kind of person who regularly rereads the accounts of healing in the New Testament, reads books about healing, goes to conferences on healing, seeks individual supervision, shares with others involved in the ministry of healing, and so on. Some "jobs" around the church can be done by people with relatively low commitment or sluggish spiritual lives. Healing is not one of them.

What about people who offer themselves for the team who fall far short of these six criteria? We would be doing them a disservice if we, out of misplaced love or affirmation, put such people on the team. Much experience has shown the damage that can ensue—harm to those who ask for healing and to the reputation of the healing ministry. While we are not to invite them to be on the team, we are not simply to turn them away, either. They desire a good thing, however troubled they may be personally, or however confused they are in their motives.

I have told such people that I really appreciate their offer to help and that they may eventually be able to do fine ministry in healing, *but not right now.* I tell them that I would like to work with them on those things that are holding them back, to bring them to a place where they would be ready to serve. I make them no promises for future healing team membership, but I do offer my help to assist them in their own healing and growth.

Some people have reacted to my offer with inappropriate hurt or anger, thereby demonstrating a problem area. Others have accepted the offer of help. It was, in some cases, the occasion of reaching them when before I had not been able to find a way. After various lengths of time, some of them grew to the point that it was appropriate for me to invite them to be on the team. Their struggles with personal issues made most of them highly sensitive and most effective in their ministry to others.

You may have noticed that I did not list a "gift of healing" as one of the main criteria for selection. At the initial stage of team formation, this is not as crucial as the other criteria. God can still use these people in healing, of course, simply because they are believers. And often, with the humble service they are offering and their desire to grow, God will say to them, "You have proven faithful in small things. I will now gift you in healing, that you may prove faithful over larger things." (See Luke 19:17.)

Part of the reason we do not select just those with demonstrated gifts of healing for the team is this: How would we know who they are unless they are already ministering healing? To cut through this "Which came first, the chicken or the egg?" dilemma, we do not base a person's selection on the demonstration of a 1 Corinthians 12 spiritual gift of healing but on a Mark 16:18 promise that God can use any believer, at least to some degree, in healing.

It has also been my experience that some persons who have a demonstrable gift for physical healing also cause great harm because they are not submitted humbly to God or the church's leadership.

I suggest that your initial team membership number between four and eight people. More may well be ready, particularly in larger congregations. But since much of a team member's initial training is one-on-one supervision, four to eight is about all a supervisor will be able to handle effectively. After several months of working with them in their apprenticeship, they will be far enough advanced not to need such close supervision. At that time you can take a second group and work intensely with them, making use of people from the first group to help.

TRAINING THE HEALING TEAM

Once you have selected the initial team, how do you go about training them? You need three things:

1. Study

Building on the general congregational study of healing already mentioned, much more learning is needed. First, do a careful study of each of the healings Jesus performed. (A list of these appears in Appendix 3.) In its training course for new members, the Order of St. Luke directs people to ask several questions about each Scripture passage. (These questions are listed in Appendix 4.)

The answers to these questions are important. No matter how good the books and tapes of the experts on healing are, our primary source must always be the Scriptures. Have each person go through the passages on healing individually, writing out the answers to the questions. Then get them together to share what they discovered.

Once this inductive study of Scripture is completed, do a systematic, topical study of the ministry of healing. You can do this by reading the earlier chapters of this book aloud in the group, by using other books, or by listening to a series of teaching tapes on healing. Periodically the leader should stop to make sure people understand what they are reading or hearing. The leader should formulate discussion questions about the material and pose them to the group. Some of the material covered may be review, and some of it may be too advanced for immediate implementation. In any case, it is wise at this stage to get a big-picture overview of the subject.

2. Spiritual direction

In some churches this is called "discipling." Each member of the healing team should start meeting regularly with a spiritual director. Spiritual direction is one of those marvelous blessings God has given to the Church. It almost died out at one point, but it is now making a strong comeback. Spiritual direction is not to be confused with teaching, counseling, confessing sins, or training for ministry. Rather, spiritual direction is assistance to help us reflect on and grow in our walk with God. The spiritual director helps us examine our prayer life so it can be improved. The director will talk with us about our struggles with temptation and sin, about our sensing (or not sensing) God's presence in our lives, about our hearing (or not hearing) God speaking to us, and about how and in what ways we are sensing God at work in us and through us. We might describe a spiritual director as a coach of the soul, whose task is to help us grow in our personal relationship with God. Good teachers can help us intellectually; good trainers can help us functionally; good counselors can help us emotionally; but a good spiritual director helps us spiritually, in the narrow, technical sense of that word.

The criteria for a spiritual director include the various qualifications of a good confessor described previously on pages 81–83, with one addition: a giftedness in guiding the growth of one's personal relationship with God. Some wise, godly people make wonderful teachers, confessors, or preachers, but not necessarily good spiritual directors. In your quest to find one, ask your devout friends if they have a spiritual director and if you might contact him or her. Their spiritual director may be able to become yours as well. If not, he or she would likely be able to recommend someone. Make certain that the person to whom you are entrusting the care of your soul is spiritually mature and theologically orthodox. Ask questions of the person you feel might become your spiritual director, and check him or her out with others whom you respect. Many people attempt to pass themselves off as spiritual directors when they really have no business doing so.

You may find, after several sessions with your spiritual director, that while this person may be a good spiritual director in general, he or she is not right for you. If this is the case, try another. Spiritual directors understand the need for directees to make a change. Make sure, however, that the reason you are changing directors is not because your director has zeroed in on issues with which you do not wish to deal.

If your spiritual director is not your pastor, the two should be in occasional contact. This is not to find out the details of what was discussed. If that were so, few people would talk with the candor necessary for adequate direction. Rather, it is so your pastor will be certain you are making the regular, good-faith effort at direction necessary for anyone rendering ministry, and so that he will be able to assist in your spiritual growth.

Why is spiritual direction so important? For one reason, a ministry of wholeness centers, as we have seen, in a personal relationship with God. If you are to help others come more fully into wholeness, the matter of your own personal wholeness is key. If your spiritual journey is not progressing, you need someone to help you discover why it is not. If it is growing, but in an eccentric way, you need assistance in discerning how to refocus it. Even if it is going well, you need someone to help you keep it that way.

As you pray with others, you may become aware of God speaking to you, perhaps in an unfamiliar way. You may sense God's presence or believe Him to be absent. You may experience a spiritual "high" or what some have called "the dark night of the soul." Ministry opens up new vistas in your relationship with

God. If you are to take advantage of these opportunities, you need the wisdom of a wise spiritual coach.

Second, the task of ministry makes you vulnerable. The devil is threatened by Christians growing spiritually and bearing good fruit in ministry. He will try to attack you in various ways. He will send you various temptations; will seek to make you lazy, discouraged, or proud; will put in your mind dark and lurid thoughts; or will so stir up unresolved issues in your life that your focus will become yourself and not God and His work. A good spiritual director will bring you comfort, reassurance, and practical help when you are assaulted by the evil one, and he will bring the occasional challenge when you are being stubborn.

Supervision

When people ask for prayers for healing, they are often at their most vulnerable. Something is wrong in their lives or in the life of someone they love. As a result, they are more likely at this time than at any other to be wounded by someone ministering in a careless manner. For this reason, many people who believe in healing and have spent time studying it are reluctant to pray for the sick. While they see the need, they are afraid of hurting the very people they want to help. Such caution is not only understandable, but also it is very wise. With careful supervision, however, they can render ministry that both gives help and avoids harm.

Two essential components to supervision make it likely that a new team member will render sound ministry.

The first is for the apprentice not to minister alone but with someone experienced in ministry. (If the pastor perceives the need for supervision in beginning a ministry of healing, someone from another healing team may be borrowed for a while.) The one experienced in praying for the sick offers prayer while the apprentice watches and prays silently. After a while, the apprentice takes the lead while the supervisor watches (while also praying quietly). When ministry is done this way, the apprentice can take those tentative first steps in ministering knowing that someone more experienced will intervene if the apprentice forgets what to say, offers inappropriate ministry, or if something should go wrong.

Second, after the service is over, the supervisor reviews what the team member has done in ministering. This review session will usually be brief, as the team has spent quite some time praying before the service and attending and ministering at the service itself. More extensive review occurs later. This review can take place in either a one-on-one session, at a team meeting, or, preferably, in both. Several kinds of issues are discussed.

THE ISSUES IN REVIEW

Theological issues

Several theological issues are raised when one is ministering, such as: "Why is this person suffering? He seems to be such a fine man." "When I was praying, I felt heat in my hands [or heat coming from a certain place on the sick person's body]. What does this mean?" "I did not see anything happen. Is this ministry real?" These and other questions may arise in the mind of the apprentice. They may also be asked by the person for whom we are praying. Having done our introductory studies in Scripture and in books and tapes, we now return to the sources for answers to these questions. Theology, which can be dry when done by itself, now takes on life and meaning when we see its relevance to questions that come up.

Practical issues

When one does ministry, all sorts of practical questions arise, such as, "What do I do if someone starts crying?" "If I believe that her need is other than, or in addition to, the one she stated, do I pray for that, too, and if so, how?" "If the power of the Holy Spirit comes down in such a way that the person for whom we are praying is noticeably affected, what do we do?" "If I am in the hospital praying and the nurse comes in, how do I explain what I am doing and ask them to give us a few minutes?"

Questions arise regarding confidentiality. How much do we tell our supervisor? If he or she happened to be present when the ministry took place, there is no problem. But if we are reporting on something that took place when our supervisor was not there, how do we get the critiquing necessary for our growth as ministers of healing while respecting the confidentiality of the ones ministered to? There are two ways.

One is to change the superficial, irrelevant details of the story. This disguises the identity of the individual. If we are presenting for supervision the case of a twenty-eight-year-old businessman, for example, we could change it to a fifty-four-year-old housewife. There are two occasions, however, in which this will not work. One is if those details are germane to the situation. Some stories cannot be reworded to protect confidentiality without causing the feedback we need to be off-target. The other, much more common, especially in small churches, occasion is that no matter how we change the details, people know whom we mean.

The other way is to ask the person's permission. If we tell the person that we, for the purpose of our own growth and for the sake of those we will minister to in the future, need to discuss the case with the person supervising us, permission is often given. Many times, when we need to present a case to the whole team, the matter for which we are praying is not particularly embarrassing and permission will be readily forthcoming. If we are unable to get permission to share one particular case with the group, we may be able to get permission for another one.

Personal issues

As we minister, we get in touch with unresolved hurts or guilt from the depths of our own souls. As for hurts, I remember praying with another person for a man whose son had drowned. No sooner did he tell us his story than my prayer partner burst into tears. She too had lost a son in a drowning. She thought she had worked through her loss adequately, but it became apparent that more grief work was necessary.

As for guilt, the request that a group of us pray for a man dying of liver cancer raised guilt feelings in one of the members of the team. She wondered if she had done enough to pray for and visit her grandmother when she was dying of cancer.

In both cases, being involved in ministry brought to the surface issues that had been repressed, ignored, or insufficiently resolved. They became the focus of supervisory sessions. In both cases, the individuals involved were grateful that those matters were identified so that they could be dealt with. We should be aware that when we are ministering, many such issues will surface. While this may be distressing emotionally, it is a wonderful opportunity to resolve those matters that, while not conscious to us, nevertheless do affect us.

Spiritual issues

Because the ministry of healing is just that—a ministry—it does not leave us unaffected spiritually. How do we discern the voice of God from other voices speaking to us? Is what I am experiencing a gift of the Holy Spirit, and if it is, how do I use this gift? What is God teaching me about Himself and myself in this? How do I deal with the personal, spiritual issues that are arising in me? Such issues might include an awareness of my need to pray better and more often, a conviction of a particular sin, a new awareness of God, and so on. Because theological, practical, personal, and spiritual issues are all interconnected, they should be raised in supervisory sessions even though we will also discuss them with our spiritual directors.

At first we may be surprised at how many things there are to discuss. It must be for this reason that God blesses the new team member with only a few people seeking prayer. Much time is needed at the beginning to address the various issues that ministry raises. I have seen ministries of healing go very wrong because time was not spent at the beginning doing the careful reflection necessary.

I have also heard from people how the time of apprenticeship became the time when they grew the most spiritually. One woman put it this way: "My prayer life and Scripture reading took on an urgency, as did the resolving of various personal issues in my life. In order to help people, I had to take my walk with God seriously. I was forced to grow up spiritually, and I did!"

While some of the healing team may always be "general practitioners," others may sense a calling or find a particular giftedness in ministering to one kind of person, in using particular gifts of the Spirit, or in one sub-specialty of healing. In those cases we will encourage them to further prayer, reading, and even apprenticeship to a person with a recognized, effective, and balanced ministry in that particular aspect of Christian healing.

DEPLOYING THE TEAM

A healing team can be deployed in several ways. We will look at three of them.

1. Hospital or home visitation

Two team members (any more than two quickly tires the person being visited) visit a sick person "on location" and pray for the specific problems. They must remember that while friendly chitchat is certainly welcome, the main purpose of the visit is prayer so that, by the grace of God, the sick person will improve in health and be drawn closer to God. They should also remember that anyone sick enough to be housebound or hospitalized has a limited amount of strength. The tone should be gentle. The visit should be brief.

Wise is the pastor who takes along his apprentices when making such visits. Not only are there more people praying, but also the apprentices have the chance to learn by observation and supervised participation.

2. "Altar rail" ministry

In a growing number of churches, healing prayer is offered at a prayer station in one corner of the church, in a side chapel, or in a separate room. This ministry (as I mentioned earlier) is brief, no longer than a few minutes per person. The person desiring prayer states his or her concerns in a sentence or two, and the members of the team respond. While the problem is being presented, the team members engage in active listening—that is, listening carefully to make sure not only that they have gotten the surface details correct, but also that they are perceiving any underlying patterns. They ask God quietly for wisdom on how to proceed.

Team members lay their hands on the sick person's head or, unless it would be embarrassing to do so, on the affected part of the person's body, asking God to heal the distress. The prayer will be short, lasting no more than a minute or two. The prayer may be something like this: "Heavenly Father, Karen has come asking You to heal her of her painful leg cramps. We ask You to take the problem away. Karen, in the name of Jesus, be healed! Amen." Anointing with oil, usually by making the sign of the cross on the person's forehead, may also be done.

The ministry is brief, and yet God honors it. Over the years I have seen many people healed in this manner. I believe it is the best way to start a person off in the ministry of healing. No personal counseling is done, no theological answers are given, and, important to the apprentice, no previous experience or expertise is needed. All that is required is a belief that God can heal and a desire to be an instrument through which God can work.

Several issues arise in conjunction with altar rail ministry.

The first is the wisdom of ministering as a team and not as individuals. While God can certainly use an individual to minister, it is wiser for a team to minister. There are several reasons for this. As more people pray, added faith is present. A greater variety of spiritual gifts is present, as are wisdom and experience. While a group can go wrong in ministry, it is less likely than for an individual ministering alone. A group also offers a lessened danger of ego. When an individual prays for someone and that person is healed, he has the tendency, even though he knows better, to take the credit for the healing. Not only does this rob God of the glory due only to Him, but also it tempts us to imagine ourselves superstars. When several people minister, it is impossible to know who it was that God chose to use as the instrument for the healing to happen. And finally, it is unwise for a variety of reasons to have someone minister solo to someone of the opposite sex. Having a second team member present helps alleviate this problem.

A second issue of altar rail ministry is the spiritual phenomena that sometimes accompany a time of prayer. Someone being prayed for may be overcome by the power of the Holy Spirit in such a way that he or she falls to the floor. Another phenomenon is heat in our hands or in the place of illness in the person for whom we are praying, or both. Sometimes this is a sign that God is using a particular person on the team in a special way that day. That team member might be the one to take the lead in ministry. The heat may occur in a place in the sick person's body other than where the team was devoting its attention. This may indicate additional need for prayer. Another manifestation is a sense of tingling or shaking in us or in the sick person, or both. There may be, additionally, a sense—gentle or overwhelming—of the presence of God.

These phenomena do not always accompany a time of prayer. Their presence does not necessarily mean that a team member is spiritually mature, although many of the great healers, saints, and mystics throughout the ages reported these phenomena. Nor does their absence necessarily mean faithlessness on the part of one praying. Sometimes they may even be counterfeits of Satan to get us distracted or puffed up with pride. Just be aware that they sometimes occur, ask God to show you what they mean, and resolve that you will not be distracted by them.

A third issue that arises in altar rail ministry is the sense that God is speaking to us about the person with whom we are praying. God may be giving us discernment about the person's life. He may be giving us words of knowledge or wisdom about his situation. Such insights could either be in words, in pictures, or in a general sense that in some way God is guiding our thoughts. Often such communication from God shows either a key to the healing we are seeking, an additional problem for which we need to pray, the pathway to future spiritual growth, or all of these.

While such divine guidance has been part of the experience of the Church since her beginnings, and while old manuals on prayer and spiritual direction describe these things in detail, they are new to many.[1] As the Church rediscovers what they mean, we need to exercise caution. We want to test such purported communication to make sure it has indeed come from God. We test by making sure that such words are in conformity to Scripture, as 1 John 4:1 tells us. We test ourselves to see if, when we get a "word," it bears out in reality. If I believe a person has a gallbladder problem, for example, and a medical examination confirms this, I will be more confident that I can hear God speaking words of knowledge than if it is not borne out by the evidence. If God is giving us such words and we are hearing Him correctly, we will want to make use of this information in ministry to the sick. As we do, however, we must keep a few things in mind.

First, we should use such information only after addressing the particular problem that those being prayed for first mentioned. Why? For one reason, while what they said may not actually be important, *it is important to them at this time.* They may not hear anything else we say if we are not directly focusing, at least at first, where they are focusing.

Second, they may realize that they have other, more urgent problems, but they will not trust us with them until they see how we do with a problem that is relatively safe to share.

Third, if those with whom we are praying have never heard of God's supernatural impartation of information, or if their only experience has been negative, we could frighten them with a bold announcement that we know personal information. It could be startling for someone to hear a blunt pronouncement: "God just gave me a word for you, sister. He told me your problem is you won't forgive your mother." That is not ministry; that is assault! It would be much better to say, "As I was praying for you, I came to wonder if perhaps some of your need may be for reconciliation with your mother. Could that be on target?" Remember, if God prods but does not force, then we too should prod but not force. If this woman does not want to deal with the problem of unforgiveness, we must respect that. Then again, maybe we did not hear God correctly ourselves.

Yes, we should be careful in how we use words from the Lord. We do not, on the other hand, want to let our caution immobilize us. While misuse of something from God can be harmful, not to use it may block the healing someone needs. We should not only share whatever comes to us in prayer, but also we should ask the one being prayed for if anything came to his or her mind while the prayers were being offered. Always remember, the sick person is not passive in the process of healing. By encouraging him to pray and listen carefully for the voice of God, we are helping not only his physical well-being but also his spiritual growth to further, fuller wholeness.

Remember that various spiritual manifestations such as falling over in the power of the Holy Spirit, heat, tingling, or words from the Lord can be—and historically have been—expressed in a variety of ways. We can respect but need not copy the particular cultural style of Pentecostals in order to honor the way God is working. A healing team can also be deployed in a style of healing ministry that many call "prayer counseling." We will examine this in the next chapter.

DISCUSSION QUESTIONS

1. What is the reason or theory for having a designated healing team?

2. Using one-word characteristics, write the minimum requirements for a healing team member.

3. Read Luke 8:40–48. Answer the questions on this passage listed in Appendix 4.

CHAPTER 13

Ministering Healing by Prayer Counseling

PRAYER COUNSELING IS a style of ministering healing different from hospital or home visitation or ministry at the altar rail. In this format, the healing team takes much more time with people and examines their needs more extensively. The setting in prayer counseling is more akin to pastoral counseling than to a service of worship. Prayer counseling is not a better way of ministering healing; it is just different. One way of ministry may be called for at onetime, a different way another time.

Prayer counseling gives the team the chance to work in considerably more depth. Because of the vital interconnectedness of body, soul, and spirit, the approach is whole-person in orientation. Prayer counseling makes use of all of the "sub-specialties" of healing ministry: laying on of hands, confession, inner healing, deliverance, counseling, guidance about nutrition and exercise, and so on. Each of these sub-specialties has an integrity of its own. In prayer counseling they are all brought together and made use of as appropriate.

Prayer counseling may require one or several sessions to examine all aspects of a person's life, from diet, to exercise, to sleep patterns, to emotional hurts, to involvement with the occult, to spiritual strengths and weaknesses. In addition to being therapeutic, it can be preventative; presenting our lives before the Lord for improvement and scrutiny can keep any number of problems from happening. While those with a single problem may find it sufficient to be prayed for briefly at the altar rail, those whose problems are undefined or complicated may need a more thorough diagnostic ministry.

Some people come because they have been referred to the team by the clergy or by professional counselors. Godly pastors and trained, qualified Christian counselors are usually in such demand that they are more than happy to refer to capable lay ministers those whose problems are less severe than those needing in-depth professional care. Others come because of friends' references.

Some people come because they have been prayed for at the altar rail repeatedly, and nothing seems to happen. In those cases, we may sense that the causes of their disease are more complex or deep-rooted than can be ministered to in a few minutes.

Finally, some people come not because anything dramatic is wrong, but just to bring their lives before the Lord to be looked at by faithful ministers. Just as having annual physical examinations is advantageous, so are sessions like this from time to time. As one's life is looked at, a number of minor things can be addressed before they become major.

It is important to conduct the prayer counseling sessions in a place where you will not be disturbed and with sufficient time for the sessions not to be rushed. It is a good rule of thumb, however, that no session last longer than an hour and a half. Any longer and the counselee gets tired and perhaps overwhelmed by having to deal with too many issues at once. Often the sessions are shorter.

Prayer counseling can be informal as a few members of the healing team meet to talk with someone desiring help. In the course of the conversation, various issues are brought up and addressed. Done in this way, prayer counseling is more like an extended version of ministry at the altar rail. With no time pressures, conversation can be relaxed and the time of prayer more extended.

There are advantages to longer soaking prayers. Sometimes the blessings of healing need to soak in gradually, just as water from a gentle rain takes time to soak into the ground. I am often surprised, when watering my garden, that even after watering for some time, the soil is still dry at a small depth under the surface mud. Clearly, to reach the roots of some plants, much more watering is needed. No rule of thumb determines how long is enough, except that we often underestimate how long a time of prayer is needed.

If the person desiring ministry is known to the team, the initial time of light conversation before ministry begins can be brief. Fewer questions need to be asked. The sessions could take place in the person's home. If the person desiring ministry is not known to the team, however, other dynamics come into play.

First, the initial time of light conversation needs to be somewhat longer so the counselee can relax and become comfortable with the team members. This is important so trust can be established. As the team members get to know the counselee, they begin to understand his or her inner dynamics. Counselees sometimes have difficulty expressing their inner feelings or are honestly unaware of them. By getting to know the people we are counseling, we can help them express what they are feeling and become aware of what is going on inside.

Second, more attention needs to be given initially to discovering the various roots of the counselee's problems. The diagnostic checklist in Appendix 2 may prove helpful here. The purpose is to get, as thoroughly as possible, a look at the life of the person we are trying to help.

It could be that only a few issues stand out as needing attention. In that case, ministry can be accomplished in one or two sessions and with the two or three people from the team who are present.

If it looks as though several problems will need addressing, however, a more thorough approach is called for. One person from the team should be assigned as "case manager." This term is borrowed from social work. It refers to the person who, in the multiplicity of various helping persons, makes sure that the person being helped gets the assistance needed in a well-integrated fashion and does not feel chopped up among various specialists. The case manager takes notes on what is done in each session and makes sure that if additional assistance is needed, such persons are brought on board. The case manager also makes sure that all the aspects of ministry are well coordinated. With many ministering according to their specialties in the ministry of healing, this is quite important.

In these cases, the team may need to be augmented by other individuals from the team or even by individuals who are not part of your church's healing team. The fact is, no one minister of healing can adequately handle the whole variety of issues a seriously hurting person has. As the apostle Paul points out in 1 Corinthians 12:4, there are a variety of gifts. While God occasionally uses an individual in gifts in which he or she seldom ministers, God normally makes use of several individuals ministering together, each with his or her own contribution to the healing process.

Third, it is wise to conduct a prayer counseling session with a person not known to the team in the church and not in a private home.

Before ministry begins, it is important to determine if the person we are counseling actually wants to be healed. Jesus asked this of the man at the pool of Bethesda (John 5:6). If someone does not want to be healed, you are wasting your time and his. Some people so enjoy being ministered to that they refuse to be healed. They tenaciously cling to their problems so that others will keep ministering to them. We can actually harm them by reinforcing and rewarding their neuroses if we play along! This is not to say that they do not have a problem. They obviously do. But their need is for someone to go to the root of the real problem, not the one they present to us. Their need may be for someone to "tough love" them into responsible behavior, not to affirm their dead-end expressions of self-pity or victimization. If you are not experienced enough in prayer counseling to discern this, or if you are but the counselees are not willing to let you expose their real problems, no progress can occur.

It is essential that the counselee does his homework. The ministry of prayer counseling requires his or her active participation. It is *his* life that is in need. We cannot take what is there and overlay wholeness on top. The counselee needs renewing from within, which cannot happen without his or her active participation. At the end of each session, the team should assign the counselee some homework. At the next session, begin by asking how the homework assignment went. If little or nothing was done, stop the session immediately and tell the counselee that you cannot resume until the homework assignment is completed.

It may sound cruel to break off ministry if the person refuses to let us work on a deeper problem. But remember, our purpose is to bring people into wholeness. Sometimes we may be so eager to be active in ministry that we care more for the good feeling of ministering than we do for the welfare of the other person. It may be that we have to be strict for them to take the process seriously. If they do not, others who are serious about healing need our time.

Prayer, of course, is an essential component of prayer counseling. The team should pray together before the counselee arrives. Each session should begin with prayer, inviting the counselee to pray as well. We should ask God to guide, direct, and protect the session, and to pour His love and grace upon the counselee and His wisdom and power upon the members of the team.

The team should not only encourage the counselee to pray as team members pray at various points in the counseling session, but also instruct the counselee how to do it if he or she is not able to do so. Not only are we prayer partners with those we are trying to help; we are also spiritual coaches. The point is not to make them dependent on us, but rather to present them mature in Christ (Colossians 1:28). After praying for the counselee for a while, we can stop to ask if he or she feels any different. While emotional and spiritual change often come gradually, there are times when the breakthrough is rapid. Suddenly the counselee becomes aware that a burden has been lifted or a fear has left.

When a healing has indeed taken place, we should stop to praise and thank God. God did something, and realizing this causes faith to grow. It will be easier to believe Him for the other needed healing to take place. Or, if a partial healing has occurred, we thank God for what He has done and ask Him to complete His work.

Let me give you an example of how a series of prayer counseling sessions might take place with a person whose problems are complex in nature. For this example (based on real life), I will call the case manager Doris, her church Morningside United Methodist Church, and the person needing ministry Andrea.

Andrea was referred to Morningside Church by a friend who knew that the Lord was doing good things there. Andrea's request for ministry was passed on by the church secretary to the head of the healing team, who passed it in turn on to Doris, one of the team members. Doris called Andrea. They chatted on the telephone for several minutes so Doris could sense if Andrea was serious about being helped, determine whether Andrea's problems were within the range of what the healing team could handle (or if a referral to a Christian counselor was necessary), and establish the beginning of a relationship. A time for the first appointment was set.

At the first session, Doris, Andrea, and Michael, another member of the team, spent several minutes getting to know each other. After a time of prayer, Doris explained the process of healing through prayer counseling. Doris then asked Andrea to repeat the reasons why she was seeking ministry. Andrea said there was not anything in particular that stood out; she just did not feel right.

As Doris went through the diagnostic checklist (again, Appendix 2), several problem areas became apparent. Andrea's problems were: (1) stomachaches; (2) difficulty in praying (when she tried to pray, which was not that often); (3) the matter of having stolen a few things at work; (4) fear that her father would die and that she would be left all alone; and (5) an admission that she had been to several séances.

Doris first got Andrea's promise that she would get a complete physical and tell her physician of the stomach complaints. Doris did not know if the stomach problem might be reflux, ulcers, cancer, or something else. She told Andrea that sometimes a physical problem can come from a variety of sources. "In any case," she said, "the problem needs to be addressed."

Michael pointed out that God could heal the problem miraculously, through medicine, or through the process of prayer counseling. They stopped at this point to pray for healing, and then suggested that until the problem ceased, it would be wise to talk with her doctor.

Then Doris addressed the matter of stealing. She told Andrea that while God is loving and forgiving, we must turn from our sins, make restitution for what we have done wrong, and reaffirm our desire to obey Jesus as Lord over our lives. She tried to help Andrea understand that it is not only individual acts that concern God, but the whole orientation of our lives. The ultimate question is not "Did I do a particular thing wrong?" but "Am I actively trying to make Jesus Lord over my life?" Doris said that it would be important for Andrea to conduct a thorough examination of her life in accordance with the revealed will of God in Scripture. She could do that with a layperson in an informal manner or with a minister or priest as a formal confession. In either case, it needed to be done. As neither Doris nor Michael were ordained nor gifted in helping people to examine their lives and repent of their sins, she said she would be happy to arrange for Andrea to see either a pastor or a person on the healing team who was gifted in these matters.

Andrea admitted that this would probably be a good idea, yet questioned what relevancy it had to her stomach difficulties. Doris took some time to explain the interconnectedness of body, soul, and spirit. She told Andrea how her stomach problem could have come from any number of sources, including guilt about having stolen. Doris noted that no matter the cause of her stomach problems, Andrea needed to confess her sin of stealing and make restitution. Michael added that while we do not always know what the cause of a problem is, the thoroughness of prayer counseling often gets to the roots.

Time for the first session was up. While Doris, Michael, and Andrea would have liked to continue, they had been at it for almost an hour and a half, and Andrea had homework to do. She had to get her complete physical, she needed to make thorough confession of her sins and start figuring out how to go about making restitution, and she needed to do the Scripture reading Doris had assigned her. Doris and Michael prayed again for her. They made an appointment to meet again. As they were leaving, Michael reminded Andrea that even if the stomach problems were to go away in the meantime, she should still keep their next appointment for two reasons: first, God had a wonderful supply of blessings to give Andrea, and second, she could grow further in the knowledge that Jesus was her Lord. The urgency of these two things should not be short-circuited in case the problem that brought Andrea to prayer counseling was removed.

Two weeks later, Andrea came back. Doris first asked her if she had gone to the doctor. Andrea replied that her doctor was heavily booked up but that she had made an appointment with her for later that week. Andrea volunteered that she had met with Pastor Jim, the associate pastor of Morningside Church. She and Pastor Jim had examined a number of areas in her life that needed change, and she said that they would be examining them further to see how she could do just that. Doris said she would need to be in touch with Pastor Jim, not to find out specific details, but so that the people working to help Andrea would be working in harmony. Andrea agreed to write a one-sentence note authorizing Doris, Michael, and Pastor Jim to share necessary information.

In the two weeks between appointments, Doris had been praying for wisdom as to what issue in Andrea's life to tackle next. Was it Andrea's fear of being left alone? If it were fear, was the fear emotional in origin, was it a demon of fear, or both? If both, which should be addressed first? If fear were not the issue to be addressed next, was it Andrea's involvement with the occult? Doris knew that there is no automatic, textbook answer to the question of the order in which ministry should be done. Waiting for a word from God was crucial. Doris knew, further, that if inner healing was next, she would need to pray to discern who on the team gifted in inner healing would be the right one to minister to Andrea. She also knew that if deliverance prayer were to happen next, she would want to know who should supplement her own gift in that area.

Doris came away from her time of waiting for the Lord's answer with some sense of God's direction, but nothing clear-cut. This used to trouble Doris, but over the years of ministering healing she had come to believe that while sometimes one proceeds with clear, unmistakable guidance from the Lord, at other times one proceeds on the basis of education and experience. She was no longer embarrassed if she had to admit a different tack was needed because the one she was on was not getting results. She smiled, realizing it was exactly the way her cousin Ed, a physician, worked.

Just as Doris was about to start the second session, Andrea said, "Can we talk about the best way for me to make amends for the things I stole from work?" Doris knew that sometimes the minister of healing has to set the agenda, but at other times the person to whom we are ministering directs it. This was one of those times.

Talking and praying through the issue of restitution took so much time that there was little time left for anything else. Doris felt that to begin to work now on something else would be unwise as it would be rushed. She asked Andrea how she was doing on her Scripture reading. Andrea admitted she had put it off for no good reason. Doris laughingly scolded Andrea, telling her that Scripture study was as important as taking the pills the doctor gives us. Andrea agreed to do better. Doris told Andrea that they would be working on issues raised by her involvement in the occult at the next session.

"Oh, I wasn't in the occult," said Andrea. "I'm not into any of that Satan stuff I've seen on TV."

Doris knew this was not the time to point out that there are many seemingly harmless things that are occultish and against God. Instead she asked Andrea to read a small introductory book on spiritual warfare so that Andrea would know what the next session would be about. She agreed. An appointment for two weeks later was made.

Just as Andrea was going through the doorway, Doris yelled out, "Oh, I almost forgot! How's your stomach?"

"Good!" Andrea replied. "Haven't had a problem in over a week."

With a smile on her face, Doris asked, "Then why did you come back?"

"Because," Andrea replied thoughtfully, "I see how important getting everything in my life in order is. I want it for God, and I want it for me. I want to get the garbage out and the good stuff in. And I know you care about me."

Andrea called Doris four days later to tell her there was some good news and some bad news. The good news was that her efforts at restitution went well. Her boss was amazed that she went to him, confessed what she had done, and laid a check covering what was stolen on the table between them.

He was so amazed he said he would not prosecute her for theft, something for which Andrea was prepared even though she was praying hard that it would not happen. The bad news was that her doctor found she had a moderate case of esophageal reflux but that it could be controlled with diet modification and could be alleviated with medication if it got too bad.

Doris rejoiced with Andrea. She did not remind her of her other homework, hoping that the good feeling Andrea had over making restitution would be all the encouragement she needed.

Ten days later the three of them met again. As always, they began with prayer and discussed how things had been going since the last visit. Andrea had been doing her Bible studies and had even gone with a girlfriend to a midweek prayer meeting at a charismatic Presbyterian Church. But no, she had not read the book on spiritual warfare.

"Please don't take this as rejection, Andrea," Doris said. "But it's important that you have a basic understanding of the spiritual world—of good and evil spirits and how these things work—before we work on your deliverance. We can reschedule the appointment for a week from now."

Andrea understood and thanked Doris for being "professional."

"We do not like to use the word *professional* in terms of ministry," Doris replied. "But I know what you mean."

A week later they met again. Andrea had read the book. There were parts of it she did not understand, and a few places where she thought the author was being unnecessarily narrow. The most important thing she derived from the book, however, was that there is a spiritual battle going on and she had innocently opened herself up for possible harm.

Doris told Andrea that sometimes she discerned the presence of the demonic. Andrea now knew enough to know what those words meant and was concerned. "No," Doris responded, "I don't sense anything with you. That doesn't mean there isn't anything to deal with, however. No one's discernment is 100 percent accurate. But not to worry; God is stronger than any evil power."

Michael first led Andrea in a prayer of renunciation of Satan and all his works. (See Appendix 5.) Then he asked Andrea if she had ever accepted Jesus as her Savior and Lord. Andrea replied that she remembered doing that when she was confirmed in the Episcopal Church as a teenager. When Doris asked if she had understood what her vows meant and if she was genuine in her commitment, Andrea replied, "Yes, very much so. I guess I drifted away from it over the years, but at the time our priest explained thoroughly why we need a Savior and how Jesus is Savior and Lord." Doris led Andrea in a prayer of rededication. (See an example in Appendix 5.)

Then Doris and Michael asked the Holy Spirit to fill spots made empty by any departing evil spirits. (See what Jesus said about this in Matthew 12:43–45.)

When that was over, Andrea asked, "Is that it?" Doris did not know what Andrea meant, so Andrea explained, "I was expecting shouting and screaming on your part and me speaking with a deep bass voice and all that!"

"Oh, no!" Doris hastened to reply. "Do not believe everything you see in those movies. Some of it is exaggerated, and even the parts that are true occur in only a small percentage of the cases. Often when I pray for deliverance, nothing noticeable happens. But people comment that heaviness lifts from their spirits and they find prayer, worship, and Bible reading to be much easier. Sometimes troublesome thoughts go away, too. Other times there are a few outward manifestations of the demonic, like twitching or jerking of the person's body as I command the evil spirits to leave. I never raise my voice because, for one thing, the demons are not deaf; for another, they respond to the authority God grants believers; and third, why scare people unnecessarily? Sometimes when I pray there are probably no evil spirits present. What I am doing, then, is saying, in effect, 'I do not know if you are there, but if you are, get lost in Jesus' name.'" They both laughed.

Doris instructed Andrea what things are demonic, occultic, and New Age, and, therefore, forbidden by God and harmful to us. After this, Doris gave Andrea some help on how to win in her battle over temptation. Her homework assignment for Andrea was basic Christian discipleship teaching on spiritual growth, prayer, worship, and Scripture study. They agreed to meet three weeks later.

After the usual pleasantries, now growing a bit longer as the three had grown in their friendship, was the time of prayer. For the first time, and quite spontaneously, Andrea offered a brief prayer. She was pleased at that, yet admitted it lacked the formal structure of Doris' more experienced words. Doris and Michael assured Andrea that God looked first on the heart and last on the form.

Doris did two things she had not done before. First, she asked Andrea if she was worshiping regularly on Sunday. Andrea gave Doris a look as if wondering if the price of her healing was to join Morningside Church! Doris understood immediately and told Andrea that while of course they would welcome her with open arms at Morningside Church, she did not have to attend there as long as she was worshiping in a church that believed the Bible to be the Word of God. Andrea said that because of her work schedule, Sunday was impossible, but that she had not missed a Wednesday night prayer meeting at the Presbyterian Church in two months.

Second, Doris asked if she could discuss what had been happening during their sessions of prayer counseling to her healing team meeting. "From time to time we each need to make a presentation to the group of the work we are doing. This helps us all learn, and it particularly benefits the person making the presentation, because anything we may be doing wrong as we minister is examined and corrected."

Andrea was a bit concerned. "You won't...I am not sure what I mean, but you won't..."

"Blab all your secrets?" Doris offered. "No, of course not. Remember the word *professional* you used last session? While you'll remember I do not like the word, you could say that we are certainly as discreet as any professional counselor or physician. And if there are parts of what we have been discussing that you do not want shared, please tell me, and I'll work around those."

"No, I trust you, Doris. You have my permission to discuss my situation with your colleagues."

Michael asked Andrea about her fears of abandonment and of losing her father. "The fears are still there," Andrea responded. Michael explained that sometimes fears, or other unwanted emotions, disappear at a session of deliverance. "Other times they do not. This is either because the need for deliverance is much deeper, which I do not sense here, or else the fears were caused by something other than evil spirits. My sense is that what's needed here is inner healing." They took several minutes to explain what that was.

"We are not particularly gifted in that area," Michael explained. "We do have someone on our healing team named Marcy who is not only gifted in inner healing but also has positive results in matters of women and their fathers. I would like to bring her into our work, if you do not mind."

"Please do, but on one condition," Andrea responded. "I want you two present when these 'inner healing' things occur."

Doris laughed. "Don't worry. Inner healing doesn't bite, and you are not made to look foolish. It *would* make it easier if we were there, because our desire is not only to be your friend and do our part in helping you toward wholeness, but remember, I am the one who coordinates the efforts of the others who are helping you. By being there, we could be plugged in firsthand. But you need to know that we will be saying and doing very little except praying and making occasional observations. Marcy will be doing more of the direct ministry."

Andrea felt comfortable with that, although she was surprised to learn that the ministry of inner healing usually takes much longer than that of confession or deliverance.

In Andrea's case, it did take longer. In fact, Andrea, Michael, Doris, and Marcy worked at it for a total of eleven sessions.[1] They prayed for God's wisdom and guidance prior to the first session, and God did not let them down. In the middle of the first session, Marcy felt she had gotten a word of knowledge that Andrea had been left behind somewhere, and that was the source—or at least a source—of her fear of abandonment. Although Andrea did not recollect an incident, her father did. When she was a little girl, they had gone to the mall together, and she had disobeyed him by wandering off. They wondered aloud together if that was why she was so fearful whenever her dad, a salesman, went away on a business trip. Andrea marveled at how much a blessing the gifts of the Holy Spirit are.

At each session of inner healing they asked Jesus to remove Andrea's fears about being abandoned. They suggested that several times during the day she picture in her mind's eye Jesus standing next to her. Once Andrea, with childlike giggles, shared how funny she thought it was that Jesus went shopping with her to Kmart.

In addition to ministering inner healing, Doris, Michael, and Marcy made sure that Andrea was growing spiritually. They checked in occasionally with Pastor Jim to see how Andrea was doing in matters of repentance. Whenever it seemed that Andrea was becoming a passive recipient of their ministry, they made her take responsibility not only for her healing, but for her growth in Christ as well.

They showed her how the various parts of healing interconnect, not just in theory, but in real life, and not just at the beginning of ministry, but at all times. This careful instruction bore fruit in the sixth session of inner healing when Andrea suddenly realized she had been blaming her father for her being lost at the mall.

"You know, I love my father, but I haven't stopped blaming him for that. And I used to tell him he was selfish for going on his business trips without taking me."

"Here's what I suggest," responded Marcy. "You are learning how to pray out loud and informally. Let us have a prayer in which you ask God to forgive you for whatever resentment you harbored or still harbor against your father." After this was done, they talked about whether it was necessary for Andrea to ask her father's forgiveness for what she did as a child.

The outcome of the sessions of inner healing was that Andrea was set free. Her reflux still kicks up from time to time, usually after a big dinner. But she is a new person in several ways. She has grown much closer to the Lord, and she is more whole emotionally and spiritually. At last report, Andrea was taking a healing ministry training course so she could find out how God could use her in ministry to others.

The expression of the healing ministry called prayer counseling can take place in any church in which there are godly people who take it seriously and believe God can use them in service to others. While not as exciting, perhaps, as the sudden dramatic healings that take place at a healing service, it is an opportunity to apply the riches of Christ's transforming power to people in ways that are thorough, deep, and lasting.

DISCUSSION QUESTIONS

1. What kinds of situations do you perceive as appropriate for prayer counseling, rather than one of the other forms of ministry?

2. Read the Diagnostic Checklist in Appendix 2. Ask yourself the questions, and honestly record the answers. Record any conclusions about your own wholeness.

3. What are the essential ingredients of prayer counseling?

4. In ministering to an individual, list the advantages and disadvantages of team ministry.

CHAPTER 14

Being and Staying Well

BY MARY GRACE PEARSON, DO

BEING WELL IS more than being healed, and health is more than not being sick. Often we settle for the absence of sickness rather than the abundant life Jesus came to bring us (John 10:10). In this chapter we will discuss how to be well and how to seek the abundant life—physical, emotional, and spiritual—that Jesus promised us.

PHYSICAL

We often shrug off exercise and diet as the field of health nuts. Nonetheless, in pursuing health we need to examine these issues carefully. Most people who attempt to diet or exercise their bodies into shape fail, and they fail for the same reasons. Because of their failures, they dismiss these disciplines of life as impossible. Why do people fail?

1. Unrealistic goals

Many people expect to lose thirty pounds in one month. Or they imagine themselves exercising their bodies into figures that sixteen-year-olds would be proud of—in a few weeks! This is why fad diets and paid weight-loss plans are popular and ultimately fail.

2. Unrealistic plans

Some of us make dramatic resolutions about exercising an hour every day. We plan on waking up at 5 a.m., going for a three-mile jog, lifting weights, and dancing through an exercise video as soon as we get home from work. Many will stop after they are thrown off their carefully planned schedule one too many times after getting home late from work or staying up late with a sick child. An unrealistic plan ultimately dooms us to failure.

3. Lack of persistence

We get bored. We get tired. We get discouraged at our lack of results. And we realize that ultimately we are more comfortable watching baseball than playing it. We binge or forget to exercise, then abuse ourselves instead of saying, "Whoops, guess I'll try harder next time."

So how can we overcome our inclinations to overeat and underexercise?

Any change we make in our lives must be based in the Lord. "Unless the Lord builds the house, those who build it labor in vain" (Psalm 127:1). We need to repent of any gluttony or neglect of the temple in which we dwell (1 Corinthians 6:19). We need to ask God's direction in our lives, especially regarding our attitudes toward food, wellness, and our own bodies. We need to ask God's help in establishing realistic goals and plans.

Now let me be clear. Realistic goals are important. Self-control is a fruit of the Holy Spirit (Galatians 5:23). Looking like a model is not. Many Christians, particularly young women, get themselves into trouble at this point. In fact, the Bible urges women in particular not to focus on outward beauty but on developing a godly character (1 Peter 3:3–4). So how do we establish realistic goals?

Diet

Food intake should be determined by our needs, not just our wants. An eighty-year-old-woman and an eighteen-year-old man will have different food requirements. Of benefit to everyone is a diet high in fruits, vegetables, complex carbohydrates, and adequate water. It is generally recommended that most people maintain a low-fat diet (a caloric intake of less than 30 percent fat). Although we do need some fat in our diet, most of us need less than one tablespoon a day! There is another benefit of a low-fat diet. Since fat is calorie-dense, fat makes you fat and low-fat foods do not! Foods that are low in fat are breads, pastas, fish, vegetables, and fruits. Butter, margarine, fatty meats (especially red meat), fried foods, and dairy products (except skim milk or foods made from skim milk) are high in fat.

There is some evidence that a diet with between 5–6 servings of fruits and vegetables a day protects against cancer. There is much evidence that a low-fat diet helps prevent heart disease. A healthy diet includes a wide variety of fresh fruits, vegetables, complex carbohydrates (bread, pasta, cereal), low-fat dairy products, lean meat, and fish. These should make up *at least 70 percent* of all the calories in your diet, preferably 85 percent. One of the many little books in the supermarkets can tell you the fat and calorie content of each food.

Some foods must be used cautiously at all times. These are caffeine, alcohol, and salt. Note that I did not say *should not be used*, merely *used cautiously*. Let me explain.

Caffeine is a stimulant chemical found primarily in coffee, colas, tea, and chocolate. It heightens awareness and alertness (thus its popularity with students, long-distance drivers, and workers on the night shift). Unfortunately, caffeine can contribute to restlessness, insomnia, rapid heartbeat, and irritability. In some people it can cause diarrhea, aggravate irritable bowel syndrome, even set off a migraine headache. There is also some evidence that women who consume coffee prior to and during their pregnancies have a higher rate of miscarriage.

In general, caffeine for most people in small amounts (less than four cups of coffee per day) is harmless. Caffeine is generally a problem only when it is consumed in excess. If you have any symptoms of irritability, restlessness, insomnia, anxiety, or rapid heartbeat, consider stopping all your caffeine intake.

Alcohol is a substance with a long history of medicinal use and social abuse. Timothy was advised by none other than the apostle Paul to take a little wine to help his stomach (1 Timothy 5:23). Some recent evidence, in fact, indicates that wine, used moderately, can help prevent heart disease. (Moderate means one or two drinks of four ounces each.) Unfortunately, some people are alcoholics and cannot use alcohol in moderation. For them alcohol becomes an addictive substance destroying liver, heart, brain—even life itself. Those who suffer from alcoholism live most productively when they abstain from alcohol use altogether. Even people who are not alcoholics can be sensitive to its side effects, including fatigue, impaired judgment, flushing, and confusion. These people may need to avoid alcohol, too, not because of an addiction but because of their sensitivity to it.

Alcohol, even white wine, is high in calories and needs to be calculated into your diet. No one should use alcohol before driving, hunting, or operating machinery. We need only to read the newspapers to see how these can be tragic combinations.

Salt is a flavoring as well as a preservative. When Jesus referred to us as the salt of the earth (Matthew 5:13), He compared us to something that improves the flavor of the world and helps keep it from rotting. In ancient and recent times, salt was used as a preservative—for example, salt cod and salt pork. Salt enhances other flavors, too, as well as provides flavor of its own. Anyone who has tried unsalted tortilla chips knows they are just not as tasty!

Unfortunately, salt has the effect of elevating our blood pressure and making us retain fluid. This is more significant for some people than for others. For someone who has a normal blood pressure and is in good general health, the occasional use of salt is probably not harmful. Anyone with fluid retention problems or heart disease, on the other hand, should probably avoid salt as much as possible. Individuals of African ancestry often have a superior salt-conserving mechanism, which makes them more susceptible to the effects of salt and more prone to elevated blood pressure and subsequent heart disease.

As with all things, our diets should be moderate. Believe it or not, the reason many people fail in their diets is that the diets are too strict. People give up on the diet because they feel it's "not worth it," or because when they are over at Aunt Tilly's house they will hurt Aunt Tilly's feelings if they don't have a slice of her double chocolate torte. Have a piece! (Have a *small* piece.) Just don't go home the next day and make some more! Have whatever you like—in small amounts. Don't cheat every day. When you fail on your diet, don't give up. Start again.

Exercise

While all of us would like to have the firm body of a professional athlete, most of us do not have eight spare hours a day to exercise. The following is not meant as a guide to start Olympic training, then; it is meant as a guide to keep you fit within the dictates of your schedule. "Not *my* schedule," you might be thinking. Yes, *your* schedule.

First, commit your course to the Lord. Ask Him for help in being physically fit. Ask Him to show you where in your schedule you can find the time to exercise.

Second, look for the "wasted" time in your schedule. What do you do during commercials? Is there time while you are on hold on the telephone? While you wait for someone to call? While you wait for the washing machine at the laundromat? While you wait in airports? Look for these time slots, whether they are minutes or hours. Doing some sit-ups and pushups or stretching exercises during commercials will keep you fit better than trotting out to the kitchen for another bag of Doritos. Stretching or doing isometric exercises will help tone you even during those brief times. Walking in the airport will help you stay limber as you await your flight.

Third, find out what kind of exercise you like to do. (It is with great difficulty that I have persuaded Mark that listening to the Red Sox does not constitute exercise!) We like to walk.

253

When that is not feasible in our New England climate, we go to the local mall to walk. Some people have a pool available to them at or near work. Others like to play racquetball or tennis in their lunch hour.

The single best thing to remember when converting from couch potatohood is that *something* is better than nothing. There are indications that even a slow-paced stroll twice a week improves fitness in sedentary individuals. So figure out what you can do—and *do* it!

Another important component of physical well-being is rest. This is probably the single most neglected aspect of well-being in America. It is a rare week that someone does not come into my office with fatigue, wondering why they cannot balance a forty-hour work week, a family, and an aggressive social life, all on four to five hours of sleep per night! Many people are proud of how little sleep they can get by on. When I was a medical resident, we looked admiringly at the person who needed the least sleep: "He only needs four hours a night. Think of all that extra time he has!"

Scripture, in contrast, says, "It is in vain that you rise up early and go late to rest, eating the bread of anxious toil; for he gives to his beloved sleep" (Psalm 127:2). We try to maximize the quality of our lives by doing more. Yet all we accomplish is ill health, snoozing during our devotions, and depending on caffeine to keep us going.

I am not proposing to set up sleep as the new idol. Any parent who has stayed up with a sick child knows there are times when sleep must be sacrificed. I am talking about maintaining a balance in one's life. What are some sensible guidelines?

The average person needs between seven and nine hours of sleep per night. Only you can determine what makes you feel rested the next morning when you get up. You should plan to get that amount of sleep at night. A lack of sleep makes us irritable, less productive, and less able to listen to God in our quiet time. To plan to get an adequate amount of sleep requires discipline. Yes, you must stop working earlier or turn off the TV earlier in the evening. You may have to settle for a less than a perfectly clean house. You may have to give up an extra meeting or night out each week. It demands self-control and a decision that God will be in control of your schedule.

Secondly, you should plan one day of rest per week. A few years ago Mark and I started taking one "play day" together a week. Ideally for us this includes sleeping late, time for prayer, some enjoyable exercise (usually a walk) and some form of play. We take turns choosing what that play is; it can be anything from hiking to attending a performance of the Nutcracker ballet. The incentive to do this for workaholics: we find that our productivity increases immensely in the remaining six days. It helps open up lines of communication between us, helps alleviate anxiety, and helps us maintain a clearer focus on our priorities.

Everyone's day off will be different. Our friends David and Audrey, who run a busy oceanarium in Bar Harbor, Maine, often turn on their answering machine and retreat to a quiet room in their house facing the ocean, a room well supplied with books and Bibles. They feel drained after the demands of their work and find it refreshing to spend their time quietly.

Jesus said, "The sabbath was made for man" (Mark 2:27), because He knew we need it! It is especially important for families with children to make this effort, because children need rest, too. There have been many articles about how many middle, upper-middle, and upper-class children are pushed, pushed, pushed to succeed, increasing their stress. The happiest times in my childhood were the family vacations, days stolen to hunt and fish with my father, and lunches with my mom. Perhaps we need rest to rediscover rest.

EMOTIONAL

We all have emotional needs, though sometimes we ignore them. This area, like every area in our lives, needs to be balanced. Some people become obsessed with their emotional needs and histories, feeding into the victimology that troubles our society. The purpose of our examining our emotional needs and histories is not to become self-centered but to become God-centered.

Emotionally we all have a history. Some of us have had a pleasant childhood, others a difficult one. All of us have come into some sorrow or loss and dealt with it in some way, either well or poorly. We have all had emotional models around us whom to some degree we have emulated. Why is it important for us to be aware of these things? Because who we have been and how our experiences have shaped us will determine our responses in the future.

If we have grown up in a family where food is considered a source of comfort, we may be prone to overeat. If we have been part of a dysfunctional family system, we may use our Christianity as a happy gloss to cover our deepest hurts, and never allow God or our church family to help us heal or cope with our other problems. We may not know how to confront other people lovingly and appropriately, and may go to the extreme of either highly emotional confrontations over trivial issues or to caving in to other people's demands. It is not within the scope of this chapter to discuss the dynamics of family life or how to deal with emotional trauma in our past. I simply want to point out that in order to have emotional health, it is critical to evaluate the health of our roots and how they affect our behavior now.

Our emotional well-being is also based in the relationships we sustain. While some of these relationships are entered into volitionally (for instance, marriage or friendship), others are mandated by circumstance. You cannot, for instance, choose your parents or your customers. Although, again, the complexity of human relationships is beyond the scope of this chapter, I would like to touch on a few aspects of human relationships that are critical to emotional health.

Communication

While we all communicate differently because of our personalities,[1] there are several common elements to good communication.

Honesty is an important element. Good communication can never be based on anything but truth. While we all want to say the most comfortable thing, that is seldom helpful and often gets us into hot water later on.

With honesty must come tact. Tact is nothing more than thinking for a moment before speaking—thinking about how we would like information to be communicated to *us*. While there are some truths that are so painful that no matter how you tell someone, he or she will be hurt (for instance, telling someone she has cancer), the vast majority of information can be communicated in such a way as to affirm the person involved and honestly communicate the information necessary.

Listening is perhaps the most important aspect of communication. We all find it difficult to listen carefully to another person for any length of time. But it is important to listen, and confirm as much with positive physical gestures such as nods and eye contact (especially when dealing with an emotionally charged issue), and by occasionally repeating and rephrasing what the other person has said: "What I hear you saying is..." This helps us to avoid misunderstanding what the other person is saying.

Attitude

It has always amazed me that people respond so differently to illness. One patient will be difficult, withdrawn, or demanding, focused on the unfairness of the situation. Another person with an identical ailment will be cheerful, joking, and grateful to God for all He has done. "It's a hard thing," they might say, "but I've had a good life, and that's more than a lot of people." This is not to say that these people do not have down times or that they do not appropriately express pain or sorrow. They simply have the "gratitude attitude." Not surprisingly, they do better overall in recovery.

If we do not have this attitude naturally or have not had it instilled in us during childhood, what can we do to cultivate it?

One thing I have had to learn—being a problem-solver by nature and vocation who tends to focus immediately on problems in any given situation—is to look for the positive aspects. I need to be intentional about expressing thanks to God *before* my petitions to God. And I need to remember to thank other people for what they do for me. It does not mean I overlook problems or pretend they are going away on their own. It simply means I am committed to looking at God's goodness and faithfulness as well as my problems. Even when it seems mechanical, I find that I begin to internalize my external positive actions and begin to *feel* more grateful.

Responsibility

Emotional health is developed and protected by an appropriate sense of responsibility. Human beings tend to make one of two errors: taking responsibility for things they should not, or not taking the responsibility that is appropriate.

Part of the normal developmental process is developing appropriate boundaries between others and ourselves. We begin to understand as small children that we are different from Mommy and Daddy. That is why two-year-olds focus on "I want to do it myself, Mommy" or on the dreaded *no* word. It is important for these little tykes to learn the *no* word, as frustrating as that is. Some adults have never really learned to say no and end up burned out and out of control because they cannot refuse engagements, responsibility, or temptation. Illness of all sorts is more likely when burnout has prepared the way. The word *no* helps us to avoid responsibility that is not ours, and to form appropriate boundaries with other people.

I must admit my frustration, on the other hand, with the three-pack-a-day smoker who curses God when he is diagnosed with lung cancer, or the fourteen-year-old girl who complains about her pregnancy with "Why did this happen to me?" How we choose to behave *does* affect our lives. We have a legitimate responsibility to take care of our bodies, minds, and souls that only we can fulfill. Denying this responsibility can only cause pain for others and ourselves. It also keep us from becoming emotionally mature.

Learning an appropriate responsibility for our own actions, and allowing others to take responsibility for their own actions, is critical to our emotional health. We also need to allow God sovereignty in situations that lie outside of our control. Much of our stress comes when we do not let God take charge of situations we cannot control anyway. When we find ourselves anxious and worried about things we cannot alter, we must remember the formula found in Philippians: "Have no anxiety about anything, but in everything by prayer and supplication with thanksgiving let your requests be made known to God. And the peace of God, which passes all understanding, will keep your hearts and your minds in Christ Jesus" (Philippians 4:6–7). Look at this passage closely. Often when we are filled with anxiety, we try to deny that the thing we fear will come upon us; or we try to ignore the anxiety; or we feel guilty for being worried. Instead, the scriptural pattern is to offer all our troubles to God and to remember to give thanks.

Why is giving thanks so important? First of all, God's Word commands it. Second, God deserves it. Third, it takes our minds off the negative and puts us into a more positive frame of mind. Fourth, it reminds us that God has done great things in the past and that He can do them again.

It is important that we do not deny the reality of our problems, but instead focus on God's power to solve them.

SPIRITUAL

Spiritual health can be found only when we are in a right relationship with God. Sin is one of the major blocks to wellness. Sin can be overcome only by:

1. Recognition of the sin

We all wear cultural blinders that make us perceive things differently than God does. Until perhaps twenty years ago, for instance, a woman in India would be burned to death when her husband's body was cremated. Most of us see that as the destruction of human life and deplore the callousness that allows or mandates such a custom. But as Americans we have become deadened to the aborting of almost two million fetuses each year. We do not get upset about divorce because it is a fact of life. We turn a blind eye when people in our churches have sex outside of heterosexual marriage. We ignore the plight of the poor and dismiss cheating on our income tax as a business ploy. Whatever our particular bias, we ignore our own sins and the sins of others.

2. Confession of sin

To recognize sin is not enough. God wants to lead us into repentance, and in order to do that we must admit to God that we have been wrong. It is often helpful to confess sins to a discreet confessor who loves God.

3. Repentance

Repentance is not only feeling sorry for or sin; it is taking steps to avoid sinning in the future. Repentance includes making restitution where possible, apologizing, retracting statements when we have slandered, repaying what we have stolen, and repairing what we have broken. Repentance means figuring out where we went wrong and how to avoid it next time. If you had sex with your girlfriend or boyfriend, maybe next time you should not stay up until midnight cuddling alone. If you were gluttonous, maybe you need to keep sweets out of your house. If you were harsh with your spouse or children, maybe you need to get more sleep. Repentance especially means drawing on God's grace and strength, because our sins are forgiven through what Jesus did for us on the cross, and our lives are changed to the degree we allow Him to change us.

Spiritual health is more than just confessing our sins and altering bad behavior. It is also developing a new set of healthy behaviors.

Spending time with God is the basis of the Christian experience. Whatever else we do, we will never be successful as Christians if we do not spend intense time with God. We can do God's will and emulate His character only as much as we know Him. How do we get to know God?

Youthful fans of famous basketball players are careful to watch every game of their idol. They pour over the "stats" of their player (the statistics, if you don't have teenagers) and of every player on the team. They know what strategy he employs and how he overcomes his rivals on the field or court. The Christian should study his or her Bible just as assiduously, for this is the record of how God has acted in the past. It contains His game plan for the present and for the future. And it contains precious promises we can cling to.

If you are a serious basketball fan, you would jump at the chance to see your favorite team. Utter delight would include receiving your players' autographs, and ecstasy might include a few minutes talking with them. Christians have the great privilege and comfort of being able to talk to God at any time, to dwell in His presence. We can share our sorrow and our joys. We can request His guidance on any matter. We are even so privileged through the presence of the Holy Spirit in our lives as to get an occasional glimpse of heaven as God reveals Himself to us and acts through us. As we grow in God, we can learn how to open ourselves more fully to God and to be a better vessel of His love.

So far we have spoken only of our individual relationship with God. We do not have a relationship with God in a vacuum; however, because we were made to dwell in community, we have a corporate relationship with all believers. We need each other as a church community, and church community needs us. Although we may find that we feel more "holy" when by ourselves, community life can be the fire that purifies us and keeps us humble.

When I was small I got a rock tumbler for my birthday. I was excited to select different stones and place them in the tumbler over several days with varying degrees of sand. The abrasion of the sand and the constant friction of the other stones rubbed away the rough spots on the stones and eventually polished them to a finish almost like glass. So community life is with us. If we avoid our troubles (the sand) or the pressures of other personalities (the other stones), we may be more comfortable but we will be incomplete. Comfort is no indicator of Christian growth (Matthew 16:24), nor is it necessarily an indicator of emotional well-being.

Mark likes to write surrounded by radio talk shows or with the television on. He can tolerate the distraction of multiple phone calls or interruptions of all sorts. I, on the other hand, must have as close to absolute silence as I can get in an imperfect and noisy world. Part of our growth as individuals is accepting our differences. To me it is incredible that anyone can think coherently under the circumstances Mark writes, much less produce an intelligent article. To Mark it is unbelievable that I would want that much silence, much less require it.

The second (and more difficult) part of our growth is sacrificing our own desires and working in such a way as to accommodate each other (Ephesians 4:1–4). I often get up earlier than Mark, for instance, in order to have my silence. When he sees I am in the middle of a good writing session, he keeps his radio low and the TV off. I try to schedule my quiet sessions, on the other hand, when he is not around, knowing that silence (or, to me, relative quiet) is difficult for Mark to sustain. It is easier to be critical of each other's styles than to be sympathetic and supportive. But working toward a higher level, self-sacrifice, demonstrates a desire to grow in Christ and in our relationship with one another.

Let me be clear that not all compromise and self-sacrifice are of God. We can never condone what God has condemned. To pat someone on the back, for instance, and say it is OK to have sex outside of marriage is not loving. Love so cares about the other person that only God's will for that person is good enough. Tolerance will condone because it is based on seeking the other person's approval. (When we feel we must have other people's approval, incidentally, we are demonstrating some emotional damage and dysfunction that we should pay attention to and seek healing for.) Tolerance does not lie down and die for another person. Love does. We can never have corporate health as a Christian community if we try to substitute anemic tolerance for love just because it is more comfortable.

Few of the issues in the Christian community, on the other hand, are issues of right and wrong. Most of them (like the "best" writing environment) are matters of preference, the kinds of things we can compromise on. Recognizing the difference is an important step in Christian maturity.

In our search for wellness and health, we must sometimes accept discomfort. Spiritual and emotional health, like physical health, involve exercise and self-denial. But being healthy does not consist only of painful choices. Rather, it consists of reeducating ourselves to choose what is best for us. It is for this reason that our entire pursuit of health must be conducted under God's direction, for He alone knows what is best for us. In order to be well, we must walk in His ways.

DISCUSSION QUESTIONS

1. Discuss several ways in which taking preventative measures physically, emotionally, and spiritually is good stewardship.

2. Share your successes and failures in dieting.

3. What are some of the dietary and nutritional programs being recommended that are dubious, if not dangerous? What makes a program sound?

4. In recent years there have been numerous books, articles, and television programs about the traits of a dysfunctional person, family, or church. In what ways are these views compatible with biblical teaching? In what ways have they become the latest pop psychology or fad?

5. What are some of the roadblocks you have encountered in trying to spend regular quality time with the Lord? How did you work around those roadblocks?

6. In what ways are we actually unloving to people when we tolerate their sin?

Epilogue

G OD LOVES US, in deed as well as in word. He who did not spare His only Son, but gave Him up for our redemption, continues to make available His blessings to us at our points of need—and that includes healing of body, soul, and spirit. He does not give these blessings reluctantly or grudgingly. His desire to bless is greater than our desire to be blessed! As we are healed, we enter more fully into our heritage as His sons and daughters; we grow closer to Him in love, gratitude, and obedience; and we are motivated and equipped to serve the world in His name. (See John 21:15–17.) What a privilege!

The extraordinary thing is that God has chosen to carry on His work of healing through ordinary folk like ourselves. Empowered by His grace, led by His Spirit, instructed by His Word, and submitted to His elders, we can be used to accomplish His purposes. The result? God's name is glorified, His people are blessed, His Church is edified, and His kingdom is extended.

My prayer for all who read this book is that you will be made whole and that you will minister this wholeness to others.

Being Overcome by the Power of the Holy Spirit

A PHENOMENON SOMETIMES ENCOUNTERED in a service of healing is that of people falling over backwards when someone prays for them. Popularly referred to as "being slain in the Spirit," it is not the same as fainting. The person has not lost consciousness. Rather, he or she is coming into a state of great peace and, often, close fellowship with God. A person may rest in this state from just a few minutes to more than an hour.

As with any other spiritual experience, it is authentic and helpful when it is a work of God, but harmful and destructive when people are manipulated, worked up emotionally, or deliberately pushed over. The presence or absence of this phenomenon neither validates nor discredits either the person ministering or the person being ministered to, unless there is a deliberate attempt to force it to happen or to block it from happening. In the former case, people can become disillusioned about the movement of the Holy Spirit in general. In the latter case, a blessing from God might be thrown away and one of the vehicles for healing set aside. In short, we are neither to force it nor prevent it.

Possible scriptural references to this phenomenon are Acts 9:4, where we are told Saul was knocked to the ground by a powerful intervention of God, and John 18:6, where we read that the Roman soldiers fell to the ground. This group was not falling at the feet of Jesus to worship Him, nor were these tough men shrinking back in fear. Rather, at this moment of betrayal, when the stage was set for the Son of God to go to the cross to make atonement for human sin, the presence and power of God must have been so strong that the soldiers could not stand.

There are many references to this experience throughout the history of the Church. I have chosen just three to illustrate how this experience is neither new nor the property only of Pentecostal groups. Notice that the references come from different centuries, different countries, different denominations, and different places in the Church hierarchy.

First, St. Teresa of Avila, a sixteenth-century Spanish Roman Catholic nun. She wrote this about the phenomenon:

> The soul becomes conscious that it is fainting almost com-
> pletely away, in a kind of swoon, with an exceeding great
> and sweet delight. It gradually ceases to breathe and all
> its bodily strength begins to fail it....He can apprehend
> nothing with the senses, which only hinder his soul's joy
> and thus harm rather than help him. It is futile for him to
> attempt to speak: his mind cannot form a single word, nor,
> if it could, would he have the strength to pronounce it. For
> in this condition all outward strength vanishes, while the
> strength of the soul increases so that it may have the frui-
> tion of its bliss. The outward joy experienced is great and
> most clearly recognized.[1]

Second, George Whitefield, eighteenth-century English Anglican (Episcopalian) priest. The following account was given of what happened at a large outdoor service at which Whitefield was the speaker:

Some were struck pale as death, others were wringing their hands, others lying on the ground, others were sinking into the arms of their friends.[2]

Third, Charles G. Finney, nineteenth-century American Presbyterian layman (and lawyer by trade). The following account was given by Finney of a service he was leading in Utica, New York. The circumstances of those being overcome by the Holy Spirit were not, he commented…

cases of objectionable excitement.…Manifestly, there is no such effervescence of the sensibility as produces tears, or any of the usual manifestations of an excited imagination, or deeply moved feelings. There is not that gush of feeling which distracts the thoughts; but the mind sees truth, unveiled and in such relations as really to take away all bodily strength, while the mind looks in upon the unveiled glories of the Godhead. The veil seems to be removed from the mind, and the truth is seen much as we suppose it to be when the spirit is disembodied. No wonder this should overpower the body.[3]

What is God's purpose in causing people to be overcome by the power of the Holy Spirit? Those who have experienced it testify that it is an occasion of blessing. Many speak of spiritual and emotional refreshment. Some receive healing. Some sense God speaking to them. Some receive visions. Some liken the inner cleansing that occurs to a "spiritual sauna." A reasonable hypothesis is that this experience provides a moment of rest when one's customary defenses and controls are lowered and one becomes more receptive to the Lord's activity. God can use the experience, too, to gain a person's attention, to let him know the reality of divine power.

There are many different ways in which falling under the power of the Spirit happens. Some people fall straight back, smoothly, and easily. Others seem to resist what is happening, stop, step back a bit to catch themselves, and then drop suddenly. Others drop straight down into a heap. Occasionally someone falls forward into the one praying for him. People can experience this phenomenon even at a distance from the person praying for them. It can happen to a person individually or as part of a group. Often one is "slain" in response to the laying on of hands or by being touched with holy water, anointing oil, or similar sacraments.

In the service I led for several years in Malden, Massachusetts, we gave the title "catcher" to those whose primary task was to stand behind persons being prayed for in case they should come under the power of the Holy Spirit. The catcher's job was to lower them to the floor so they would not be hurt. Some do not see the need for a catcher, believing that God will not allow a person to be hurt by falling over when He pours the Spirit down upon him or her. While this is often true, it is not *always* true. I have seen people hurt and have heard of this happening from others. Just as Jesus would not tempt His Father by jumping from the pinnacle of the temple, we should refuse to tempt God by not providing a catcher.

Robert Shelton, who served as our trainer and supervisor of catchers, has offered this helpful advice on what to do if you are ever called upon to be a catcher:

> There is an art to catching, and it is easily learned. Never attempt to hold a person up, because the person "slain" becomes dead weight and awkward to hold. Catch the person under the armpits and step backward so that you may lay the person out flat without dropping or hurting him. Try never to drop a person on his buttocks since this could lead to a nasty injury to the coccyx bone at the base of the spine.
>
> While lowering the person, be careful of your own back. Remember to use your arm and leg muscles and not your back muscles when you are lowering someone.
>
> Be aware of the clothing that people are wearing, for several reasons. One, silky clothing makes it hard to hold

people. They could slip from your grasp. Two, be aware of the state of the person's clothing so that there is no embarrassment when he or she is at rest on the floor. Three, be careful not to damage the clothing; tearing is possible.

Remember one more thing: the catcher is also one of the pray-ers for the relief or healing of the person. You have as much input to the person as the rest of the team. You might pray in silence or aloud just like the rest of the team.

Good catching, and be careful!

Once people have been overcome by the Spirit and safely settled on the floor, we have found it unwise to attempt to rush them back to their feet. For one thing, this might be difficult, as they are in a physically unstable state. More importantly, to get them up too soon would interrupt whatever it is that God is trying to do. Until such point as they try to get onto their feet, the whole team, or one team member detached for this purpose, should continue to pray alongside them. This prayer, however, should be very quiet. I have experienced occasions when I could not hear what God was trying to say to me because the team members were praying too loudly over me. When the people on the floor attempt to get to their feet, help them, remembering to bend your knees so as not to hurt your back. Notice whether they are sufficiently recovered to get back to their seats without further help, and, if not, offer them that help.

APPENDIX 2

A Diagnostic Checklist

THE FOLLOWING CHECKLIST has been prepared to help you find possible causes of an illness and in keeping good physical-emotional-spiritual health for yourself and those to whom you minister. The fact that this list is lengthy should serve as a warning to avoid simplistic judgments as to why a person is sick. To assist yourself and others in coming to and maintaining health, an honest, Holy Spirit–assisted use of this list on a regular basis is strongly suggested.

A. Physical condition

1. Do you maintain a balanced diet of basic food groups?

2. Do you take in too many or too few calories on a regular basis?

3. Have you been checked for nutritional deficiency in a particular mineral? For allergies?

4. What is the amount and quality of your sleep?

5. What is the amount and regularity of your exercise?

6. Do you smoke? Do you drink more than eight ounces of wine, two beers, or two mixed drinks each day? Do you use any other "social drug"?

7. Has there been a recent occurrence of physical trauma: a fall, strain, bump, or accident?

8. Do you regularly have physical, dental, and eye examinations?

9. Are there hereditary illnesses, conditions?

10. Have you been chaste/monogamous? If you are married, has your spouse?

11. Are you on any medications? Do you take them as prescribed?

B. Spiritual practice

1. Do you read the Bible each day? Do you submit to what God tells you to believe?

2. Do you try, with God's help, to live an obedient life, surrendering control of your will to God and seeking to bring your actions into conformity with God's will?

3. Do you pray regularly? Does your prayer life include several modes of prayer, such as adoration, meditation, confession, intercession, petition? Do you take time to be still in God's presence?

4. Do you worship regularly with other Christians?

5. Do you have regular fellowship with other Christians?

6. Do you receive regular individual spiritual direction or guidance?

7. Do you confess your sins to God regularly, either directly or to another person? Are you too hard on yourself? Too easy? Do you find it difficult to accept God's forgiveness? Do you want to be forgiven but are unwilling to change? Do you let God examine your whole life, or do you hold some things back? Do you forgive others?

8. Do you regularly receive Holy Communion?

9. Do you have a good balance of emphasis in your spiritual practice among doctrine (study of Scripture and Christian books), discipline (obedience to God's commands), and devotion (adoration, praise, worship, meditation, silence before God)?

10. Are you trying to grow spiritually in your own strength, or are you asking God to grow you through grace?

11. Is your spirituality authentically yours (God makes people with different spiritualities, temperaments), or are you trying to be like someone else?

12. Most importantly, are you trusting Christ as your hope for heaven, or are you "trusting in your own righteousness"?

C. Psychological/emotional health

1. Past

   a. Are there people, places, or periods of your life that you have blotted out or that you avoid or deny?

    b. Does the recollection of certain people, places, or events produce great feelings of shame, guilt, fear, hurt, anger, or rejection?

2. Present
    a. Are there recurrent problems with social interactions, close relationships?

    b. Are you afraid to be alone? Do you always want to be alone? Can you be by yourself and enjoy it (solitude vs. loneliness)? Do you enjoy only being by yourself and not being with others?

    c. Are you constantly dependent on others to validate or approve you? Do you accept yourself?

    d. Are you afraid to share intimate inner knowledge with anyone? Do you share too readily, indiscriminately?

    e. Are there things you should be able to do that you cannot do, for reasons that are difficult to articulate?

    f. Can you be assertive (standing up for your rights while respecting those of others), or are you generally passive or aggressive?

    g. Do you have violent mood swings?

    h. Are you happy with who you are while acknowledging and acting on the need for improvement?

    i. Do you compare yourself favorably or unfavorably to others?

    j. Do you always go along with the group? Always insist on your own way? (That is to say, are you a compulsive "people-pleaser" or one who is rigid and inflexible?)

    k. Do you generally make yourself the focus of attention/subject of conversation (whether positively or negatively)? Or do you avoid being the topic of discussion at all costs?

    l. How do you deal with criticism? Do you automatically disagree/defend yourself or agree/put yourself down?

    m. Do you generally resolve arguments by giving in? By trying to win at all costs?

3.   Future
    a. Are you anxious and fearful about the future?

    b. Do you have goals for the future that are realistic for your age, gifts, background? Are you making steady progress toward those goals? Are you able to reassess and redefine goals when appropriate? Do you live from crisis to crisis?

    c. Does your existence consist of "hours of boredom, moments of panic"?

D. Occult involvement

1.   Is or was there involvement by your parents or grandparents in witchcraft or the occult?

2.   Have you ever been involved in occult or New Age practices? (See Appendix 5 for a list of these.) If so, have you renounced them?

3.   Is it particularly difficult for you to pray, praise God in worship, receive ministry, honor the name of Jesus?

4.   Do you feel more than a normal compulsion to do wrong things? To take the Lord's name in vain?

5. Do you feel as though you have one or more extra personalities within you?

6. Do you hear voices or have dreams that are generally terrifying or hostile?

Healings Recorded in Scripture

HEALINGS IN THE OLD TESTAMENT

1. Abimelech healed; Abimelech's wife and female slaves healed of barrenness	Genesis 20:1–18
2. Abraham's wife Sarah healed of barrenness	Genesis 21:1–7
3. Moses healed of leprosy at the burning bush	Exodus 4:1–7
4. Moses' sister, Miriam, healed of leprosy	Numbers 12:1–15
5. Moses successfully stops a plague	Numbers 16:41–50
6. Snakebites healed in the wilderness	Numbers 21:4–9
7. Manoah's wife healed of barrenness	Judges 13:2–24
8. King Jeroboam's paralyzed hand healed by "a man of God"	1 Kings 13:1–6

HEALINGS IN THE
OLD TESTAMENT—CONTINUED

9. Elijah restores to life a widow's son	1 Kings 17:17–24
10. Elisha restores to life the son of a Shunammite woman	2 Kings 4:8–37
11. Elisha heals Naaman of leprosy	2 Kings 5:1–14
12. Isaiah heals King Hezekiah of a boil and prolongs his life	2 Kings 20:1–11; Isaiah 38:1–8
13. Job healed of leprosy and of various losses	Job 2:7–8; 42:10–16

HEALINGS BY JESUS IN THE NEW TESTAMENT

1. Multitudes healed and delivered at Galilee	Matthew 4:23; Mark 1:39; Luke 6:17–19
2. Leper healed	Matthew 8:1–4; Mark 1:40–42; Luke 5:12–15
3. Centurion's servant healed of paralysis	Matthew 8:5–13; Luke 7:2–10
4. Peter's mother-in-law healed of a fever	Matthew 8:14–15; Mark 1:30–31; Luke 4:38–39
5. Multitudes healed and delivered from demons	Matthew 8:16–17; Mark 1:32–34; Luke 4:40–41
6. Gadarene demoniacs delivered	Matthew 8:28–34; Mark 5:1–15; Luke 8:26–33
7. Paralytic man healed and forgiven	Matthew 9:2–8; Mark 2:3–12; Luke 5:17–26
8. Jairus' daughter restored to life	Matthew 9:18–19; 23–25; Mark 5:22–24, 35–43; Luke 8:41–42, 49–56
9. Woman healed of hemorrhage	Matthew 9:20–22; Mark 5:25–34; Luke 8:43–48
10. Two blind men healed	Matthew 9:27–30
11. Mute, demon-possessed man healed and delivered	Matthew 9:32–33
12. Multitudes healed	Matthew 9:35

HEALINGS BY JESUS IN THE
NEW TESTAMENT—CONTINUED

13. Healing cited to convince John the Baptist that Jesus was the Messiah	Luke 7:19–22
14. Man with a withered hand healed on the Sabbath	Matthew 12:10–13; Mark 3:1–5; Luke 6:6–10
15. Multitudes healed near Capernaum	Matthew 12:15; Mark 3:9–11
16. Blind, mute, demon-possessed man healed and delivered	Matthew 12:22; Luke 11:14
17. Multitudes healed in the desert right before Jesus fed the 5,000	Matthew 14:13–14; Luke 9:11; John 6:2
18. Multitudes healed at Gennesaret as they touched the fringe of Jesus' garment	Matthew 14:34–36; Mark 6:55–56
19. Daughter of Syrophoenician woman delivered	Matthew 15:22–28; Mark 7:24–30
20. Multitudes healed on a mountain near the Sea of Galilee	Matthew 15:29–31
21. Epileptic boy healed, delivered	Matthew 17:14–18; Mark 9:14–27; Luke 9:38–43
22. Multitudes healed in Judea beyond the Jordan River	Matthew 19:1–2
23. Two blind men healed near Jericho	Matthew 20:29–34
24. Blind and lame people healed in the temple	Matthew 21:12–14
25. Man with an unclean spirit delivered	Mark 1:22–26; Luke 4:33–36

HEALINGS BY JESUS IN THE
NEW TESTAMENT—CONTINUED

26. A few in Nazareth healed	Mark 6:5
27. Deaf and mute man healed	Mark 7:31–35
28. Blind man at Bethsaida healed	Mark 8:22–26
29. Blind Bartimaeus healed	Mark 10:46–52; Luke 18:35–43
30. Multitudes gather to be healed after Jesus healed the leper	Luke 5:15
31. Young man at Nain restored to life	Luke 7:11–16
32. Bent-over woman with a spirit of infirmity healed	Luke 13:11–16
33. Man with dropsy healed	Luke 14:1–4
34. Ten lepers healed	Luke 17:11–19
35. Severed ear of Malchus healed at Gethsemane	Luke 22:50–51
36. Nobleman's son healed	John 4:46–53
37. Infirm man at Bethesda healed	John 5:2–15
38. Man blind from birth healed	John 9:1–11
39. Lazarus restored to life	John 11:1–44

HEALINGS BY JESUS IN THE
NEW TESTAMENT—CONTINUED

40. Jesus raised from death by God the Father	Matthew 28: 1–10; Mark 16:1–14; Luke 24:1–43; John 20:1–29

HEALINGS THROUGH THE DISCIPLES OF JESUS

1. Internship of the Twelve	Matthew 10:1–8; Mark 3:13–19; 6:7–13; Luke 9:1
2. Internship of the seventy	Luke 10:1–9
3. The apostles perform signs and wonders on the Day of Pentecost	Acts 2:43
4. Peter and John minister healing to a man lame from birth	Acts 3:1–16
5. The apostles perform signs and wonders in Solomon's Portico	Acts 5:12–16
6. Philip casts out demons and ministers healing to paralyzed and lame people in Samaria	Acts 8:5–7
7. Ananias ministers healing to Saul (Paul) for his blindness	Acts 9:10–19
8. Peter ministers healing to the paralyzed Aeneas at Lydda	Acts 9:32–34
9. Peter is used to restore Tabitha (Dorcas) to life at Joppa	Acts 9:36–41
10. Paul and Barnabas minister by signs and wonders	Acts 14:3
11. Paul ministers healing to a crippled man at Lystra	Acts 14:8–18
12. Paul casts out evil spirit from a young woman at Thyatira	Acts 16:16–18
13. Healing and deliverances ministered by Paul at Ephesus	Acts 19:11–12
14. Eutychus restored to life through Paul's prayers	Acts 20:7–12

HEALINGS THROUGH THE
DISCIPLES OF JESUS—CONTINUED

15. Paul is healed from venomous viper bite at Malta	Acts 28:1–6
16. Paul ministers healing at Malta to the father of Publius, who suffers from a fever and dysentery	Acts 28:7–8
17. Other people on Malta are healed through the ministry of Paul	Acts 28:9

Study Questions About Scripture Passages on Healing

The facts of the incident

1. Describe the person in need (including age, sex, and social status).

2. What was the apparent need?
    a. How was this expressed by the person involved?
    b. How was it expressed by others?

3. What was being sought? By whom?

4. Did Jesus say what the cause of the person's problem was? If yes, what was the cause?

5. Who took the initiative in effecting a healing?
    a. The person in need? If so, how?
    b. Others? If so, how?
    c. Jesus? If so, how?

6. Processes involved leading to healing:

   a. What did Jesus say?

   b. What did Jesus do?

   c. What did Jesus tell the person in need to do?

   d. What did Jesus tell the others to do?

7. Reactions to the healing:

   a. How did the person in need react?

   b. How did the others react?

   c. Did Jesus say anything about the healing after it was accomplished, and, if so, what?

Your personal evaluation

1. After reading the record, what do you think was the matter with the person in need?

2. Attitude toward ministry:

   a. What was the attitude of Jesus concerning a ministry of healing to the person in need?

   b. What was the attitude of others concerning the possibility of healing?

   c. What was the attitude of the person in need?

3. The place of faith and love in effecting a restoration to health:

   a. What attitude does Jesus tell the person in need he will have to assume if he expects to be healed?

b. Did the person in need give any verbal expression of faith?

c. Did any others give any verbal expression of faith?

d. Identify all nonverbal evidences of faith in the narrative.

e. How did Jesus manifest His faith or express His love?

4. What were the evidences of healing?

5. Why do you think Jesus performed this healing?[1]

Statements and Prayers

A statement of dedication or rededication to Christ as Lord and Savior

> *Heavenly Father, I admit to You that I am a sinner. I have sinned in thought, word and deed, and by what I have failed to do. I acknowledge that I cannot earn my salvation but need Jesus to be my Savior. I know that He died on the cross to pay the penalty for my sins. I now ask Jesus to be my Savior and to take away the penalty of my sins so that I can have fellowship with You, both now and in heaven. Thank You, Jesus, for being my Savior. By Your grace I wish to live in conformity to Your will and make You the Lord of my life. Amen.*

A prayer of confession of sin

> *Heavenly Father, I acknowledge that I have sinned in thought, word, deed, and by failure to do that which You have called me to do. In particular I acknowledge my sins of _____, I acknowledge my ongoing orientation of _____, and I admit my fascination with _____. Lord God, I know these things are wrong, and I ask Your forgiveness. I thank You that Jesus paid the penalty for my sins at Calvary and*

that His blood can wash me from my sins. I claim His atoning work for me right now. And I ask the Holy Spirit to give me grace to turn from these sins, orientations and fascinations, that I may live from now on in holiness of life. Through Jesus Christ, my Lord and Savior. Amen.

(In the blanks you may add specific sins and orientations that are not in keeping with the will of God, and fascination with actions, attitudes, or orientations that are not of God.)

A statement of renunciation of occult practice

Lord Jesus Christ, I acknowledge that there are spiritual powers in the universe that are in rebellion against You. Through my ignorance and willfulness I have given these a place in my life. I have called out to various "spiritual powers" I have participated in spiritual practices You have forbidden, such as _____. I turn my back on them and renounce any place they have in my life. I command, in the name of the Lord Jesus Christ and in the power of the cross, that any spiritual entities not submitted to God leave me. I ask the Holy Spirit to come and fill any place in my spirit made empty by their departure. And I ask, Lord Jesus Christ, that You give me grace to live only for You and to be kept steadfast in my walk with You. Through Jesus Christ, my Lord and Master. Amen.

(In the blank mention any involvement in the worship of, devotion to, calling out to, or following of any spiritual entity other than the God of Scripture; or any involvement in such occult practices as tarot cards, Ouija boards, meditation that is not the historic Christian kind of meditation, séances, contacting the dead, palm reading, water-witching, mind reading, channeling, magic [other than sleight of hand or card tricks], use of crystals for healing or magic purposes, casting spells, using a crystal ball, manufacturing or using magic potions, astrology, etc.)

A statement of renunciation of Satan and of commitment to Jesus Christ as Lord and Savior

Question: Do you renounce Satan and all the spiritual
forces of wickedness that rebel against God?
Answer: I renounce them.

Question: Do you renounce the evil powers of this world
that corrupt and destroy the creatures of God?
Answer: I renounce them.

Question: Do you renounce all sinful desires that draw
you from the love of God?
Answer: I renounce them.

Question: Do you turn to Jesus Christ and accept Him as
your Savior?
Answer: I do.

Question: Do you put your whole trust in His grace and
love?
Answer: I do.

Question: Do you promise to follow and obey Him as
your Lord?
Answer: I do.[1]

Exorcism of persons

*You evil spirit, I command you in the name of the Lord Jesus
Christ and by His cross and precious blood to depart from
this person. I command you to go directly to Jesus for your
future fate, and I forbid you to harm anyone along the way.
Lord Jesus Christ, please fill with the Holy Spirit the places
in [name] now made empty by the departing of these evil
spirits. Amen.*

■ ■ ■

I exorcise you, every unclean spirit, in the Name of God the Father Almighty, in the Name of Jesus Christ His Son and our Lord and our judge, and by the Power of the Holy Spirit, to be gone from this image of God [name] whom our Lord in His goodness has called to His Holy Temple, that he [she] himself [herself] may become a temple of the Living God, and the Holy Spirit may dwell in him [her]. Through the same Christ our Lord Who will come to judge the living and the dead and the world by fire. Amen.[2]

Exorcism of places

Deliver, O Lord, this place [or house, dwelling, church] from all presence of the evil one, all evil spirits, all noises, feelings, senses, phantasms, and presences. Make them depart from here and go to the place you have assigned them, never to return. Bring peace to this place, O Lord, and fill it with Your presence. Through Jesus Christ, our Lord. Amen.

■ ■ ■

Pour Your blessing on this place [or house, dwelling, church] and make it a place set apart for You. Drive far from it, O Lord, the presence of any spirit not submitted to You. In Your mercy, place Your warrior angels as a hedge to guard and defend all in this place [or house, dwelling, church] and keep us safe from the evil one and all his minions. Indwell it, Holy Spirit, that all who enter [or enter and dwell, or enter and worship] here may be drawn closer in knowledge, faith, and love to You, the Father and our Lord Jesus Christ. May the Lord bless and sanctify this tabernacle of His servants and grant them the riches of the kingdom of heaven. In Jesus' name. Amen.

Commendation of the soul of someone known to have died in the faith of Christ

Into thy hands, O merciful Savior, we commend thy servant [name]. Acknowledge, we humbly beseech thee, a sheep of thine own flock, a sinner of thine own redeeming. Receive him into the arms of thy mercy, into the blessed rest of everlasting peace, and into the glorious company of the saints in light. Amen.[3]

Commendation of the soul of someone who has died and his faith is known to God alone

We commend, O merciful Lord, the soul of [name], departed. We commend him [her] to Your merciful and wise judgment, knowing that Your judgment is true. Through Jesus Christ our Lord. Amen.

Clinical Evidence for Healing

The question is often raised why, despite the large percentage of the population claiming faith in God, there is
a limited number of clinical studies relating the impact of
religion on objective health measures. One reason may
be funding. Pharmaceutical companies fund research
experiments because positive outcomes are necessary for
approval of their products. Few religious organizations
have the resources to devote to such studies. Another
reason may be residual effects of the so-called Enlightenment period. "Scientists of that era flushed with enthusiasm for their new discoveries, wished and needed to
unshackle themselves from the church.... The burgeon-
ing successes of the scientific method created new ten-
sions in the relationship between religion and medicine,
leading eventually to a split in which religion was forced
to restrict itself to the role of caretaker of the soul, while
the role of medicine became that of caretaker of the body,
and later, the mind. Faith, by its very nature, was deemed

to be unobjective and not verifiable, and hence, unscientific and not worthy of data-based research."
—FROM THE INTRODUCTION TO *THE FAITH FACTOR:*
AN ANNOTATED BIBLIOGRAPHY OF CLINICAL
RESEARCH ON SPIRITUAL SUBJECTS,
BY DALE A. MATTHEWS, MD,
DAVID B. LARSON, MD, MSPH,
AND CONSTANCE P. BARRY, MPH

This two-volume study is the best collection of summaries of articles from various research journals on the relationship between religion (or faith) and physical and emotional health. For further information, consult the publishers: National Institute for Healthcare Research, One Colonial Pl., 2111 Wilson Blvd., Suite 1130, Arlington, VA 22201.

What follows are citations of a few of the articles from research literature.

1. A study on "The Impact of Religion on Men's Blood Pressure" noted that the self-perceived importance of religion was directly associated with lower blood pressure. *Journal of Religion and Health* 28 (1989): 265–278.

2. The study "Religious Belief, Depression and Ambulation Status in Elderly Women with Broken Hips" found that belief in God and frequency of church attendance was significantly related to post-operative ambulation status and inversely correlated with level of depression in the study group. *American Journal of Psychiatry* 147 (1990): 758–760.

3. A study of nearly 100,000 people noted that frequency of church attendance is associated with significant reductions in morbidity and mortality from a variety of disease conditions. *Journal of Chronic Diseases* 25 (1972): 665–672.

4. "The Effect of Prayer on Well-Being" notes a strong and positive correlation of religious practice with multiple measures of well-being. *Journal of Psychology and Theology* 19(1) (1991): 71–83.

5. Religious commitment is positively associated with psychological adjustment and life satisfaction according to the study "The Relationship Between Religion and Mental Health/Distress," published in *Review of Religious Research* 31(1) (1989): 16–22.

6. The article "Does Religion Influence Adult Health?" noted that the greater the practice of one's religion, the better one's health. *Journal for the Scientific Study of Religion* 30(2) (1991): 193–202.

7. Religious commitment and prayer for healing were demonstrated to produce long-term success for those quitting smoking in the study "Factors Determining the Success of Nicotine Withdrawal: 12-Year Follow-up of 532 Smokers After Suggestion Therapy (by a Faith Healer)," published in *The International Journal of the Addictions* 22(12) (1987): 1189–1200.

8. The article "Frequency of Church Attendance and Blood Pressure Elevation" demonstrated that frequency of church attendance is inversely related to blood pressure regardless of age, sex, socioeconomic status, and body mass. *Journal of Behavioral Medicine* 1 (1978): 37–43.

9. High religious involvement is associated positively with lower rates of alcohol and drug abuse among those with mood disorders in the study "Alcohol and Drug Abuse in Patients with Affective Syndromes." *Comprehensive Psychiatry* 26(3) (1985): 283–295.

10. Religious orthodoxy is often attacked for the harm it is believed to cause individuals. The study "Relationship Between Religious Orthodoxy and Three Mental Health Factors" demonstrated, however, that religious orthodoxy was negatively correlated with hostility and had no negative associations with a person's anxiety or self-esteem. *Psychological Reports* 38 (1976): 756–758.

11. Orthodox religious belief and practice is correlated positively with greater life satisfaction in older people in the study "Religion, Age, Life Satisfaction, and Perceived Sources of Religiousness: A Study of Older Persons." *Journal of Gerontology* 40(5) (1985): 615–620.

12. Sometimes those hostile to religion assert that religious commitment is a, if not the, cause of psychopathology. The study "Psychopathology and Religious Commitment" demonstrated, however, that mental illness and the strength of religious commitment are inversely related. *Review of Religious Research* 12(3) (1971): 165–175.

13. A lengthy article in *Prevention in Human Services* reviews various research articles on the relationship between religious practice and physical health. The authors, J. S. Levin and H. Y. Vanderpool, demonstrate how, in various ways, faith has a generally beneficial role. *Prevention in Human Services* 9 (1991): 41–64.

14. Another article that reviews various studies is "Religious Domains and General Well-Being." Authors M. M. Poloma and B. F. Pendleton note how religious commitment and general well-being are positively associated. *Social Indicators Research* 22 (1989): 1–22.

Some observe that several of the above studies, while involving scientific investigation, are still somewhat subjective in their approach. There have been, however, studies that have been conducted using more objective clinical research methodologies.

- A recent study combining direct prayer with medications on rheumatoid arthritis patients has been reported in the article, "Effects of Intercessory Prayer on Patients With Rhuematoid Arthritis," by Dale A. Matthews, M.D., Sally M. Marlowe, N.P., and Francis S. MacNutt, Ph.D. The conclusion was that patients receiving in-person intercessory prayer showed significant overall improvement during one-year follow-up. The article is found in the December 2000 issue of *Southern Medical Journal*, pages 1177–1186.

- A true double-blind study that positively correlates prayer—done without the patients' knowledge—is outlined in "Positive Therapeutic Effects of Intercessory Prayer in a Coronary Care Unit Population," by Randolph C. Byrd, M.D. The article is found in the July 1988 issue of *Southern Medical Journal*, pages 826–829.

■ ■ ■

New Creation Healing Center, led by my wife, Dr. Mary G. Pearson, is a Christian, whole-person healing facility combining the scientific practice of medicine, intentionally Christian psychotherapy, and prayer. Dr. Mary Pearson is the author of the following two case studies:

- "Obtunded White Female with End Stage Alcoholic Jaundice" by Dr. Mary G. Pearson

A fifty-year-old white woman, whom the author met on the third day of hospitalization for advanced alcoholic jaundice and metabolic encephalopathy. Her total bilirubin was 22.8 mg/dl, direct bilirubin 17.6 mg/dl. The patient had profound electrolyte abnormalities and was jaundiced and obtunded. Her liver extended down to her iliac crest, and was deemed by all physicians involved in her care to have a very poor prognosis, and death was believed to be imminent. Discussion of "Do Not Resuscitate" was initiated with her son, who insisted on a full code status.

At this time the author approached obtunded patient, prayed for her, and encouraged her to seek God. Patient did not respond at this time.

The following day the patient was responsive, and her liver enzymes began to normalize. By the sixth day of hospitalization her mentation was normal. Patient allowed the author to pray with her. Patient fully recovered, having completely normal liver enzymes. She remains sober ten years later, despite a thirty-year history of chronic alcoholism.

Patient remains open to healing prayer, and is aware of her miraculous healing.

- "Healing of White Female with Malignant Lymphocytic Small Cell Disease" by Dr. Mary G. Pearson

Sixty-two-year-old white female noted an enlarging node in her left cervical chain. For several months prior to this she had been experiencing night sweats and chills. She had lost 40 pounds on an intentional weight loss program. Lymph node aspirate revealed malignant small cell lymphocytic disorder. A flow cytometry was not ordered initially. When the patient sought oncologic evaluation she was told she had either non-Hodgkins lymphoma or chronic lymphocytic leukemia but that there was nothing that could be done at this stage, and that she would have to have the cancer become more aggressive before chemotherapy would be of benefit. Furthermore, the patient was told a definitive diagnosis could not be obtained without a flow cytometry. The patient's CBC was normal, and CT scan of the neck revealed only local enlargement lymph glands in the left cervical chain.

At this point the patient sought healing prayer and was anointed by a priest, a bishop, her husband, and other lay people.

She was profoundly reluctant to allow the cancer to progress without a definitive diagnosis or any treatment and returned to her ENT who agreed to remove the previously aspirated lymph node so that flow cytometry could be performed. This lymph node and an adjacent lymph node were removed and found to be completely benign. The patient recognizes her miraculous healing and gives complete credit to her Lord and Savior, Jesus Christ. She remains cancer free one year later.

The Service of Holy Communion
As a Service of Healing

EVERY SERVICE OF Holy Communion is a healing service. In this section we will look at the various parts of the Communion service and how they relate to the ministry of Christian healing. It is my hope that every time you are at a service of Holy Communion, you can find in it a means to your healing—physical, emotional, and spiritual.

OPENING ACTS OF PRAISE

Nearly every Communion service, unless it is a quiet, early Sunday morning or a daytime midweek service, begins with a hymn or several songs of praise. Such acts of praise serve to get us in touch with God, who dwells in the praises of His people (Psalm 22:3, KJV). Besides opening us to God, praise serves to strengthen our faith. Our orientation is upward, toward Him from whom all blessings flow, and away from ourselves, giving God the freedom to work in us and helping us to get out of the way. Our thoughts can focus on the words of the songs, which often build our faith by describing who God is, how much He loves us, and what He does. Often, long before specific prayers for our needs, God intervenes when we forget about our needs and focus on Him.

THE MINISTRY OF THE WORD

In most Communion services, the time of praise is followed by a time of reading from the Scriptures and a sermon based on them. This relates to Christian healing in at least two ways.

1. As we hear about the promises of God

God makes many promises to us, and the reading of Scripture reminds us of them. Even though the promises may not specifically relate to healing, we are reminded by statements of promise and by stories of how those promises were received over the centuries by His people that God offers us His very best. Confident that God wants to bless us, we can approach Him with our needs of the present.

2. As we hear about the commands of God

God calls us to discipleship, lived out as we bring before Him all aspects of our life. Much spiritual sickness comes because of our sin. When we sin, we place a barrier between ourselves and God, and our relationship with God suffers. Although not all physical or emotional sickness happens because of our sin, some does, as we have already seen.

When we hear what God expects of us as the Word of God is read and preached, we have an opportunity for repentance, for receiving divine forgiveness, for coming into restoration of fellowship with God, and for healing.

THE RECITATION OF THE CREED

The Creed, either the Apostles' Creed or the Nicene Creed, is a summary statement of the basics of the Christian faith. Unless we consider ourselves above God and above the collective wisdom of the Church throughout the centuries, we will never pick and choose among the articles of the Creed, believing only what we wish. Our attitude must always be, "This is what You have revealed, Lord. I receive it by faith. Please help me understand what it means and apply it to my life."

Nor must we adopt the attitude of, "I do not care about doctrine; I just want to praise the Lord." Jesus said it is the truth that makes us free and that we are to love the Lord with our minds (Mark 12:30; John 8:32). Wrong belief leads to painful experiences.

The Creed relates to healing in this way: it points us to God and away from any of the other spiritual beings in the universe. Many of these spiritual beings are in open rebellion to God, and our relating to them, whether intentionally or by a lazy, fuzzy understanding of who God is, can be very harmful, even though initially it may even bring a measure of healing. In this day of increased Satanism, New Age occultism, and so-called alternative Christian spiritualities, a proper understanding of who God is (and is not) is very important.

THE PRAYERS OF THE PEOPLE

During the time of congregational prayer, we have an opportunity to pray for the needs of the world, the universal Church, other people, and ourselves. In many churches a list of names of sick parishioners is read. In some churches this list is reproduced in the Sunday bulletin for people to take home and use in daily devotions.

In some churches opportunity is given for people to speak prayer concerns aloud. What an opportunity to take to the throne of grace the needs of loved ones, and to do it with the prayer support of our fellow worshipers! When praying aloud for someone during a church service, therefore, make sure you speak loudly enough that you can be heard by others.

CONFESSION AND ABSOLUTION

One of the causes of our physical, emotional, and spiritual sickness, as we saw earlier, is our own sin. The time of the confession in the Communion service is a time to acknowledge our sins before the Lord so that they can be forgiven and their consequences removed.

We should never rely *solely* on such general confession. The liturgical formula for confession is, by necessity, general and brief. Our time of doing real business with the Lord is beforehand. The liturgical formula of confession, however, is a helpful reminder that we have already confessed and can approach God with our needs with our guilt taken away. Sometimes it serves as a reminder of what we yet need to do.

Absolution is a time when God's ministers pronounce forgiveness in His name to those who vow to turn from their sins. It is a reminder that "if we confess our sins, he is faithful and just, and will forgive our sins and cleanse us from all unrighteousness" (1 John 1:9). Satan is the "accuser of our brethren" (Revelation 12:10). He will try to get us to believe that our sins are such that God will never forgive us, much less bless or heal us. The absolution is a good reminder that what Jesus did on Calvary is sufficient atonement for sin. If we confess with purpose of amendment of life, God forgives, no matter what Satan may say or what thoughts he may try to put into our consciences.

Some clergy, in pronouncing absolution, make the sign of the cross over the people. This is a wonderful visual reminder that between our sins and the just judgment of God stands the atoning, forgiving cross of Christ. Many people make the sign of the cross over themselves as an acknowledgment of what Christ has done in forgiving our sins.

THE EXCHANGE OF THE PEACE

In many orders of service, right after the absolution comes the exchange of the peace. (In the Roman Catholic liturgy this occurs immediately before the people come forward to receive Communion.) "Passing the peace" is a reminder that while Christianity is a *personal* relationship with God, it is not a *private* one. During the exchange of the peace we may discover we are not comfortable greeting certain individuals. In fact, we may find ourselves trying to figure out how we can greet our friends while avoiding certain others. This could be God's way of telling us that there is some work of reconciliation yet to be done, either right then or soon after. We are not required to have every member of the church as our close friend or to agree with them on everything. We *are* called to be at peace with them, insofar as it lies within us (Romans 14:19; Hebrews 12:14). To be at enmity with another person often manifests itself in spiritual, emotional, or even physical sickness.

THE OFFERTORY

For many of us, the offertory is simply a time to put our offering envelope in the plate and sit back and listen to an anthem from the choir. It is, however, much more than that. The money we place in the plate is not our dues for belonging to the organization. It represents the offering of our whole selves, our treasure, yes, but also our time, our talents, our very being. We are not giving God money to buy favors from Him. We are surrendering ourselves to God, who gives His blessings as grace—free and unmerited favor.

THE PRAYER OF CONSECRATION

There are at least two ways in which the prayer consecrating (or setting apart) the Communion elements relates to the ministry of healing.

1. It reminds us of what Christ did for us on Calvary.

On Calvary Jesus offered His life in atonement for sin. Because of our sin, we are estranged from God, a spiritual sickness with eternal consequences. Our lostness makes us susceptible to various other bad fruits of human fallenness, emotional and physical sickness. On the cross Jesus paid the penalty for the sins of those who would put their trust in Him. Thus we have access to the throne of grace from which all blessings come.

As one historic prayer of consecration puts it, "Through faith in His blood, we and all Thy whole Church have remission of our sins *and all other benefits of His passion*."[1] Those who make Jesus Christ their Lord and Savior are offered healing for their spiritual sickness and other blessings as well, including physical and emotional healing.

2. The Communion elements are consecrated to be the body and blood of Christ and to be vehicles for the mediation of grace.

From her earliest days the Church has believed that the Communion elements are means of bestowing God's grace. God uses material things to flesh out spiritual reality. One man asked me once, "How could God bestow blessing through a piece of bread and a sip of wine after certain words were said over them?" I asked him if he had any difficulty in accepting the truth that the second Person of the Godhead lived on earth as a human being with flesh, blood, and bones. He got the point. The God who took flesh also uses material objects as some of the ways He comes to us and bestows blessings.

Just as Jesus is not a *symbol* for God but is literally God made flesh, so too do the Communion elements do more than just *symbolize* spiritual reality. They *are* spiritual reality—the body and blood of Jesus—and they convey spiritual blessing. I have known people to be healed of various physical, emotional, and spiritual ailments as they took Holy Communion. Many of them were not even thinking about their need for healing as they received the elements.

HEALING MINISTRY WITH A PRAYER TEAM

Although this is not part of the Eucharistic liturgy as such, a growing number of churches have teams of people available in a side chapel or in a corner of the main church to pray for people right after they receive Communion. With the reminder of what Christ did for them at Calvary fresh in their minds, and with His body and blood just consumed, they are ready to meet God in a focused, intentional prayer for healing.

CLOSING PRAYERS AND DISMISSAL

In the closing prayer we thank God for what He has done for us—whether invisible manifestations of His grace, in ways we will not discover until later, or in general ways of blessing us—and we ask Him to strengthen us for service in His name. One prayer often used contains these words: "Send us out to do the work You have given us to do." Part of that work is to minister healing through leading people to salvation in Christ (*always* the most important healing a person can receive), by praying for or with people to be healed, and by working for the healing of society.

Such words of dismissal as, "Let us go forth in the name of Christ," or "Go in peace to love and serve the Lord," or "Let us go forth into the world, rejoicing in the power of the Spirit," give us our marching orders, and the name under which and the power by which we minister. As we understand the tremendous healing power of the Eucharist and that every Communion service is a healing service, we will want to receive Communion more often. And as we understand that Communion was the service observed every Sunday by the Church since the days of the apostles, we will join the ranks of the many who are demanding that every Sunday service be a service of Communion.

May Christians Judge?

C HRISTIANS ARE CONSTANTLY being told, "Do not be judgmental." The text cited is Matthew 7:1: "Judge not, that you be not judged."

We recognize that the judgmental attitudes we all slip into are not in keeping with Christian love. But are not there times when we simply have to judge? We would evaluate potential babysitters for our children to make sure they were reliable and mature. In the same manner, we would not blindly accept any teaching that comes along but would test it to see if it is from God. (See 1 John 4:1.)

Far from forbidding us to judge, the Bible even exhorts us to do this: "Do you not know that the saints [that is, God's people] will judge the world?...Do you not know that we are to judge angels? How much more, matters pertaining to this life!" (1 Corinthians 6:2–3). God is not self-contradictory. How then do we reconcile these seemingly conflicting statements?

The Greek of the New Testament makes it clear that two different types of judgment are meant. The judgment that is wrong—the judgment that Matthew 7:1–2 rules out—uses the Greek word *krino*. It means to pass judgment on, to condemn. The judgment that is right uses several other Greek words: *dokimazo,* *anakrino,* and *diakrino.* The meaning is to test, investigate, search out, weigh, examine or discern. There are a number of ways we can test ourselves to see if an attitude or action is judgmental (wrong) or discerning (right).

1. *Judgment forms opinions on first impressions, on hearsay, or on secondary evidence. Discernment withholds forming an opinion until it checks things for accuracy and does it firsthand with the person involved.*

Judgment is quick to believe something because it appeared that way on the surface, or because someone else said it was so. Discernment goes to the person directly and seeks clarification. How many times have I passed judgment on the basis of what someone told me, only to discover that things were not as they had been related to me? We hear and see selectively, and we inadvertently garble what others tell us. Jesus' message in the temple needs to be grafted onto our hearts: "Do not judge by appearances, but judge with right judgment" (John 7:24).

2. *Judgment condemns others without getting oneself in order. Discernment examines self first before presuming to go to others.*

It is often the case that those sins we hate in others are our own worst faults! Paul told the Romans that "in passing judgment upon [others] you condemn yourself, because you, the judge, are doing the very same things" (Romans 2:1). Jesus tells us in the Sermon on the Mount that we should first take the log out of our own eye so that we can see clearly to take the speck out of our brother's (Matthew 7:3–5). Jesus' statement does not mean we are not to point out to other people their faults. What He means is for us to get our own spiritual house in order first. As a result, when we go to others, it will be with the humility of one who has "been there." On such occasions we will have love in our "tough love."

3. *Judgment has as its purpose destruction. Discernment has as its purpose restoration.*

From time to time Christians, especially those in leadership positions, are called on to deliver a strong word of correction to those under them. Paul told Titus to watch out for those dwellers of Crete over whom Paul had appointed him bishop. In strong language Paul referred to them as "liars, evil beasts, lazy gluttons" (Titus 1:12). Titus was told to rebuke them sharply. The difference between judgment and discernment is not always sharp rebuke versus tender words. The difference has to do with motive. Titus was told to rebuke them not in order to tear them down, but so "that they may be sound in the faith" (Titus 1:13).

Before you go to other people to point out their faults, ask yourself why you are going. Is it to tear them down or to build them up? When we tear down, we glare, use harsh words, put the other persons down, and are not interested in what they have to say. Our emotions are out of control. When we go to build up, we choose our words more carefully, are in control of ourselves, have the desire to see the others do well, and sometimes even have tears in our eyes. Since we cannot always gauge ourselves accurately, before we speak a hard word to someone, it may be helpful to check our motive out with someone who will be honest with us.

4. Judgment condemns the person involved. Discernment condemns the action, but loves the person.

One day when Jesus was teaching in the Temple, a woman who had been caught in the act of adultery was brought to Him (John 8:1–11). He was asked, "What do you say about her?" He was being presented with the opportunity to be either judging or discerning. In saying, "Go and do not sin again," Jesus made it clear that her actions were out of the will of God. Yet He refused to condemn the woman.

Before we go to other people to point out their faults, we need to make sure of two things. First, we must make sure that their actions are actually sins according to Scripture. On the one hand, we may gloss over or excuse things that the Bible condemns. In that case we may tolerate or even applaud behavior that God wants stopped. When we do this we are not being loving to others. We are failing to sound a needed, though unpleasant, warning. On the other hand, we may deem as sin something that is merely a difference in personality or culture. In that case we may condemn an action that is not against God's will.

Second, we must take care to distinguish between condemning persons and condemning sin. If you are having a difficult time doing this, take some time to reflect on how you appreciate being loved by those who talk to you about your sins. In addition, take some time to pray lovingly and positively for the person you are going to confront.

5. *Judgment deals with matters publicly. It gossips and seeks to make others judge the person. Discernment deals with the matter privately. It goes to the person directly and involves no one else, until bringing in others is appropriate.*

Jesus care fully outlined the procedure we must follow when we act on what we perceive are the sins of others. In Matthew 18:15 He said, "If your brother sins against you, go and tell him his fault, *between you and him alone*" (emphasis added). If he refuses to hear, the next verse tells us to involve one or two others, so long as they are people who are already involved ("the evidence of two or three witnesses"). We are not to go get people who were not present at or involved in the particular offense, tell them our version of the story, and get them to take up our cause with us.

Even if we are able to withstand the obvious temptation to line up otherwise uninvolved people, we must guard against the more subtle temptation to phrase our gossip as a "prayer request": "Please pray for John. He's in need of God's help because of his sin of…."

6. *Judgment is nosy. It butts in where it has no business, and it speaks at times and in ways the Lord has not led. Discernment is needful. It is involved only when it has the right to be, and when and how the Lord directs.*

It is not always up to us to take up another person's cause and get angry for them. It is often our job to help others deal with their problems in the proper way. People with spiritual discernment know, moreover, that some revelations are for keeping, not for sharing. That is to say, on some occasions we are allowed to recognize the faults of others, not to go to them but to hold them before God in prayer.

A FINAL NOTE

Why is it so important that we distinguish between judging and discerning?

1. Because we all need help getting rid of judgmental thoughts or deeds. By familiarizing ourselves with what constitutes being judgmental, we will better be able to identify such actions and attitudes and, with the Lord's help, take corrective action.

2. So we will not go to the opposite extreme. Many people who will not take a stand on anything, or who cannot assert scriptural truth with conviction, act that way because formerly they were judgmental. But one extreme is just as bad as the other. To be able to avoid being judgmental can help us from swinging to the opposite error.

3. To protect the biblical ministry of building up one another into maturity. Often our discerning words to other people strike raw nerves in them. They do not want to deal with their sins, so they attack the person who brought them a discerning word as being judgmental, harsh, critical, and unloving. In other words, "If you do not like the message, attack the messenger." For many, they attack with a misuse of the word *judgmental.*

Often the effect on those bringing discerning correctives is devastating. They do not want to be judgmental, and they certainly do not want to be yelled at. Thus, they reason, maybe they had better stop saying anything. This is detrimental to the church because it means there will be little or no building up one another into maturity, no nipping sin in the bud. After a while, we become a church of wimps, and Satan wins a victory.

In this time of great theological and moral crisis in churches, it is crucial that we know we are doing God's will when we take biblical stands in appropriate ways. God's truth done in God's love is what is needed now.

Case Study Review Questions

WE SHOULD BE careful to remember that no matter how tired we are, or how distracted by our own cares, or how many people to whom we have ministered on a particular day or through the years, each person deserves our best. One way to keep this in mind is to remember that every person to whom we minister is precious to God and should be precious to us. In addition, each time we minister to someone, we are presented with a situation that can be reviewed and discussed (but only in an appropriate manner) with our prayer partners and with those supervising us.

We find that Jesus trained His disciples and sent them out (Matthew 10:1). Nevertheless, they did not get it right all the time and needed their ministries reviewed (Matthew 17:14–21). Similarly, from time to time it is helpful for us to review our ministries by selecting an occasion of ministry to a person and making it a "case study." The purpose is to review occasions of ministry to see if we made some mistakes that need to be rectified, to learn how we can do better the next time, and to identify what spiritual and personal issues have come to the surface. Far from depersonalizing those to whom we minister, such case studies help us to be even more helpful to them. Here are several points to ponder in your review.

PRACTICAL

1. Did the person to whom you were ministering cry when you prayed? Did you have facial tissues handy?

2. Was he or she overcome by the Spirit? Were there trained "catchers" ready? Did you have something handy with which to cover those lying in a way that would have embarrassed them?

3. Was the deployment of the teams such that there was sufficient privacy for prayer?

4. Did you encounter a "problem person" (for example, someone who tried to tell you his life story when only a brief description of the immediate problem was appropriate, or who insisted you pray longer than the appropriate amount of time)? How did you handle the situation? On further reflection, how will you handle it in the future?

5. Was there someone who so lost composure as to embarrass himself or significantly disturb others? How should this situation be handled?

6. If you sensed there were various gifts of the Spirit (such as prophecy, a word of knowledge, or a word of wisdom) to be manifested, what did you do? Were there practical problems in using them? Did the people for whom you prayed seem comfortable with the manifestations of the Spirit?

7. Were there logistical problems in praying together with others on your prayer team? Was there someone clearly in charge? Did he or she know what to do and do it confidently, yet gently? Did each person on the team know his or her role and yet have sufficient freedom to minister as the Spirit led?

8. Did you have enough time with each person, or did you feel rushed? What could be done about this?

9. Did people who wanted prayer need to stand while waiting their turn?

10. How did people who could not get to the altar for prayer signal their needs so that a healing team could go to them in their pew?

11. Was the prayer team physically comfortable during the prayer session? If not, how could the situation be altered?

THEOLOGICAL AND SPIRITUAL

1. Were theological questions raised by the people to whom you were ministering, questions for which you did not have a biblically sound, brief answer? What were those questions, and what are you doing to find out the answers?

2. What theological questions arose in you?

3. Are you actively seeking the gifts of the Spirit? Do you sense God starting to use you in various of the spiritual gifts? What have you experienced so far? What are you doing to make sure you are staying theologically sound in your understanding of them? What are you doing to make sure you are staying balanced in your use of them?

4. Did you find your confrontation with human pain and misery affecting your relationship with God? In what way? If negatively, what are you doing about it?

5. Because of your ministering healing, have you noticed increased temptation or the experience of those "little nastinesses" Satan throws at those trying to roll back his rule? How can you prepare better spiritually for next time?

6. Have you added to or altered your prayer practice because of your experiences in ministering?

7. Did you sense the move of the Spirit in you? In the others on the team?

PSYCHOLOGICAL

1. Were you "appropriately compassionate"? (Or were you too emotionally caught up with the problems of the people to whom you ministered? Were you too detached?)

2. Did the needs of a particular person or persons remind you of loved ones who had suffered similarly? Were you aware of your emotional response to the remembrances during the time of ministry?

3. Did they remind you of needs or hurts you have experienced personally?

4. Did they remind you of painful things you had repressed from conscious thought?

5. Were you aware of "projection"—that is, saying or doing things that are directed more appropriately toward yourself than to others?

6. Were you aware of the emotional issues of your own future illness and death?

7. Did you feel discouraged about people returning for prayer over unresolved issues or problems? How did you handle it?

Notes

THE GOD WHO HEALS

1. The Lausanne Committee for Evangelism, a distinguished international group representing the evangelical Protestant segment of the Church, commented recently on the place of healing in the life of the church: "Jesus did more than preach the kingdom; he demonstrated its reality with signs of the kingdom, public evidence that the kingdom he was talking about had come. We believe that signs should validate our evangelism, too..." (*Evangelism and Social Responsibility: An Evangelical Commitment*, Lausanne Occasional Paper No. 21 [Grand Rapids, MI: 1982], 31–32). This statement is significant coming from a wing of the Church not usually participant in the ministry of healing.

2. Lesslie Newbigin, *The Household of God* (Norwich, UK: SCM Press, 1947).

CHAPTER TWO
WHY DID HEALING DECLINE?

1. John Wesley, "The More Excellent Way, Sermon 89," *John Wesley's Works*, vol. 7 (N.p.: n.d.), 26–27.

CHAPTER THREE
OBJECTIONS AND ANSWERS TO THE MINISTRY OF CHRISTIAN HEALING

1. St. Augustine, *The Confessions of St. Augustine*, Book I.

2. John Polkinghorne, *Science and Creation* (Nashville, TN: Abingdon Press, 1988).

CHAPTER FOUR
WHY ARE SOME PEOPLE NOT HEALED?

1. This example comes from Oscar Cullman, *Christ and Time* (New York: Gordon Press Publishers, 1977).

2. See Appendix 6, "Clinical Evidence for Healing," for a few case studies demonstrating this.

CHAPTER FIVE
SIN, SICKNESS, REPENTANCE, HEALING

1. But as examples of sickness as punishment, please note how the Lord sent a plague on the people because they made the golden calf (Exodus 32:35); how He promises to make sick the false prophetess Jezebel and strike dead her children for encouraging people to commit fornication (Revelation 2:20–23); and the dire consequences of partaking of the Lord's Supper in an unworthy manner (1 Corinthians 11:27–30.) On occasion God may do such a thing; He has every right to. On other occasions God may send sickness for the greater good of getting our attention so that we will turn to Him in repentance and faith. Paul's temporary

blindness on the road to Damascus is an example of this (Acts 9:8–9).

2. John Donne, "Devotions Upon Emergent Occasions," *Meditation XVII*, 1624.

3. For a helpful book on how church discipline, done correctly, is a great blessing to God's people, see John White and Ken Blue, *Healing the Wounded: The Costly Love of Church Discipline* (Westmont, IL: InterVarsity Press, 1985).

CHAPTER SIX
THE HEALING OF MEMORIES

1. Mark Albrecht, *Reincarnation* (Westmont, IL: InterVarsity Press, 1987).

2. Leanne Payne, *Restoring the Christian Soul* (Grand Rapids, MI: Baker Books, 1996).

CHAPTER 7
SATAN, DEMONS, TEMPTATION, AND OPPRESSION

1. See http://www.svol.org/~hinojosj/quotes/quotes.txt.

2. C. S. Lewis, *The Screwtape Letters* (San Francisco: HarperSanFrancisco, 2001), from the Preface.

3. Allan Bloom, *The Closing of the American Mind* (New York: Simon and Schuster, 1988), 25–26.

4. Paul Zahl, *The Anglican Digest*, Midsummer 1988.

5. At the signing of the Declaration of Independence, "The Quotable Franklin," The Electronic Franklin, http://www.ushistory.org/franklin/quotable/quote71.htm. "Franklin and the Declaration: A Fourth of July Celebration," The Electronic Franklin, http://www.ushistory.org/franklin/declaration/.

6. M. Galanter, D. Larson, and E. Rubenstone, "Christian Psychiatry: The Impact of Evangelical Belief on Clinical Practice,"

American Journal of Psychiatry 148 (1991): 90–95.

CHAPTER EIGHT

CHRISTIAN HEALING AND THE NEW AGE MOVEMENT

1. Werner Erhard, *If God Had Meant for Man to Fly He Would Have Given Him Wings*, booklet available from the est Foundation.

2. *Meditations of Maharishi Mahesh Yogi*, page 178, as quoted on "Answers to Quotes of Man Being God," Let Us Reason Ministries, http://www.letusreason.org/WF31.htm.

3. For a good understanding of how spiritual renewal must be grounded in personal reform, see Benedict J. Groeschel, CFR, *The Reform of Renewal* (Ignatius Press, 1990).

4. Robert Todd Carroll, *The Skeptic's Dictionary*, skepdic. com, s.v. "Ramtha (aka J. Z. Knight)," http://skepdic.com/channel. html.

CHAPTER NINE

THE SACRAMENTS AS VEHICLES OF HEALING

1. Michael Scanlan and Ann Therese Shields, *And Their Eyes Were Opened: Encountering Jesus in the Sacraments* (Ann Arbor, MI: Servant Publications, 1987).

2. I demonstrate the way different personality types often prefer different styles of worship, Bible study, prayer, and Christian service in my book *Why Can't I Be Me?* (Chosen Books, 1992). See especially chapter seven.

3. Scanlan and Shields, *And Their Eyes Were Opened*.

4. Ibid.

5. Theodore E. Dobson, *Say But the Word* (Mahwah, NJ: Paulist Press, 1984).

6. For a fuller treatment of the various aspects of how the service of Communion can work for healing, see Appendix 7. For

a book-length treatment, see Rev. Robert De Grandis, SSJ, *Healing Through the Mass* (Williston Park, NY: Resurrection Press, 1992). Although Roman Catholic in orientation, there is little in the book that would not apply equally to people of nearly all Christian groups.

7. Scanlan and Shields, *And Their Eyes Were Opened*.

8. The book is entitled *Christian Initiation and Baptism in the Holy Spirit: Evidence from the First Eight Centuries* (Collegeville, MN: The Liturgical Press, 1991). A brief summary is the mini-book *Fanning the Flame*, same publisher and date.

9. Scanlan and Shields, *And Their Eyes Were Opened*.

10. Ibid.

11. Ibid.

12. Ibid.

13. Ibid.

CHAPTER TEN

MINISTERING HEALING USING THE SPIRITUAL GIFTS

1. Dennis Bennett, *Nine O'Clock in the Morning* (South Plainfield, NJ: Bridge-Logos, 1970).

CHAPTER ELEVEN

HOW TO INTRODUCE A HEALING MINISTRY INTO YOUR CHURCH

1. It is quite possible for a person to assent to particular Christian truths while having a basically secular worldview. For a discerning presentation of the importance of a consistently Christian worldview, see Harry Blamires, *The Christian Mind: How Should a Christian Think?* (Ann Arbor, MI: Servant Books, 1978). Blamires' tutor at Oxford was C. S. Lewis, some of whose brilliance rubbed off onto his pupil.

CHAPTER TWELVE
THE SELECTION, TRAINING, AND
SUPERVISION OF THE HEALING TEAM

1. A classic example is *Interior Castle* by St. Teresa of Avila. *The Spiritual Exercises of St. Ignatius* is ideal for the study of discerning God's guidance through the movement of the heart and mind in prayer. Thomas Green's *Weeds Among the Wheat* is an excellent modern counterpart. A modern-day mystic, Carlo Carretto, provides a "little course" in understanding mystical encounter and guidance in all of his books, but perhaps especially in *Why, O Lord?*, *Blessed Are You Who Believed*, and *The God Who Comes*.

CHAPTER THIRTEEN
MINISTERING HEALING
BY PRAYER COUNSELING

1. Those offering ministry need to discuss the progress of the ministry from time to time with their supervisor. A good rule of thumb is to evaluate after five or six sessions before deciding to continue. If little progress is being made, one needs to ask why. Sometimes it is because we are not gifted in the area needing attention. Sometimes it is because a specially trained, professional counselor is needed. Sometimes it is because our original diagnosis was incorrect. We also have to be aware that our need to be needed can so get in the way that we get people dependent on us and ask them to keep coming back.

CHAPTER FOURTEEN
BEING AND STAYING WELL

1. See *Why Can't I Be Me?* by Mark A. Pearson for a thorough discussion of how different personality types communicate differently.

APPENDIX 1
BEING OVERCOME BY THE POWER
OF THE HOLY SPIRIT

1. Chapter 18, *The Life of St. Teresa of Avila*, translated and edited by E. Allison Peers from the critical edition of P. Silverio de Santa Teresa, CD, accessed at Eternal Word Television Network Web site, http://www.ewtn.com/library/MARY/AUTOTERE. HTM.

2. James Paterson Gledstone, *The Life and Travels of George Whitefield, M.A.* (London: Longmans, Green, and Co., 1871), 215, as quoted by Richard Riss, "The Manifestations Throughout History," St. Louis Catch the Fire Conference, May 3–6, 1995, http://www.evanwiggs.com/revival/history/riss2. html.

3. Charles G. Finney, "Letters on Revivals—No. 8: Excitement in Revivals," *The Oberlin Evangelist*, May 7, 1845, http://www.charlesgfinney.com/1845OE/45%20let_art/450507_ let_on_revival_8.htm.

APPENDIX 4
STUDY QUESTIONS ABOUT
SCRIPTURE PASSAGES ON HEALING

1. These study questions are from the Order of St. Luke and used with gratitude.

APPENDIX 5
STATEMENTS AND PRAYERS

1. Service of Holy Baptism, *Book of Common Prayer*, 302–303.

2. From the *Rituale Romanum*.

3. *Book of Common Prayer*, 483.

APPENDIX 7
THE SERVICE OF HOLY COMMUNION
AS A SERVICE OF HEALING

1. *Book of Common Prayer,* 335, emphasis added.

RESOURCES

HERE ARE JUST two of the many organizations you can contact for help in growing in your ministry of healing:

Institute for Christian Renewal

Led by the Rev. Canon Mark A. Pearson, the Institute exists to assist individuals and local churches in experiencing the riches Christ offers and in serving effectively in His name. The Institute has a variety of resources for training and equipping people in the ministry of Christian healing, and sponsors Canon Pearson as he travels to churches around the world to conduct healing missions and training programs.

You can contact the Institute at:

Institute for Christian Renewal
148 Plaistow Rd.
Plaistow, NH 03865
(603) 382-0273
E-mail: i4cr@verizon.net

In the latter half of 2005, the Institute will be moving to its new home on Route 125, Kingston, NH, 03848. Please call information in area code 603 for the new telephone number.

The International Order of St. Luke the Physician

O.S.L. is an international, interdenominational fellowship of clergy, medical people, and laity dedicated to the ministry of Christian healing. In existence for the better part of the twentieth century, O.S.L. is considered one of the oldest and best ministries in this field.

You can contact O.S.L. at:

The International Order of St. Luke the Physician
P. O. Box 13701
San Antonio, TX 78213
(210) 492-5222
E-mail: OSL2@satx.rr.com

ALSO BY MARK A. PEARSON

Why Can't I Be Me? Understanding How Personality Type Affects Emotional Healing, Relationships, and Spiritual Growth. Grand Rapids, MI: Chosen Books, 1992.

Chapter 4, "Gifts of Healing," in *The Gifts of the Spirit*, Jack Hayford, John Wimber, and Reinhard Bonnke. Lake Mary, FL: Creation House Books, 1992.

The Basics of the Faith. Dallas, TX: Latimer Press, 1994.